# Christian Citizens and the Moral Regeneration of the African State

In recent years the rapid growth of Christian charismatic movements throughout sub-Saharan Africa has drastically reconfigured the region's religious landscape. As a result, charismatic factions play an increasingly public role throughout Africa, far beyond the religious sphere. This book uses a multi-disciplinary approach to consider the complex relationship between Charismatic Christianity, especially in the form of Pentecostal-charismatic Christianity, and the socio-political transformation taking place throughout this region.

Each of this text's three main sections helps in understanding how discourses of moral regeneration emanating from these diverse Christian communities, largely charismatic, extend beyond religious bounds. Part 1 covers politics, political elites and elections; Part 2 explores society, economies and the public sphere; and Part 3 discusses values, public beliefs and morality. These sections also highlight how these discourses contribute to the transformation of three specific social milieus to reinforce visions of the Christian citizen.

Examining contemporary examples with high quality scholarly insight, this book is vital reading for academics and students with an interest in the relationship between religion, politics and development in Africa.

**Barbara Bompani** is a Reader in Africa and International Development at the Centre of African Studies at the University of Edinburgh. Her work focuses on the intersection between religion, politics and development in sub-Saharan Africa. For many years her research has investigated the relationship between religious organisations and their activities and socio-political action in post-apartheid South Africa. Since 2012 she has been involved in a research project that investigates the role of Pentecostal-charismatic churches in framing the public and political discourse around morality, sexuality and nationhood in Uganda. She published (with Maria Frahm-Arp) *Development and Politics from Below. Exploring Religious Spaces in the African State* and several peer-reviewed articles and chapters in edited volumes.

**Caroline Valois** is a postdoctoral fellow at Stellenbosch University in the Department of Sociology and Social Anthropology. With a PhD from the Centre of African Studies at the University of Edinburgh her research focuses on Christianity, namely Pentecostal or Charismatic movements, sexuality and public health. Her work has been published in peer-reviewed journals like *the Journal of Eastern African Studies* and *Critical African Studies* as well as edited volumes including *Christianity and Controversies over Homosexuality in Africa* edited by Ezra Chitando and Adriaan van Klinken.

# Christian Citizens and the Moral Regeneration of the African State

Edited by
Barbara Bompani
and Caroline Valois

Routledge
Taylor & Francis Group
LONDON AND NEW YORK

First published 2018
by Routledge
2 Park Square, Milton Park, Abingdon, Oxon OX14 4RN

and by Routledge
711 Third Avenue, New York, NY 10017

*Routledge is an imprint of the Taylor & Francis Group, an informa business*

© 2018 selection and editorial matter, Barbara Bompani and Caroline Valois; individual chapters, the contributors

The right of Barbara Bompani and Caroline Valois to be identified as the authors of the editorial material, and of the authors for their individual chapters, has been asserted in accordance with sections 77 and 78 of the Copyright, Designs and Patents Act 1988.

All rights reserved. No part of this book may be reprinted or reproduced or utilised in any form or by any electronic, mechanical, or other means, now known or hereafter invented, including photocopying and recording, or in any information storage or retrieval system, without permission in writing from the publishers.

*Trademark notice*: Product or corporate names may be trademarks or registered trademarks, and are used only for identification and explanation without intent to infringe.

*British Library Cataloguing-in-Publication Data*
A catalogue record for this book is available from the British Library

*Library of Congress Cataloging-in-Publication Data*
Names: Bompani, Barbara, editor, author. | Valois, Caroline, editor, author.
Title: Christian citizens and the moral regeneration of the African state / edited by Barbara Bompani and Caroline Valois.
Description: New York : Routledge, 2017. | Includes bibliographical references and index.
Identifiers: LCCN 2017034105 | ISBN 9781138242739 (hardback : alk. paper) | ISBN 9781315277653 (ebook)
Subjects: LCSH: Pentecostalism—Africa, Sub-Saharan. | Citizenship—Religious aspects—Pentecostal churches. | Citizenship—Africa, Sub-Saharan. | Political participation—Religious aspects—Christianity. | Political participation—Africa, Sub-Saharan. | Economic development—Religious aspects—Pentecostal churches. | Economic development—Africa, Sub-Saharan.
Classification: LCC BR1644.5.A35 C47 2017 | DDC 289.940967—dc23
LC record available at https://lccn.loc.gov/2017034105

ISBN: 978-1-138-24273-9 (hbk)
ISBN: 978-1-315-27765-3 (ebk)

Typeset in Sabon
by Apex CoVantage, LLC

# Contents

*Acknowledgements* vii
*List of contributors* ix

Introduction: Christian citizens and the moral regeneration
of the African State 1
BARBARA BOMPANI AND CAROLINE VALOIS

PART 1
Regenerating politics: nationhood, political elites
and the elections 19

1 'Good Christians, Good Citizens': Pentecostal-charismatic
 narratives of citizenship, public action and national belonging
 in contemporary Uganda 21
 BARBARA BOMPANI

2 Vox Dei, Vox Populi: Pentecostal citizenship and political
 participation in Nigeria since 1999 35
 ASONZEH UKAH

3 Election prophecies and political stability in Ghana 49
 EMMANUEL SACKEY

4 Democratic backsliding, religious institutions and the
 constitution of citizenship in sub-Saharan Africa 63
 ELIZABETH SHERIDAN SPERBER

## PART 2
## Regenerating society: economies and the public sphere 81

5 Heavenly commonwealth and earthly good: contemporary African
Pentecostal-charismatic discourses on responsible citizenship 83
J. KWABENA ASAMOAH-GYADU

6 Forging economic citizens: financial integrity and national
transformation at Watoto Church in Uganda 99
CAROLINE VALOIS

7 Pentecostals and developmental citizenship in Ethiopia 115
EMANUELE FANTINI

## PART 3
## Regenerating morality: values, public beliefs and morality 131

8 Sexual citizenship in postcolonial Zambia: from Zambian
humanism to Christian nationalism 133
ADRIAAN VAN KLINKEN

9 'I will make you into a Great Nation, and I will Bless
you': citizens, traitors and Christianity in Kenya 149
GREGORY DEACON

10 Citizenship beyond the State: Pentecostal ethics and political
subjectivity in South African modernity 163
MARIAN BURCHARDT

11 Moral models, self-control and the production of the moral
citizen in the Ugandan Pentecostal movement 177
ALESSANDRO GUSMAN

*Index* 193

# Acknowledgements

Working on a multi-disciplinary and multi-sited study that aims to shed light on the increasingly public role that Charismatic Pentecostalism plays in shaping African political imaginaries, posed several intellectual challenges to the editors as well as to the contributors. Engaging with the variety in the case studies, in the terminology and in conceptual assumptions dictated by disciplinary belongings has been an adventure as well as a journey. We, though, felt that the time was right to make a collective effort to engage with the emergence of those religious groups who are predisposed to shape the present to re-appropriate hope for a future that had hitherto been considered to be lost and distant from their theological and moral worldviews, across sub-Saharan Africa as well as in Latin and North America or in the Pacific.

In this book project we brought together academics at different stages of their careers, from diverse scholarly traditions and from a range of disciplines in order to interrogate the growth of Pentecostal public engagement and its efforts to shape the African political realm. This presented a challenge but also allowed different perspectives and multiple angles to be brought to bear to test the strength of similar conclusions. And we are convinced that this strategy has paid off.

Research and preparation for this book spans the past few years and we have many people we are obliged to thank for their support and many contributions, without which this project would not have been possible. First and foremost, we wish to extend our heartfelt thanks to the contributors whose ideas fill the proceeding pages, your contributions have been invaluable and your willingness to take on board our guidance generous.

We would like to thank the Centre of African Studies at the University of Edinburgh and the Department of Sociology and Social Anthropology at Stellenbosch University, where we are based, for intellectual and institutional support. We also thank all of the participants that informed the case studies for their cooperation and invaluable contributions.

Henry, Caroline's new-born baby arrived during the home stretch and brought a lot of joy, and perhaps a few challenges, to the final round of editing to the book project. Many thanks Henry for making those last few months so special!

We would like to thank the reviewers for their very productive comments and for encouraging us to push our conceptualisations further; and the editors at Routledge for their confidence in our proposal and the collaboration that made this work possible.

And finally, we would like to thank you the readers for taking the time to read this book and hopefully joining us in reflecting on the dynamic role that religion plays in shaping the material and what was considered 'the secular' in new and creative ways.

Barbara Bompani & Caroline Valois
Edinburgh & Cape Town, May 2017.

# Contributors

**J. Kwabena Asamoah-Gyadu** is Fellow of the Ghana Academy of Arts and Sciences is Baëta-Grau Professor of Contemporary African Christianity and Pentecostal/Charismatic theology at the Trinity Theological Seminary, Legon, Ghana. He has researched and written extensively on contemporary Christianity in Africa, Christianity and healing, and Pentecostalism including African immigrant churches in both Europe and North America. He is author of *Contemporary Pentecostal Christianity: Interpretations from an African Context* and *African Charismatics: Current Developments within Independent Indigenous Pentecostalism in Ghana*. He is co-editor of *Pentecostal Mission and Global Christianity* and *Babel is Everywhere! Migrant Readings from Africa, Europe and Asia*. His co-edited book *Christianity in Sub-Saharan Africa* is forthcoming.

**Barbara Bompani** is a Reader in Africa and International Development at the Centre of African Studies at the University of Edinburgh. Her work focuses on the intersection between religion, politics and development in sub-Saharan Africa. For many years her research has investigated the relationship between religious organisations and their activities and sociopolitical action in post-apartheid South Africa. Since 2012 she has been involved in a research project that investigates the role of Pentecostal-charismatic churches in framing the public and political discourse around morality, sexuality and nationhood in Uganda. She published (with Maria Frahm-Arp) *Development and Politics from Below. Exploring Religious Spaces in the African State* and several peer-reviewed articles and chapters in edited volumes.

**Marian Burchardt** is a Researcher at the Max Planck Institute for the Study of Religious and Ethnic Diversity in Göttingen, Germany. His research is chiefly concerned with the links between diversity, power and subjectivity in the age of globalisation, and especially with how they play out through spatial practices. He is also the author of *Faith in the Time of AIDS: Religion, Biopolitics and Modernity in South Africa*, and is a co-editor of *Beyond Neoliberalism, Multiple Secularities Beyond the West, After Integration: Islam, Conviviality and Contentious Politics in Europe*, and *Topographies of Faith: Religion in Urban Spaces*. His work on religion

x  Contributors

and diversity in Africa and Europe has appeared in *International Sociology*, *Comparative Sociology*, *Sociology of Religion*, *The Journal for the Scientific Study of Religion*, *Current Sociology* and *The Journal of Religion in Africa*.

**Gregory Deacon** (independent) gained his PhD from SOAS (University of London) and was a British Academy Postdoctoral Research fellow in African Studies at the University of Oxford and a Junior Research Fellow at St Antony's College. His work looks at Kenyan, neo-Pentecostal Christianity, its socio-economic role, interaction with traditional understandings of the spirit world, and its role in nation building. His publications include 'Allowing Satan in? Moving Toward a Political Economy of neo-Pentecostalism' (with Gabrielle Lynch) in the *Journal of Religion in Africa*; 'Kenya: A Nation Born Again' in *PentecoStudies*; 'Preaching Politics: Islam and Christianity on the Kenya Coast' (with George Gona, Hassan Mwakimako and Justin Willis) in the *Journal of Contemporary African Studies*.

**Emanuele Fantini** is Senior Researcher at IHE Delft Institute for Water Education in the Netherlands. His research interests cover: water, politics and development in Ethiopia; the role of soft power, popular culture, religion in transboundary water conflicts in the Nile basin; citizenship, contestation, human right to water; media studies, and visual research methods. Between 2010 and 2015 he conducted extensive field research on the Pentecostal presence in Ethiopian public spaces. Among his publications: (with J. Haustein) "Introduction: The Ethiopian Pentecostal Movement – History, Identity and Current Socio-Political Dynamics" and "Transgression and acquiescence: the moral conflict of Pentecostals in their relationship with the Ethiopian State" both in *Pentecostudies*, "Go Pente! The Charismatic Renewal of the Evangelical Movement in Ethiopia" in E. Ficquet and G. Prunier (eds.) *Understanding Contemporary Ethiopia*.

**Alessandro Gusman** is Research Fellow and Adjunct Professor of Medical Anthropology at the University of Turin in Italy. His research focuses on the presence of Pentecostalism in Uganda and, more recently, on Congolese churches in Kampala. Among his publications: *Strings Attached. AIDS and the Rise of Transnational Connections in Africa* (co-edited with Nadine Beckmann and Catrine Shroff); "The Abstinence Campaign and the construction of the Balokole Identity in the Ugandan Pentecostal movement" in the *Canadian Journal of African Studies*; "HIV/AIDS, Pentecostal Churches, and the Raise of the 'Joseph Generation' in Uganda" in *Africa Today*.

**Emmanuel Sackey** is currently a PhD candidate in Development Sociology at the University of Bayreuth, Germany. His research interests revolve around Disability and Politics, Social Conflict, Civil Society and Development in Ghana. His publications include "Disability and Political

Participation in Ghana: An Alternative Perspective" in the *Scandinavian Journal of Disability Research*, "The Media, Propaganda and Political Conflict in Ghana" (forthcoming) in *African Studies Working Papers*, Bayreuth: BIGSAS and "Good Governance, Civil Society and the Resurgence of the Disability Movement" (forthcoming) in *Diversity Reader*, Bayreuth: BIGSAS.

**Elizabeth Sperber** is an Assistant Professor of Political Science at the University of Denver. She specialises in comparative and international politics, with regional expertise in sub-Saharan Africa. She is currently completing a book manuscript about the rise of new religious movements (e.g., Pentecostalism) in sub-Saharan Africa since the end of the Cold War. She also served as a Mellon Graduate Fellow at the Interdisciplinary Centre for Innovative Theory and Empirics at Columbia University, and has published work in journals such as *Politics and Religion*, the *International Journal of Social Policy*, the *American Journal of Public Health*, and *the Journal of International Affairs*, among others.

**Asonzeh Ukah** is a sociologist/historian of religion; he is affiliated to the Department of Religious Studies at the University of Cape Town. His research interests include Religious Urbanism, sociology of Pentecostalism, and religion and media. He is the Director of Research Institute on Christianity and Society in Africa (RICSA), University of Cape Town, South Africa, and Affiliated Senior Fellow of Bayreuth International Graduate School of African Studies (BIGSAS), University of Bayreuth, Germany. He has published widely in English, German and Portuguese; he is the author of *A New Paradigm of Pentecostal Power* and co-editor of *Bourdieu in Africa*.

**Caroline Valois** is a postdoctoral fellow at Stellenbosch University in the Department of Sociology and Social Anthropology. With a PhD from the Centre of African Studies at the University of Edinburgh her research focuses on Christianity, namely Pentecostal or Charismatic movements, sexuality and public health. Her work has been published in peer-reviewed journals like *the Journal of Eastern African Studies* and *Critical African Studies* as well as edited volumes including *Christianity and Controversies over Homosexuality in Africa* edited by Ezra Chitando and Adriaan van Klinken.

**Adriaan van Klinken** is Associate Professor of Religion and African Studies at the University of Leeds. His research focuses on contemporary Christianity in Africa, specifically in relation to issues of gender and sexuality. He is the author of *Transforming Masculinities in African Christianity: Gender Controversies in Times of AIDS* and co-editor of *Public Religion and the Politics of Homosexuality in Africa and Christianity* and *Controversies over Homosexuality in Contemporary Africa*. Furthermore, he has published his work in several peer-reviewed journals and edited volumes.

# Introduction
## Christian citizens and the moral regeneration of the African State

*Barbara Bompani and Caroline Valois*

This book is concerned with the increasing public and political role played by charismatic Christianity, and in particular Pentecostal-charismatic Christianity, in sub-Saharan Africa and the implications for the state, the nation and understandings of participation and citizenship in African contexts. The rapid growth in recent years of Christian charismatic movements throughout the continent has drastically reconfigured the region's religious landscape (Anderson 2014). Initially marginal, Pentecostal-charismatic churches have grown steadily over the past three decades and now represent the fastest growing Christian movement worldwide (Davie 2010). Riding the wave of this precipitous growth charismatic factions play an increasingly public role throughout sub-Saharan Africa and far beyond the religious sphere and religious idioms. As a result, these religious voices, ideas and actors are having a profound impact over politics and society throughout Africa.

While the plurality and incongruity of Pentecostal-charismatic (PC) Christianity cannot be understated, given their lack of a consistent theological approach and the variety of ways in which they organise and manifest themselves, this book highlights some of the emerging traits that unifies this diverse and often contradictory movement to offer a new understanding of Pentecostalism based on its heightened politicisation.[1] Fully embracing the movement's incoherence and complexity, we offer a definition of Pentecostal-charismatic Christianity that focuses on its political engagement in sub-Saharan Africa. As a result, different forms of Pentecostal-charismatic Christianity are brought together for consideration. In doing so, the collected chapters demonstrate the movement's evolution from a more apolitical (Yong 2010) prophetic theology of individual empowerment to a political theology intent on refashioning the nation (McDougall 2013; O'Neill 2010; Robbins 1998). Employing this understanding of Pentecostal-charismatic Christianity the book will trace certain emerging consistencies within this diverse movement.

While the approaches, techniques and priorities adopted by churches are historically and often nationally contextualised and churches differ in their social and public roles, in all the African countries under analysis in this book, African Pentecostal-charismatics have created political domains and categories for moral as well for practical practices. Perhaps most notably in regard to the continent, the continuities displayed in forms of African charismatic Christianity in the public sphere come through a unified and vibrant vision of an ideal form of citizenship morally shaped through the lens of Pentecostalism. This vision, and its antithetical rhetoric to fight the perceived evils of the world (Yong 2010), has come to maintain a dominant discursive presence in the public sphere, bearing profound social implications (O'Neill 2010).

A body of growing research concerning African contexts takes into consideration the growing importance of Christian public action within diverse public spheres. Within this model, the Christian citizen inhabits a binary of moral certainty that provides a blueprint for not only other 'good' Christians to follow but more importantly for nations (Deacon & Lynch 2013). Charismatic actors envision Christian citizens capable of not only morally transforming themselves to lead more prosperous lives, but to spiritually, economically and politically regenerate the African subcontinent by incorporating the same moral parameters into all aspects of the public arena. As charismatic actors maintain more and more social influence, their vision of the Christian citizen is made increasingly visible not only in public debates, but perhaps more significantly works to inform public values and beliefs, economic perceptions and strategies in the public sphere, to the very nature of political actors and agendas throughout the region.

What began with a religious contingent has spread to the broader public. Throughout sub-Saharan Africa parallel religious, not only Pentecostal-charismatic, and secular discourses regularly call for moral regeneration, as widespread perceptions frequently point to the occurrence of what is perceived as the loss of public morality. In public discourse corruption, political, social and economic stagnation, the reconfiguration of gender roles and the rights of sexual minority groups are taken as evidence of moral decline. For example, as the chapters by Barbara Bompani (Chapter 1) and Alessandro Gusman (Chapter 11) on Uganda illustrate, religious and political agendas have become increasingly indistinguishable. The proposal and passage of 'moral' legislative initiatives – like the now overturned Anti-Homosexuality Bill that was formulated and supported by the ever more political Ugandan charismatic community – have been upheld by the political elite as a defence of God and Uganda's morality. While for charismatic actors the Christian citizen can easily transform such social woes, the impetus on moral transformation is increasingly utilised beyond the religious sphere as a panacea for all that ails the African state (Marshall 2009).

Throughout sub-Saharan Africa the political elite incrementally embody an idea of community crafted along a narrowly defined Christian morality. As a result, this not only helps to shape political discourses but also influences how political power is both obtained and maintained, to what is included and prioritised on political and legislative agendas. Yet, the focus on generating social change advocated by many Pentecostal-charismatic communities extends to an array of social realms. This particular Christian worldview is increasingly evident in public perceptions about defeating widespread corruption and reversing economic decline. Yet, perhaps the arenas that have received the most attention from the international community, press and academia is how this Christian Pentecostal-charismatic moral worldview has impacted upon public health interventions and policies (see Boyd 2015; Gusman 2009; Parsitau 2009; Pfeiffer 2004; Van Dijk 2013; Cooper 2015) – for example in HIV prevention – and the rise of discourses admonishing sexual minorities throughout sub-Saharan Africa (see Chitando & van Klinken 2016a; Chitando & van Klinken 2016b; Bompani & Terreni Brown 2015; Kaoma 2014).

This book engages in a multi-disciplinary discussion that considers the complex relationship between Pentecostal-charismatic Christianity and rapid socio-political transformation throughout sub-Saharan Africa. Evangelical movements[2] have often been world-withdrawing in order to retreat into a private world closed off from the perceived irredeemably corrupt political sphere, and one of the interests of the newer charismatic movements (not only in Africa) is that they are claiming areas which they had constantly regarded as secular. By examining how Pentecostal-charismatic communities envision the Christian citizen and what that means in terms of political participation, the construction of citizenship and the state, this edited collection explores the nature of these new political reclamations. Through this approach, the work makes a significant contribution to existing literature on African Christianity, African Politics and on Religion and Politics in the post-secular era more broadly by arguing that the rapid sociopolitical transformations taking place throughout sub-Saharan Africa can only be explained by considering the profound role of religion and new religious actors in the public sphere.

While a body of scholarly work is dedicated to the impact of Pentecostal-charismatic movements throughout sub-Saharan Africa, its focus largely concerns how belief shapes the daily lives of believers and local communities. The recent upsurge of Pentecostal-charismatic voices calling for moral, material and political regeneration across sub-Saharan Africa calls for an increased scholarly focus. Religion has profound political implications for the African context. The profound growth of Pentecostal-charismatic communities has engendered sweeping social change. In this light, this book helps explain how social and political realties are informed by religious voices in order to understand rapid transformation taking place in the sub-Saharan context.

## The rise of Pentecostal-charismatic Christianity in sub-Saharan Africa

While academic pursuits necessitate an obligatory attempt to first define the subject under consideration, it is difficult to offer an unambiguous 'definition' of Pentecostalism. As the previous section articulates the book employs a working definition of the movement through its attempts at active political participation above theological doctrine – thus allowing for consideration of its broad manifestations across sub-Saharan Africa. As a result, this book examines what Pentecostalism does, rather than what Pentecostalism is or who is Pentecostal.

Yet, for greater clarity it is necessary to first ground discussion in an overview of the historical evolution of contemporary Pentecostal-charismatic Christianity from its mainline predecessor and more encompassing charismatic forms. Between Pentecostal and charismatic churches exists tremendous diversity and often indistinguishable overlap that proves difficult to conclusively define and categorise. Perhaps more notably clear distinctions frequently prove futile as various denominations often employ terminology interchangeably within their own religious communities, for example Pentecostal-charismatic, charismatic, born-again, etc.

Among scholars it is widely accepted that the history of contemporary Pentecostal and charismatic movements can be understood in 'three waves': classical, charismatic and the third wave – the most relevant to further discussion (Bartos 2015). Today all three forms are represented throughout sub-Saharan Africa, with the latter being the most significant – both in actual numbers and in how the latest incarnation influences and continues to inform not only the broader religious sphere, but the public sphere as well.

With brevity in mind, classical Pentecostalism or mainline Pentecostal churches began as branches of North American Pentecostal churches. These churches prove more doctrinally uniform, centralised and stress important 'gifts' of the Holy Spirit like faith healing, glossolalia and other miracles. Charismatic, the second form, includes mainline denominations outside of classical Pentecostalism that incorporate the aforementioned gifts of the Holy Spirit. Lastly, the third wave proves the widest and most diverse doctrinal category encompassing the non-denominational churches that have arisen since the 1980s (Freeman 2012), namely PC churches.

The current prominence of PC Christianity throughout sub-Saharan Africa cannot be divorced from broader processes of globalisation (Anderson 2004; Casanova 2001; Robbins 2004) and neoliberal reforms (Comaroff 2009; Freeman 2012; Meyer 2007) that helped spur its profound relevance – leading scholars to initially position the movement as a global form, disseminating the West and functioning to reinforce the existing economic order.

Yet, the movement's geneses began decades earlier. Many of the earlier mainline and African independent churches (AICs) that help define current charismatic manifestations of African Pentecostalism began to take root in sub-Saharan Africa following independence achievements in the mid-twentieth century (Meyer 2004). Throughout the sub-Saharan region many mainline Pentecostal churches expanded throughout the 1960s, while charismatic forms slowly became integrated in other mainline Christian denominations. As a result charismatic versions of mainline churches exist across all Christian denominations as well as in some forms of Islam (Coleman 2000; Csordas 2007).

Prior to this time non-Pentecostal Christians who received the gifts of the Holy Spirit often left their respective churches to attend Pentecostal congregations. However, once the charismatic movement gained ground many followers maintained a more fluid membership between mainline and charismatic congregations, with many believers creating new charismatic subgroups within mainline branches (Robbins 2004). From the 1970s the charismatic movement saw a significant increase in the number of followers worldwide (Synan 1997), of which PCs comprised the largest portion. While many refused outright labels of *charismatic* or *Pentecostal* – in order to distinguish themselves from mainline denominations – PC churches proved central to the overall global proliferation of charismatic Christianity.

Notwithstanding its Western provenance, nearly a century after the movement's origins, two-thirds of the world's charismatic and PC Christians are found throughout the Global South (Robbins 2004), particularly Latin America and Africa. Today Pentecostals, and charismatics more broadly, prove to be the most rapidly growing forms of Christianity (Anderson 2004), with the PC movement promising to soon become *the* predominant form of Christianity worldwide (Casanova 2001).

Due to the movement's tremendous fluidity and the lack of consensus among scholars on what the term PC actually incorporates (Corten & Marshall-Fratani 2001; Droogers 2001) statistics vary greatly. However, conservative estimates put the number at around 250 million (Pew Forum 2011). In sub-Saharan Africa alone – where the majority of converts began to join from the 1980s onwards – Pentecostal and charismatic Christians comprise an estimated 11% of region's total population (Freeman 2012).

Throughout sub-Saharan Africa the 1980s proved a transformative time for the movement. For Gifford (1994) social fragility and collapsing economies prompted a dependence on 'new' North American–style churches. Yet, during this initial period of profound growth African churches kept politics at arm's length – maintaining a critical view of the political arena as a site of moral corruption – a tendency that has become increasingly irrelevant. Numerous scholars (Comaroff 2009; Freeman 2012; Yong 2010) link the rapid growth of African Pentecostalism with ongoing economic crisis, political instability, social upheaval and the worsening poverty that have come to characterise the past decades dominated by neoliberal socio-economic interventions. In contexts of economic and social uncertainty the seemingly limitless potential of the health and wealth doctrines espoused by local PC churches offered respite from the ambiguity of daily life for many Africans.

*Locating Pentecostal-charismatic belief*

The sheer fluidity and diversity of not only the movement's belief system but also the distinct ways in which it locally manifests itself is a constant and generates intellectual challenges for the researcher. This cannot be understated, not only with regard to other forms of Christianity but increasingly to the complex and intertwined political and social agendas throughout the Global South. Due to the absence of a single ecclesiastical body and unified doctrine, belief varies hugely throughout PC churches, more often defined by a single charismatic leader who either founded or presides over the church. For Anderson (2004:10) these churches have "defined themselves by so many paradigms that diversity itself has become a primary defining characteristic". However, certain consistencies do apply. Beyond having a similar liturgical form and similar patterns of congregational life (Meyer 1998), church doctrine incorporates a strict moral code incorporating restrictive beliefs that work to govern individual behaviour, for example abstaining from premarital or extramarital sex, drugs and alcohol – generally avoiding what is deemed secular temptations of the outside world. This is reflective of the binary frame most PC churches employ wherein 'good' forces are positioned as at odds with evil, reducing the lived experience of converts into a reality devoid of nuance, requiring a constant navigation of oppositional forces. Yet, these restrictive aspects are balanced with the promises of abundance churches pose to their congregations, offering the converted not only a spiritual rebirth but quite often restored health and financial prosperity as well.

Reflective of a belief in being 'born again' – a concept of spiritual rebirth through the conversion process – churches consistently emphasise a notion of personal, and more broadly communal, transformation. This process requires what Barbalet (2008:75) deems a "reorientation" and Maxwell (1998:352) defines as a "remaking" of the converted. For many scholars the PC focus on rebirth has led to a prevailing line of academic inquiry focusing on rupture (Engelke 2004, 2010; Marshall 2009; Robbins 2004, 2007; van Dijk 1998) and explains the mass appeal of PC churches as a result of their ability to offer the converted a 'break with the past' (Meyer 1998).

For Meyer (1998) conversion provides adherents with the ability to forge new identities through "dialectics of remembering and forgetting" the past (Meyer 1998:318). For many followers the process of rebirth enables a newfound sense of agency. Conversion has a deep impact on the lives of believers, instilling a profound reorientation of individual subjectivities, and enabling those relegated to the periphery to finally view themselves as valued members of society (Freeman 2012:13). This reorientation also brings a newly discovered optimism concerning the prospect of financial gain and restored health.

In PC discourses, financial blessing and good health serve as quantifiable evidence of fidelity to God, concrete manifestations of Divine will, while signalling the movement's significant focus on the material. Converts regularly pray for blessings of health and wealth, as Jesus desires his followers enjoy financially abundant lives and physical wellbeing (Ukah 2005). Yet, the spirit of abundance is perhaps best demonstrated within church walls. From the lavish facilities of wealth churches to the extravagant dress and lifestyles of the pastors themselves, members are expected to practice regular tithing and other monetary donations in an effort to be financially or otherwise rewarded with their own Divine blessings.

As already briefly mentioned, Pentecostal-charismatic churches initially viewed the political sphere as a demonic realm, yet, as our exploration of Christian citizenship will demonstrate the boundary between religious and political discourse is increasingly indistinguishable. For example, during the 1996 election in Ghana "those involved in political campaigns and debates also made the responsibility for the future of the nation dependent on individual believers, on their prayers and votes . . . Pentecostalists viewed good citizenship and Christian virtues as two sides of the same coin" (Meyer 2004:97). As chapters by Emmanuel Sackey (Chapter 3) and Kwabena Asamoah-Gyadu (Chapter 5) will demonstrate in the Ghanaian example Pentecostal moral character has become inextricable from nationalism and definitions of citizenship. Being a good citizen requires being a good Christian. While the Pentecostal church in the Ghanaian context was initially divorced from the political, a binate political theology grew stressing a narrative that progress could only be achieved through the incorporation of God into the political sphere (Gifford 1998).

## Christian citizens

While a growing body of work has demonstrated the political and social significance of the growth of Pentecostal-charismatic Christianity, this volume situates the debate within Marshall's consideration of Nigerian Pentecostalism – which contests accounts that locate religious change as merely a symptom of other social phenomenon but "in and of itself a mode of historical and political transformation" (2009:34). Charismatic movements employ distinct practices of subjectification aimed at governing and transforming African publics that extend beyond spiritual compliance but greatly constitute the political, economic and moral parameters of the African state. These practices rely on a vision of a Christian citizen that works to redefine the public sphere, penetrating the political and social imaginary.

A conception of Christian citizenship involves the creation of a citizenry that *actively* participates in and contributes to – politically, economically and morally – the broader polity. In the Foucauldian (1988) sense the Christian citizen exists beyond a legal distinction or set of rights, although as the various chapters will demonstrate are increasingly impacted by, but equally exist as subjective modes of being governing the self. Christian citizens are charged with not only transforming their own lives, a process that reflects the unending process of rebirth that begins with conversion, but also their broader communities and nations as well. Within this vision Christian citizens have the capacity to experience a moral transformation that enables not only a more prosperous life, but establish a citizenry equipped to spiritually, economically and politically regenerate sub-Saharan Africa.

This volume expands upon O'Neill's (2009, 2010) concept of Christian citizenship among Pentecostal-charismatics in post-war Guatemala where churches offered the moral parameters for believers to establish and perform acts of citizenship through their faith in acts of prayer and at communal church events. For O'Neill these performative practices of citizenship "place the moral responsibility for societal problems . . . onto the shoulders of the believer. This moral ownership ultimately privatized, or better yet internalizes" the social, political and economic failures of the nation while making Pentecostal-charismatic believers responsible for transforming and regenerating society at-large (O'Neill 2010:4). The conversion process and church participation work to transform the individual subjectivities of Pentecostal-charismatic Christians, experiences that shape not only belief but perhaps more significantly action – as believers are charged with direct responsibility for the fate of the nation. From the individual body of the self we are now moving into the collective body of the polity (Wariboko 2014).

Within this paradigm action is paramount. Yet, O'Neill (2009) problematises the pedagogical understanding (Glendon 1991; Kymlicka & Norman 1994) that presupposes that the relationship between Christianity and citizenship is established upon a distinct binary where churches teach believers how to be 'good' citizens within the public sphere. Significantly "the paradigm presumes no substantial overlap between Christianity and citizenship, only temporary bridges" (O'Neill 2009:338). Rather than clearly demarcated realms, understanding the fluid relationship between church and state, public and private, the global and local, individual and polity, and thought and action, helps to forge a better understanding of the complex relationship between religion and citizenship. Far from providing the precepts to merely direct action, within Pentecostal-charismatic practice thoughts often *are* active. According to O'Neill, in Guatemala Pentecostal-charismatic churches urge "congregants to pray for a better nation . . . because prayer is said to have actual effects in the world" (2009:340).

The performative dimension of Christian citizenship has served as a recent point of academic departure for many scholars. While O'Neill locates Christian citizenship as "a lived category" and PC Christianity as the agent that "teaches congregants how to participate as citizens in the public sphere" (2009:334) other scholars have explored the performative nature between PC Christianity and citizenship. Osinulu (2014:116) suggests that in Pentecostal churches come to represent a government proxy wherein a model of citizenship and "political action is mediated through religious ritual". For Marshall (2014) the ways Nigerian Pentecostals engage with the spiritual and material realms not only creates new social and political landscapes, but ideas around citizenship and collective solidarity. The demands of Christian citizenship require an unyielding and visible public presence where acts of faith are bound to performances of the miraculous that divulge PC Christianity as "a formidable apparatus for the production and consumption of pure means" (Marshall 2014:95).

More explicit work concerning the relationship between citizenship, PC Christianity and the political sphere considers the many heterogenic manifestations of PC involvement in politics throughout Latin America (Lindhardt 2016). In sub-Saharan Africa, recent scholarship by van Klinken (2016) and Ndjio (2012) highlights the convergence of citizenship with the construction of PC masculinity, a component of a broader political project intent on redeeming the Zambian nation. In Nigeria conversion is inherently political as it provides the "means of creating the ideal citizen, one who will provide a living incarnation of the *nomos* of an ordered political realm" (Marshall 2009:211).

The Christian citizen offers new ideas of citizenship within African public spheres. Not only motivated by PC principles the Christian citizen actively negotiates a role in the political through a particular set of moral parameters, reflective of PC beliefs. This active mission intends to transform African nations, develop new worlds reflective of the biblical principles espoused by PC churches while also providing a new eschatology of hope for the future of African political communities (Yong 2010:352). As a result while notions of Christian citizenship clearly define who is included in new visions of the nation, the excluded are equally demarcated. As the chapters will illustrate employing a notion of Christian citizenship not only helps to understand the growing sense of action and belonging within the polity, but also the increasing exclusion of those deemed non-citizens, exemplified in the focus on LGBTI communities by numerous legislative initiatives throughout sub-Saharan African within the past decade, highlighted in the collection of chapters in section three.

Throughout sub-Saharan Africa Pentecostal-charismatic discourse consistently positions its believers as the only righteous or moral members of society. At the same time, those who fail to comply – at least publicly – with the strict moral confines of PC Christianity are inadvertently seen as acting against the greater public good churches purport to establish. PC citizens are fundamentally moral citizens, rather than placing the emphasis on civic or human rights, the imperative is on agency and moral authority.

Yet, the relationship of the Christian citizen ultimately does not reside with the state, rather with the greater objective of establishing a biblical model of a reborn nation, thus validating their duty to act as agents of change not for the postcolonial state but the prospective nation. The focus on the reborn nation and Christian citizenry enables an understanding of the complex features of current state and nation-building processes in sub-Saharan Africa, far beyond deterministic views of the colonial and postcolonial that informed regional debates.

Rather, employing a concept of Christian citizenship allows academics to reconsider continuities and discontinuities of nation building from the perspective of how particular forms of Christianity took shape and how it was discursively legitimised giving rise to specific configurations of citizenship. This new paradigm recasts the focus away from the defining dynamics set forth by the colonial and postcolonial state (Cooper 2002; Mamdani 1996) towards new forms of nation building specific to sub-Saharan Africa.

*Locating citizenship*

As the collected chapters will demonstrate, within churches notions of Christian citizenship are both performative and rights-based, requiring a more elaborated discussion of the notion of citizenship itself. Citizenship is both a mutable and abstract concept. In most contemporary understandings citizenship is fundamentally about the relationship between the state and the individual. As the previous section addresses the notion of Christian citizenship calls into question fundamental configurations between the state and citizenry with its newfound focus on forming a reborn nation.

Two features of citizenship make the concept particularly volatile. First, in order to define who is included or extended a sense of belonging in the greater polity those who are excluded must simultaneously be delineated. This prompts an important question: how are boundaries of inclusion and exclusion determined? Second, citizenship merges individual rights with obligations to the state. The same set of expectations on which power is based underscore individual claims to certain rights (Cooper 2014). For Cooper:

> citizenship seems like a relationship of individual and state, in practice citizens act as members of communities and participants in networks, and the men and the women whose actions constitute 'the state' mobilize and organize their followers in the context of such relations. The notion of 'belonging' that is intrinsic to citizenship might crystalize around collectivities that are both smaller . . . or larger.
>
> (2014:5)

Overall, we examine citizenship as a cultural identity – rather than a firm political category – yet this construction of citizenship involves other complex dimensions and is not without profound political consequences. This reflects the way PC churches engage with a broader notion of citizenship, not as rights-based, but more as a collective sense of belonging – although this construct works to shape public impressions, the political and ultimately rights. As a political status citizenship is centred on feelings of belonging and recognition (Anderson 1991). The actual political status of citizenship, or inclusion in political process, "bleeds into the idea of citizenship as a cultural identity. If citizenship as a legal status asks who is . . . a citizen, citizenship as a cultural identity poses this question: What does citizenship look like?" (O'Neill 2010:14). Looking at citizenship as a cultural identity is fluid, and reveals how it is contextually dependent and tied to constructions of the state, and the categories that exist within, like sexuality and religion (ibid.).

For Mamdani (1996) notions of citizenship in postcolonial Africa are bound to colonial political history, where regimes of indirect rule created to address 'native populations' represent the "generic form of the colonial state in Africa" (Mamdani 1996:8). Colonial authority relied on a divide between a rights-based notion of citizenship – extended to a small minority in urban sectors – with the rural majority who were excluded from a rights-based approach to citizenship (Mamdani 1996).

The colonial legacy produced a bifurcated system of citizenship, "colonialism . . . created a sense of 'dual citizenship,' with the result that ordinary people felt little, if any, moral attachment to the legal order while they continued to respect the norms of traditional society" (Halisi 1999:2). For Ekeh (1975) colonial authorities compartmentalised the way Africans viewed the rights and obligations of citizenship. Dual citizenship is defined by the way certain communities are excluded from rights of citizenship, and how membership in other communities replace membership in the state (Halisi 1999:3). For African contexts, the colonial legacy defined "the nature of dual citizenship, as a moral concept . . . [results] in dual publics . . . dual authority . . . [and] dual citizenship" (Halisi 1999:3). Consequently, the postcolonial legacy relies less on rights-based approaches to citizenship. Yet, Christian citizenship is also a subjectivity that becomes ingrained within knowledge and belief systems, and, academically, requires more Foucauldian analyses of Pentecostal ideals of self-governance and discipline.

For O'Neill, this is expressed as a "political rationality that constantly asks: What should the good citizen do?" (O'Neill 2010:15). Modes of governmentality and discipline are integral to the construction of citizenship as a subjectivity and identity. The onus is placed on the individual to self-regulate their conduct to be 'good citizens'. In lieu of the state "simply governing its citizens, citizens . . . take on the responsibility to govern themselves – to regulate their own conduct. . . . The logic and the promise of citizenship prompt people to do things – to themselves, for their nation" (ibid.).

Throughout sub-Saharan Africa the heightened involvement of PC churches in the political sphere increasingly aligns constructions of citizenship with a narrow religious identity. Church goals to transform the nation undertake a project of nation building that requires the construction of a good, idealised citizenry. As a result, the increasing relevance of PC discourse throughout African public spheres helps to align the vantage and aims of the state alongside a theological belief system – as PC churches strive to reform nations as prosperous lands-of-plenty through an active 'moral' citizenry.

PCCs are positioned in an analytical framework as key contributors to processes of political governance – as "an imagined political community" – and national belonging by means of constructing a broader national identity (Anderson 1991:6). Yet, as numerous chapters will detail this drive proves a double-edged sword. As Pentecostal-charismatic churches find more and more political, economic and social significance within African public spheres what are the implications for those groups excluded from an increasingly contracted view of citizenship?

## Overview of the book

This book is structured into three main parts to understand how discourses of moral regeneration emanating from diverse charismatic Christian communities, largely Pentecostal-charismatic, extend beyond religious bounds and contribute to the transformation of three specific social milieus to redefine understandings of citizenship. The chapters represent the diversity of publics and political realities throughout sub-Saharan Africa. While these contexts represent profoundly diverse paths of social and political engagement, the chapters are unified by how charismatic voices promote a vision of Christian citizenship that bears significant ramifications across the political, economic and social spectrums.

Part 1 includes chapters that address how politics, the political elite and elections across sub-Saharan Africa are integral to formations of Christian citizenship. Part 2 offers a selection of chapters that consider the second integral component of Christian citizenship themes of society, economies and the public sphere. The final part offers an examination of Christian citizenship through a compilation of chapters that take on the themes of values, public beliefs and morality. While the three areas of study are interrelated distinguishing between the political, social and moral transformations encouraged by charismatic communities helps uncover the comprehensive approach advocated in church discourse towards revitalising the African state. Transformation extends far beyond the spiritual and involves an inclusive vision of society.

### Part 1: regenerating politics: nationhood, political elites and the elections

This first section assembles four essays that address the relationship between the ideal Christian citizen with politics and the political elite. Specifically, this section concerns the role of the Christian citizen in politics and how moral discourses have helped to redefine the political arena and contribute to processes of rapid social transformation. As a result Part 1 gives particular reference to the political sphere, the nation and special attention to the relationship between the political elite and the Christian citizen, as well as how Christian citizens help to shape imaginings of the state and electoral process.

The book opens with Barbara Bompani's chapter on Pentecostal-charismatic churches in Uganda and the way they performatively and creatively engage with the political. Drawing from the analysis of four churches in the capital Kampala, Bompani's work highlights how these religious bodies prophetically try to challenge the *status quo* and provide a set of orientation practices in the present in order to transform the future of the country. While the analysis of church's action and sermons clearly details an interest in shaping new moral Pentecostal citizens and new perspectives of salvation for the nation, this on the other hand highlights an exclusionary project that rejects immoral citizens from the nation-building project as well as an active intent of 'Pentecostalize' the whole community.

Chapter 1 is followed by an examination of the transformative capacity of the Nigerian Pentecostal-charismatic movement by Asonzeh Ukah. Historicizing the growth of Pentecostal-charismatic churches in Nigeria since 1999, Ukah positions religion as the primary vehicle of change throughout sub-Saharan Africa, bearing significant ramifications for African politics, society and the economy in the process. For Ukah, Nigerian Pentecostalism offers a form of political activism that transforms both civic practice and behaviour.

Following Ukah's insights on Nigeria, Emmanuel Sackey offers an analysis of the growing phenomenon of election prophecies in Ghana. The chapter examines the impact of electoral prophecies by Pentecostal-charismatic pastors on political stability. Using the prophetic declarations of Pentecostal-charismatic pastors between 2013 and 2016, Sackey argues that prophecies potentially exacerbate existing mistrust in the electoral process and identity politics.

Part 1 concludes with a chapter examining the relationship between democratisation and the growth of African charismatic and Pentecostal Christianity by Elizabeth Sheridan Sperber. Drawing on the 'Christian state' of Zambia, Sperber explores diverging visions of 'Christian citizenship' across mainline, more broadly charismatic and Pentecostal communities. Identifying the social, economic and political influence of faith-based institutions, Sperber helps demonstrate the significance of Christianity in contemporary Zambian politics as well as stretching out differences between denominations.

*Part 2: regenerating society: economies and the public sphere*

This section is a collection of three essays that examine the way charismatic discourses engage with themes of societal regeneration, the economy and public sphere. Namely Part 2 concerns the role of the good Christian citizen in strategies of economic regeneration. Charismatic discourse often positions economically prosperity as a central role of Christian citizens. As charismatic discourses have grown to include a vision for the nation the idea of economic prosperity is applied on a national level. A role of the Christian citizen is not only for individual prosperity, but to enable the nation. As a result, in charismatic circles religious belief is a central component in the ability to regenerate stagnate and dwindling economies.

Part 2 begins with an insightful examination by Kwabena Asamoah-Gyadu on Pentecostal-charismatic discourses of responsible citizenship in Ghana. Drawing on a spiritual conception of citizenship defined more by material prosperity Asamoah-Gyadu considers the implications of these increasingly dominant understandings of citizenship for the here and now. The chapter helps to bridge the narrow divide between the economic and political spheres, highlighting the fluid relationship between politics and the material and economic realms within Pentecostal-charismatic understandings of citizenship.

Caroline Valois presents a view into the economic component of Christian citizenship within Pentecostal-charismatic churches in Uganda. Drawing on a case study of a one of the largest churches in Kampala, Watoto, Valois highlights the emphasis on financial prosperity and responsibility for forging 'good' economic citizens. Arguing that economic citizenship is an integral component in a broader vision of Christian citizenship the chapter

14  *Barbara Bompani and Caroline Valois*

demonstrates how the fiscal responsibility taught at church proves an essential strategy to transforming the nation.

Part 2 concludes with an inventive examination of Pentecostals and developmental citizenship in Ethiopia by Emanuele Fantini. The chapter considers the relationship between the Pentecostal call for a national moral regeneration and the political and socio-economic transformations occurring in Ethiopia. As Asamoah-Gyadu accomplishes, Fantini uses his examination to highlight the interdependence between the political and economic in notions of Christian or developmental citizenship. Contending that Pentecostal calls for moral regeneration mirror governmental discourse on transformation, Fantini contends that the government's notion of developmental citizenship is ultimately incompatible with Pentecostal logics and works to nourish church narratives of spiritual and moral crisis.

## *Part 3: regenerating morality: values, public beliefs and morality*

The final section includes four chapters that engage with charismatic discourses and understandings of morality and values. Part 3 investigates the ways the Christian citizen has put morality and religious values at the forefront of public debate throughout sub-Saharan Africa. Eliminating immorality has served as a central element of charismatic reimaginings of the state and society. In religious discourses immorality stands as an impediment to national progress and thus relegated as a realm of concern. As a result this section engages with numerous themes immorality has come to represent throughout sub-Saharan Africa, particularly discussions that incorporate the dichotomy between what is perceived as a secular and decadent West and underlying disappointments with the post-colony.

Highlighting the interconnections between discourses centred on public morality and politics Part 3 begins with an astute examination of Zambian sexual citizenship by Adriaan van Klinken. The chapter contextualises the continuity and change in the discursive politics of sexual citizenship during two distinct periods in Zambia history. Beginning with an overview of political discourses envisioning Zambian humanism – as the national political ideology – and later the postcolonial period when Pentecostalism took on a profound public role through an ideology of Christian nationalism. In his assessment van Klinken offers a nuanced account that transcends the tendency to consider these periods through a simplistic binary.

This chapter is followed by an exploration of Pentecostal-charismatic or neo-Pentecostal understandings, historical evolution and implications for citizenship in Kenya by Gregory Deacon. In Deacon's perceptive analysis secularisation theories are inverted to unpack the nature of Christianity in Kenya. Rather than monolithic forms of Kenyan Christianity, Deacon suggests that the evolution of a 'Pentecostalized' discourse of Christianity have become bound to the nation, prompting exclusionary definitions of Kenyan citizenship within the public sphere.

Marian Burchardt follows with an ethnographic examination of Pentecostal-charismatic ethics and political subjectivity in post-apartheid South Africa. In this keen analysis modernity and citizenship are central concepts for understanding contemporary South African Pentecostalism. For Burchardt Pentecostalism both contests the more progressive politics of post-apartheid modernity – highlighted in notions of gender equality and sexual freedom – while endorsing particular notions of personhood. As a result the chapter concludes that between the boundaries of social movements and Christianity new repertories begin to emerge around the aesthetics and representations of personhood shaping contemporary South Africa.

Lastly the volume concludes with a chapter on moral citizenry in the Ugandan Pentecostal-charismatic movement by Alessandro Gusman. His account provides an analysis of movement's success, grounding it in its ability to offer alternative behavioural models of social control beyond the existing gerontocratic arrangement, while highlighting the inextricable link between the religious and political in citizenship arrangements. For Gusman Pentecostalism offers new social and political features wherein the Christian citizen learns to regulate behaviour through an ethos of individual responsibility – in order to counter the perceived moral crisis occurring in the country.

While the chapters are grounded case studies from within sub-Saharan Africa, ultimately interrogating the relationship between religion and politics is useful beyond the African context. The rise of religiously inflected moral discourses in politics have taken hold throughout the Global South as well in the Global North and has profound consequences for understanding political representation, participation, nationhood and what it means to be a citizen and feel part of a political community. Brought together those chapters make the case that understanding religious phenomena is integral to understanding current constellations of citizenship, rights and exclusion – while helping to explain the rapid social change and the rise of moral imaginings of the state beyond the sub-Saharan context.

## Notes

1 While the volume more specifically addresses Pentecostal-charismatic churches some chapters use other terminology, like Pentecostal or charismatic alone, to reflect the way the churches and/or communities under consideration self-identity. The chapters provide an overview of the significance of the Pentecostal-charismatic movement, not only on African public spheres, but other religious forms as well. The inconsistency in terminology demonstrates the limitations of more conventional definitions, the extreme diversity and indistinct boundaries of evangelical phenomena across African Christianity, while speaking to the impact religious forms have over each other.

2 Evangelical Christianity finds its origins within disparate groups of Protestant Christianity that emerged in the seventeenth and eighteenth centuries. The movement gained great momentum during the eighteenth and nineteenth centuries with the 'Great Awakenings' in the United Kingdom and North America. Evangelical

Christianity is composed by a vast umbrella of denominations that believe in the centrality of the conversion that brings salvation, in the authority of the Bible and God's revelation, and in spreading the Christian message – from which 'evangelise' and 'Evangelical Christianity'. Within this framework, since the twentieth century Pentecostals grew consistently and they are amongst the most dynamic and fast-growing groups in the Global South.

# References

Anderson, A. 2004. *An Introduction to Pentecostalism: Global Charismatic Christianity*. Cambridge: Cambridge University Press.

Anderson, A. 2014. 'The Pentecostal Gospel, Religion, and Culture in African Perspective'. In C. Clarke (Ed.) *Pentecostal Theology in Africa*. Eugene: Pickwick Publications.

Anderson, B. 1991. *Imagined Communities*. London: Verso.

Barbalet, J. 2008. *Weber, Passion and Profits: The Protestant Ethic and the Spirit Capitalism in Context*. Cambridge: Cambridge University Press.

Bartos, E. 2015. 'The Three Waves of Spiritual Renewal of the Pentecostal-charismatic Movement'. *Review of Ecumenical Studies Sibiu*, 7(1): 20–42.

Bompani, B. & Terreni Brown, S. 2015. 'A "Religious Revolution?" Print Media, Sexuality and Religious Discourse in Uganda'. *Journal of Eastern African Studies*, 9(1): 110–126.

Boyd, L. 2015. *Preaching Prevention: Born-Again Christianity and the Moral Politics of AIDS in Uganda*. Athens, OH: Ohio University Press.

Casanova, J. 2001. 'Religion, the New Millennium, and Globalization'. *Sociology of Religion*, 62(4): 415–441.

Chitando, E. & van Klinken, A. (Eds.) 2016a. *Public Religion and the Politics of Homosexuality in Africa*. Surrey: Routledge.

Chitando, E. & van Klinken, A. (Eds.) 2016b. *Christianity and Controversies Over Homosexuality in Africa*. Surrey: Routledge.

Coleman, S. 2000. *The Globalisation of Charismatic Christianity*. Cambridge: Cambridge University Press.

Comaroff, J. 2009. 'The Politics of Conviction: Faith on the Neo-liberal Frontier'. *Social Analysis*, 53(1): 17–38.

Cooper, F. 2002. *Africa Since 1940: The Past of the Present*. Cambridge: Cambridge University Press.

Cooper, F. 2014. *Citizenship Between Empire and Nation: Remaking France and French Africa, 1945–1960*. Princeton, NJ: Princeton University Press.

Cooper, M. 2015. 'The Theology of Emergency: Welfare Reform, US Foreign Aid and the Faith-Based Initiative'. *Theory, Culture and Society*, 32(2): 53–77.

Corten, A. & Marshall-Fratani, R. 2001. 'Introduction'. In A. Corten & R. Marshall-Fratani (Eds.) *Between Babel and Pentecostal: Transnational Pentecostalism in Africa and Latin America*. Bloomington: Indiana University Press.

Csordas, T. 2007. 'Global Religion and the Re-Enchantment of the World: The Case of the Catholic Charismatic Renewal'. *Anthropological Theory*, 7(9): 295–314.

Davie, G. 2010. 'Resacralization'. In B. S. Turner (Ed.) *The New Blackwell Companion to the Sociology of Religion*. Oxford: Wiley-Blackwell.

Deacon, G. & Lynch, G. 2013. 'Allowing Satan in? Moving Toward a Political Economy of Neo-Pentecostalism in Kenya'. *Journal of Religion in Africa*, 43(2): 108–130.

Droogers, A. 2001. 'Globalisation and Pentecostal Studies'. In A. Corten & R. Marshall-Fratani (Eds.) *Between Babel and Pentecostal: Transnational Pentecostalism in Africa and Latin America*. Bloomington: Indiana University Press.

Ekeh, P. 1975. 'Colonialism and the Two Publics in Africa: A Theoretical Statement'. *Comparative Studies in Society and History*, 17(1): 91–112.

Engelke, M. 2004. 'Discontinuity and the Discourse of Conversion'. *Journal of Religion in Africa*, 34(1): 82–109.

Engelke, M. 2010. 'Past Pentecostalism: Notes on Rupture, Realignment and Everyday Life in Pentecostal and African Independent Churches'. *Africa*, 80(2): 177–199.

Foucault, M. 1988. *Technologies of the Self*. Amherst: University of Massachusetts Press.

Freeman, D. 2012. 'The Pentecostal Ethic and the Spirit of Development'. In D. Freeman (Ed.) *Pentecostalism and Development: Churches, NGOs and Social Change in Africa*. Basingstoke: Palgrave Macmillan.

Gifford, P. 1994. 'Ghana's Charismatic Churches'. *Journal of Religion in Africa*, 24(3): 241–265.

Gifford, P. 1998. *African Christianity: Its Public Role*. Bloomington: Indiana University Press.

Glendon, M. 1991. *Rights Talk: The Impoverishment of Political Discourse*. New York: Free Press.

Gusman, A. 2009. 'HIV/AIDS, Pentecostal Churches, and the "Joseph Generation" in Uganda'. *Africa Today*, 56(1): 67–86.

Halisi, C. 1999. *Black Political Thought in the Making of South African Democracy*. Bloomington: Indiana University Press.

Kaoma, K. 2014. 'The Paradox and Tension of Moral Claims: Evangelical Christianity, the Politicization and Globalization of Sexual Politics in Sub-Saharan Africa'. *Critical Research on Religion*, 2(3): 227–245.

Kymlicka, W. & Norman, W. 1994. 'Return of the Citizen'. *Ethics*, 104: 352–381.

Lindhardt, M. (Ed.) 2016. *The Ways of Being Pentecostal in Latin America*. London: Lexington Books.

Mamdani, M. 1996. *Citizen and Subject: Contemporary Africa and the Legacy of Late Colonialism*. Princeton, NJ: Princeton University Press.

Marshall, R. 2009. *Political Spiritualties: The Pentecostal Revolution in Nigeria*. Chicago: University of Chicago.

Marshall, R. 2014. 'Dealing With the Prince Over Lagos: Pentecostal Arts of Citizenship'. In M. Diouf & R. Fredericks (Eds.) *The Arts of Citizenship in African Cities: Infrastructures and Spaces of Belonging*. New York: Palgrave MacMillan.

Maxwell, D. 1998. 'Delivered From the Spirit of Poverty'. *Journal of Religion in Africa*, 28(3): 350–373.

McDougall, D. 2013. 'Evangelical Public Culture: Making Stranger-Citizens in Solomon Islands'. In M. Tomlinson & D. McDougall (Eds.) *Christian Politics in Oceania*. Oxford: Berghahn Books.

Meyer, B. 1998. 'Make a Complete Break With the Past: Memory and Post-Colonial Modernity in Ghanaian Pentecostal Discourse'. *Journal of Religion in Africa*, 28(3): 316–349.

Meyer, B. 2004. 'Christianity in Africa: From African Independent to Pentecostal-charismatic Churches'. *Annual Review of Anthropology*, 33: 447–474.

Meyer, B. 2007. 'Pentecostalism and Neo-liberal Capitalism: Faith, Prosperity and Vision in African Pentecostal-charismatic Churches'. *Journal for the Study of Religion*, 20(2): 5–28.

Ndjio, B. 2012. 'Post-Colonial Histories of Sexuality: The Political Invention of a Libidinal African Straight'. *Africa*, 82(4): 609–631.

O'Neill, K. 2009. 'But Our Citizenship Is in Heaven: A Proposal for the Future Study of Christian Citizenship in the Global South'. *Citizenship Studies*, 13(4): 333–348.

O'Neill, K. 2010. *City of God: Christian Citizenship in Postwar Guatemala*. Oakland: University of California Press.

Osinulu, A. 2014. 'The Road to Redemption: Performing Pentecostal Citizenship in Lagos'. In M. Diouf & R. Fredericks (Eds.) *The Arts of Citizenship in African Cities: Infrastructures and Spaces of Belonging*. New York: Palgrave MacMillan.

Parsitau, D. 2009. 'Keep Holy Distance and Abstain Till He Comes: Interrogating a Pentecostal Church's Engagements With HIV/AIDS and the Youth in Kenya'. *Africa Today*, 56(1): 45–64.

Pew Forum. 2011. 'Christian Movements & Denominations: Global Christianity: A Report on the Size and Distribution of the World's Christian Population'. available at: www.pewforum.org/2011/12/19/global-christianity-movements-and-denominations/

Pfeiffer, J. 2004. 'Condom Social Marketing, Pentecostalism, and Structural Adjustment in Mozambique: A Clash of AIDS Prevention Messages'. *Medical Anthropology Quarterly*, 18(1): 77–103.

Robbins, J. 1998. 'On Reading World News: Apocalyptic Narrative, Negative Nationalism and Trans-National Christianity in a Papua New Guinea Society'. *Social Analysis*, 42(2): 103–130.

Robbins, J. 2004. 'The Globalization of Pentecostal and Charismatic Christianity'. *Annual Review of Anthropology*, 33: 117–143.

Robbins, J. 2007. 'Continuity Thinking and the Problem of Christian Culture'. *Current Anthropology*, 48(1): 5–38.

Synan, V. 1997. *The Holiness-Pentecostal Tradition: Charismatic Movements in the Twentieth Century*. Grand Rapids, MI: Eerdmans.

Ukah, A. 2005. 'Those Who Trade With God Never Lose: The Economies of Pentecostal Activism in Nigeria'. In T. Falola (Ed.) *Christianity and Social Change in Africa: Essays in Honor of J.D.Y. Peel*. Durham: Caroline Academic Press.

Van Dijk, R. 1998. 'Pentecostalism, Cultural Memory and the State: Contested Representations of Time in Postcolonial Malawi'. In R. Werbner (Ed.) *Memory and the Postcolony: African Anthropology and the Critique of Power*. London: Zed Books.

Van Dijk, R. 2013. 'Counselling and Pentecostal Modalities of Social Engineering of Relationships in Botswana'. *Culture, Health and Sexuality*, 15(4): 509–522.

Van Klinken, A. 2016. 'Pentecostalism, Political Masculinity and Citizenship: The Born-Again Male Subject as Key to Zambia's National Redemption'. *Journal of Religion in Africa*, 46(2–3): 129–157.

Wariboko, N. 2014. *Nigerian Pentecostalism: Rochester Studies in African History and the Diaspora*. Rochester, NY: Rochester University Press.

Yong, A. 2010. *In the Days of Caesar: Pentecostalism and Political Theology*. Grand Rapids, MI: Wm. B. Eerdmans Publishing & Co.

Part 1
# Regenerating politics
Nationhood, political elites and the elections

# 1 'Good Christians, Good Citizens'

Pentecostal-charismatic narratives of citizenship, public action and national belonging in contemporary Uganda

*Barbara Bompani*

Ugandan blogs, the Facebook pages of popular opinion-makers, Twitter handles and online newspaper fora where readers reply or comment on articles[1] are indeed valuable opportunities to observe how ordinary citizens debate, imagine, interpret and understand the state, public affairs and the future of their own country. Through the lens of Ugandan virtual life[2] it is apparent that the majority of preoccupations revolve around the prolonged failure of the State to deliver services, economic and job security, development, progress and in particular to secure a positive future for Ugandan young people (see also academic analyses such as Kobusingye 2010; Wiegratz 2010; Wiegratz 2016).[3] In this light, it is not surprising to discover that the second most popular hashtag in Uganda in 2016 was '#Ugandadecides', suggesting the sheer weight of political tweeting and discussions around the presidential elections but also concerns regarding the (mis)management and future direction of the country ('How Africa Tweets' 2016). This deep sense of dissatisfaction and preoccupation with the future is very often articulated, in virtual spaces as well as in the materiality of the everyday,[4] in terms of a lack of morality and integrity from 'corrupted and ineffective'[5] political and administrative elites. These elites do not leave much hope in terms of new, quick or straightforward solutions to the seeming impasse of the management of public affairs. This is in line with the frequently enunciated National Resistance Movement (NRM)'s rhetoric, and with many authoritative religious voices, that the nation is suffering from a lack of a strong moral fibre in order to protect its own citizens from 'immoral' dangers like corruption, greed, selfishness, lack of respect towards authority and fixed gender roles, divorce, homosexuality etc. – all dangers perceived as brought in by external Western influences attached to colonialism first and globalisation second (as will be expanded upon in the next section). These Western influences now preclude the nation (that according to this rhetoric has abandoned its own original African 'good' way of living) from flourishing and prospering.

Ultimately these rooted emotions and understandings have an impact on public action and the political imagination of a polity; and therefore need to be taken seriously by academics. What does it mean, for example, to be a citizen in a continuously underperforming African state? How do global forces, with their rapid and radical social changes brought in by neoliberal interventions,[6] shape the meaning of citizenship and a sense of national belonging for social and political communities? How do concepts such as public action and participation change across time and space? And most of all, in line with the concerns of this book, how do other spheres and actors beyond the 'purely' political participate in the construction of a sense of national belonging and citizenship when politics seems to fail to deliver? As Sanja Osha argues in his philosophical and political account *African Postcolonial Modernity* (2014), there is an urge to approach the study of political realms in new and original ways in light of the erosion of the old nation-state model and, I would like to add, in the slow erosion of trust towards the international aid assistance community,[7] taking in consideration the emergence of new actors that are shaping the political in 'non-traditional manners' (Osha 2014:7). For example, in contrast to secularist expectations that religion was retreating from the political sphere in Africa as well as in the West, academic literature has shed light on the dynamic and creative role that religion plays in the public in African countries (ter Haar & Ellis 2006; Marshall-Fratani 2009; Wariboko 2014; Ranger 2006) and how more and more religious ideas, leaders and religiously framed public action are shaping society, public policies and electoral trends (in this book, for example see Chapter 2 "Vox Dei, Vox Populi: Pentecostal Citizenship and Political Participation in Nigeria since 1999" by Asonzeh Ukah and Chapter 3 "Election Prophecies and Political Stability in Ghana" by Emmanuel Sackey). In Uganda, where religion has always been connected to the political sphere in various ways (Gifford 1998; Ward 2005), new religious actors are emerging as shapers of the political domain and producers of their own vision for the future of the country within which (religious) citizens should contribute in an active way. It is within this analytical framework that the chapter offers an analysis of Pentecostal-charismatic churches (PCCs) in Uganda as a relatively new reservoir of political creativity and a driver of citizens' public action with very specific religiously driven expectations and motivations. Moving in the space of a few decades from a publically silent religious minority[8] to a vibrant and vocal group able to influence public debates and policies, Pentecostalism, in its charismatic form, is successfully filling a vacuum in terms of providing a positive vision for the future of the country – that implies corruption, inactivity and immorality be defeated through conversion to Pentecostalism – and in publically stating solutions to address the perceived lack of morality and ethical public behaviour. It is in this light that the chapter offers an analysis of the accentuation of the 'moralisation of politics' in contemporary Uganda and provides an understanding of these new forms of 'Christian public activism' through which Pentecostal subjects are called (more than ever) to play an active role in shaping the nation and society after decades of 'secular' failures.

## Public morality and Christianity in Uganda

Not surprisingly, given their conservative theological overview, Pentecostal-charismatic public action in Uganda has been vigorous in support of morally framed campaigns and policies (Boyd 2015). For example, in the past eight years Pentecostal public interventions and battles have been strongly connected to the campaign and debates over the introduction of a new and tightened Anti-Homosexuality Bill aimed at replacing the old repressive law introduced by the British government in colonial times and severely punishing Ugandan LGBTIQ communities (Bompani & Terreni Brown 2015; Bompani 2016; Valois 2016). Similarly, Pentecostal churches were publically backing the Anti-Pornography Act that came into law in February 2014. This law was led by the Minister of Ethics and Integrity[9] Father Simon Lokodo, an ex-Catholic priest,[10] and strongly supported by the Pentecostal-charismatic community that saw in the act the possibility of better controlling public decency and morality in the country, perceived as in constant decline brought about by the increasingly secular and decadent (according to those interpretations) Global North. With the implementation of a national anti-pornography committee, the law tries to ensure "early detection, collection and destroying of pornographic materials defined as any representation through publication, exhibition, cinematography, indecent show, information technology or by whatever means, of a person engaged in real or stimulated explicit sexual activities or any representation of the sexual parts of a person for primary sexual excitement" (*New Vision* 18 February 2014). With the inclusion of the ban for women to wear short skirts, the law became known as the 'mini-skirt ban'. In a public appearance Minister Lokodo said that whenever his team arrests 'immoral people', human rights groups storm his office to ask for their release. "It is a painful fact that Uganda has lost its esteem as a God-fearing country because people have embraced with enthusiasm Western cultures that have a negative impact on our morals yet when I arrest immoral people, you talk about rights" (Minister Lokodo, The Daily Monitor 29 April 2015, Kampala). At the same event, he claimed that "rights activists have increased moral decadence" (ibid.). Pentecostal-charismatics also ferociously campaigned against the Marriage and Divorce Bill that, if passed, would cover a wide range of marriage, divorce and gender issues, including bride wealth, female circumcision and rights of cohabitating couples. The Bill caused controversy from the beginning, with some objecting to the very naming of the proposal which mentions marriage and divorce in the same breath, others arguing that it was a Bill that only favours women. A common objection was that the Bill undermined traditional and religious understandings of marriage and property relations and that ultimately it would penalise the idea of family as the core of Ugandan society. Pentecostal churches are focused on influencing the channelling of international aid and State support[11] to morally framed development and educational interventions. In fact, Pentecostal voices and campaigns frequently attack the work of secular NGOs that provide healthcare to LGBTI communities, that support birth control activities and sex education in schools' curricula (Valois 2016; Bompani 2016). For example, in her first visit to a school in 2016[12] as Education and Sport Minister Janet Museveni, considered as a sort of moral leader of the Pentecostal community in Uganda, urged the teachers to scrutinise and change the "Comprehensive Sexual Education Curriculum", in her terms defined as "containing dangerous material for the children and schools" because it "basically teaches homosexuality" (UgChristianNews 22 July 2016).

These public and highly political interventions are only the tip of the iceberg of more systematic day-to-day work of Pentecostal-charismatic communities in an attempt to fill a perceived sense of a national moral deficit. When we consider the work of those churches we always need to keep in mind their tripartite action that aims to transform at the same time the individual/self; the community/Church; and the nation perceived as an extension of the religious community. Daily efforts attempt to shape Ugandans, the Church and the country. Along with influencing politics through direct interventions, lobbying, through political connections (for example with the Museveni family through the First Lady and the President's daughter Pastor Patience Rwabogo Museveni), further work is done on a daily basis through Bible readings, cell meetings, social events, training, messages reiterated and discussed during Sunday sermons, in radio owned by Pentecostal-charismatic pastors,[13] in television programmes, in church published print and online material where morality and common goals are thoroughly articulated and through the power of praying that in Pentecostal interpretations has powerful material implications. This simultaneous three-level action clearly emerged from my analysis of the four Pentecostal-charismatic churches investigated in Kampala between 2012 and 2014.[14] The churches under analysis were: Watoto, formerly known as Kampala Pentecostal Church (KPC), with its five churches in the capital identified by their local position, Central (in Nakasero), North (in Ntinda), East (in Kazinga), South (Lubowa), West (in Kyengera) and one church in Gulu; Life Line Ministries (LLM) a much smaller affair than Watoto, situated in a low-income area of Kampala, Kinawataka, that is known in the city for its wetlands and informal settlements; Miracle Centre Cathedral (MCC) the mega church situated by the Kabaka's palace at Mengo and to the Roman Catholic Rubaga Cathedral; and Convenant Nation Church (CNC), a small but influential church situated outside of Kampala, in Bunga, a very wealthy suburb. From an analysis of those churches and their weekly work, it was evident that at the core of their action there was the preoccupation of reconnecting the entire Ugandan nation with the spiritual and the moral and guiding them towards a more prosperous and successful future. As Freston (2004) has observed, biblically the nation becomes the vehicle for reconnection with God in times of crisis and misery. In this perceived moment of degeneration and moral crisis, churches' attention seems to move away from the individual – the subject – in order to reconnect with the community – the polity.

The moralisation of the public and political spheres is not new in Uganda and it is important to understand contemporary idioms and actions within longer historical trajectories. As several authors have demonstrated (Ward 2005; Ward & Wild-Wood 2012; Peterson 2012) social transformation has always been debated in terms of moral guidance and orientating examples in the country (Peterson 2012:286) and the public sphere has always been an arena for moral judgement in times of social and political change. For example, within the perceived crisis of gender roles and 'traditional' family in the period of post-independence reconstruction, in 1964 Milton Obote appointed a commission where religious leaders were consulted to consider the laws regulating marriage and divorce (ibid 285). Even the 2014 Anti-Pornography law can be reconnected to Idi Amin's mini-skirt ban[15] issued in May 1972 (Decker 2014) when the then dictator legislated to instil discipline and morality within the framing of a new cultural nationalism that proposed specific ideas of how Ugandan women should be and perform in public. This was followed by the wig ban and, in 1975 when times became more turbulent, by the banning of makeup and skin lightener that in Amin's words were changing "the natural beauty of women" (Decker 2014:65).

In line with these historically rooted articulations, in the present religious and political leaders respond to a new profound sense of social anxieties with a new wave of public moralisation (Sadgrove et al. 2012). While Christianity has always been at the core of this morally framed public action, what Pentecostal churches are offering in contemporary Uganda is a more meticulous and proactive engagement than other churches. While also the Catholic and Anglican Church promote these morally framed public policies at different levels, their open support and public presence is considerably limited compared to Pentecostal voices while day-to-day their work within their religious communities is not as engaged and cannot be compared with the systematic project of influencing and shaping new moral citizens and their actions.[16] This can be extrapolated from a comparison of sermons and church material and activities in mainline churches and Pentecostal-charismatic churches with their transformational emphasis and focus on changing the self. Generally mainline churches are commonly perceived as less powerful in combating the devil of immorality and other evil forces that are negatively affecting the country as one of the interview testifies:

> I was born into an Anglican family and grew up in this faith. I was 27 when I embraced salvation in Jesus Christ, and this happened just a year after getting married. The reasons I left the Anglican Church were because I believed that they were not powerful enough. I had encountered the devil, and realised that the Anglican Church was not powerful enough to counteract the work of the devil. There was a battle within my heart – I saw the devil and it frightened me. It was quite terrifying. I knew then that the devil was powerful and so I was looking for a greater power to stop the devil. When I encountered the Pentecostal movement, I knew for the first time how to defeat the devil – it was none other than through Jesus Christ.[17]

Drawing from the strength derived from spectacular growth, from their success in occupying influential public spaces, from their theological urgency of combating evil forces that are forbidding the country to prosper, Pentecostal-charismatic churches are shaping Ugandan citizens in new ways and with new energies while echoing and connecting with the past.

## Becoming Christian citizens

In 2015–2016, the year preceding the Ugandan national elections, one of the most popular shared motivational flyers on Facebook discussion pages run by Pentecostal-charismatics was a motto reciting: "Changing a nation does not start with the President, it starts with the Church".[18] Although this message was shared in online Pentecostal circles beyond Uganda, it perfectly epitomises the emphasis placed on the role of the Church as a community of churchgoers in transforming the polity. So much so that for example President Museveni frequently applauds church efforts in supplementing the government "in the social and economic transformation of the country" (for example, see *New Vision*, 10 December 2012). This resonates with what is discussed in Pentecostal-charismatic churches' sermons, weekly cell and Bible meetings, church print material, religious leaders' public interventions and other spaces aimed at encouraging church members to become active transformative citizens through the lens of Pentecostalism.[19] For example, on a Sunday sermon at the Covenant Nation Church founded by Patience Rwabogo Museveni, one of the daughters of President Yoweri Museveni and frequently attended by Janet Museveni and other influential leaders, the pastor commented on the need to be 'offensive' citizens:

> It is time for us to be on the offensive. We need to send those down the valley and over the mountains. Amen. The days of us being on the defensive are over. We have a Ministry of Defense but we at CNC [Covenant Nation Church], are the Ministry of Offence. Our mandate is that we are the gatekeeper Church, we are forerunners. This is very powerful. We have been called to the nations. Those are not defensive people, those are offensive people being called to go out, to be out-goers. The Lord is very organised. He is very systematic. It is one step at a time, he opens our eyes. He gives us a vision. Then the mission is how to get to that vision.[20]

The formulation of this new political theology of (offensive) action attests to a significant turn in Ugandan Pentecostalism that only recently, over the past decade, moved from being a publically silent community, to a vocal and influential one with the ambition to change the whole nation. This sheds light on an important change. If past analyses defined Pentecostalism as concerned with individuality (for example Martin 2002; Corten & Fratani 2001; Maxwell 1998; Comaroff & Comaroff 2000),[21] it is clear that the Ugandan Pentecostal imaginary and actions has evolved and recently moved away from the individual to the political community, from the microsite of single bodies to the macro-politics of the social body as Nimi Wariboko similarly wrote in relation to the Nigerian context (2014:113). In Ugandan Pentecostal's view, the perceived sense of degeneration, corruption, immorality and lack of progress testifies that evil forces hold sway over the collective and this therefore requires new forms of action and public interventions over the polity. Corrupted powers, in Pentecostal understandings, influence and erode the spiritual and material life of the community (Wariboko 2014:146). Politics, being a force, is related to the spiritual dimension. Therefore, changing the political sphere (an extremely powerful force) requires a collective effort.

Through the testimonies collected in religious sites, one is left with little doubt that the Devil is tirelessly working to appropriate the Ugandan spheres of power and it is in this warfare against malevolent forces that Pentecostal citizens are called to battle in order to regain the space potentially corrupted and corrupt by political engagement.

> It is time for us to enter the territory of our worship. This is warfare. How many of you know about airspace? The Central Aviation Authority requires that you tell them of your whereabouts and when you are entering different nation's airspace. This is an international requirement. And every country in the world has specific spots where you can't fly over – like here, you can't fly over State House and in America it's the White House and in Britain you can't fly over Buckingham Palace. Let me tell you – this place [Uganda] is a no fly zone for the devil! You and me have the capacity to tell the devil – this is a no fly zone! I really want to tell you guys that when you get back to your homes and offices, make it, tell the devil, this is a no fly zone![22]

This new concern for the 'body of the nation' calls for action and causes a sense of theological urgency in fighting corrupt forces that manifest in material ways in the public with the intent to affect the divine project of converting Uganda into a godly, and therefore functional, country. Mostly, converting the nation becomes a necessity against the dominant evil of immorality (as outlined in the previous section) which is paralysing the country against which no other intervention has worked so far. "If we put Jesus in this nation, we will be sorted! We will have no corruption".[23] But it is also a necessity in biblical terms if the country wants to reconcile with the divine (O'Neill 2010). In these new interpretations, the effort of saving Uganda takes place at the intersection between Christianity and politics in the way public participation is shaped through the lens of Pentecostal understandings. Pentecostal-charismatic congregants constantly work through Christianity to interpret and make sense of the everyday; therefore, they interpret politics and social realms through Pentecostal-charismatic lenses and they define and perform their same citizenship through Christianity. Being Ugandan citizens comes through being Pentecostals. In this imaginary, the nation becomes a projection, an extension, of the religious community, of the Church. It is not sufficient to reach personal salvation in this new Pentecostal dispensation. Personal salvation can only be reached through national salvation with the nation becoming an extension of the Church and a sum of the individualities.

Although the postcolonial state has not fully delivered its promises of progress and advancement for everyone, nonetheless full citizenship can be realised through the Holy Spirit. Through the blood of Christ, there will not be second-class citizens, but a community of moral and saved subjects. In this way, Pentecostalism in Uganda not only formulates a critique of the nation-state from the holy position of Christian citizens (Robbins 1998), but actively produces citizens involved in finding Christian solutions to address those societal problems and fight evil powers. These new moral citizens will obey the law, pay taxes, be good neighbours, work for the common good of the community, become new incorruptible leaders. "Let me say that being a good abiding citizen means to teach others moral values, to give to church, to give taxes to the country, to pay heed to the leaders. Good governance comes from the Lord, so if you're a Christian then you will be a good citizen, and have a good country".[24]

This change towards a strategy of collective action does not come through a contestation of the existing political structures, as for example political parties, but through the Pentecostal idea of transformation and domination of the self (Coleman 2004). There is no need to introduce new political institutions, new development interventions and new alliances with the Global North; change can take place from within and throughout the Ugandan people. Through the transformation of people into trustworthy, hardworking and morally impeccable Christian agents, Pentecostalism becomes a secure and reassuring coherent political project. Forging highly moral citizens equipped to address the battle against evil powers that try to appropriate the country is the way forward. This leads to spiritually shaped action as one of the participants explained: "The church has teachings about how to be a good citizen, and if we are all like this, then we can be a better country together. We can build for a better future on these Christian teachings".[25]

Indeed, Pentecostals are frequently represented and discussed in the public as 'moral agents' who can be trusted and who can deliver. For example, in an interview a Ugandan journalist noted:

> There is a crop of Pentecostal women in particular who are very keen on these churches. It offers them something that the traditional churches [meant as mainline churches] cannot offer, and perhaps that is something to do with support for women in positions of leadership. There is Allen Kagina, Ondoa, Musisi. There is an increasing belief that these people [Pentecostals] can be looked to get things done, but they can get things moving, especially because they are seen as trustworthy people.[26]

And again: "there is an increasing belief that public service offices should be occupied by born-agains [Pentecostals]. It has happened hugely at the Uganda Revenue Authority. The president is convinced that born-again people do not steal".[27]

It is in this way that Pentecostal individual stories of positive transformation are used to show how individual experiences can transcend into the collective with Pentecostalism providing spiritual and physical healing at an individual as well as at a collective level. The subjective break with the past, so central to Pentecostal theology (Meyer 1998), transmutes into a break for the entire unity of citizens. The only way ahead is 'winning the country for Jesus through the Holy Spirit' and transforming Uganda into a Pentecostal nation through its citizens:

> The Lord spoke to me. He said that the Uganda which is going to fulfil its destiny and inherit all its promises is not the Uganda you are seeing right now [. . .] The Lord said that the Uganda will be a nation that is reborn [Pentecostal]. He showed me that being born again [Pentecostal], that experience which we think is limited to an individual can be stretched to a nation, a nation can be reborn can be born again. Uganda will be an Uganda that will be born again.
>
> [Pentecostal][28]

These new Pentecostal aspirations are not merely shaping debates around the best way to govern the country (Robbins in Tomlinson & McDougall 2013:198), but they create a framework for action – an aggressive action as Comaroff (2009) would say. Through individuals working on the self and the community on the collective, Pentecostal citizens work to reconquest the public from evil forces. Churches work in several ways and at several levels on the transformation of the congregants (Bompani 2016), while most of them also run programmes to shape the leaders of the future. For example, Watoto runs the School of Community Leadership, a leadership course to become professionals with a Christian ethos and influence local communities accordingly. The course is specifically designed for leaders and professionals in corporate organisations, government, NGOs and church. There are also specialised external training institutions not directly connected to churches but run by famous Pentecostal-charismatic figures. Examples of training agencies that form future leaders within Pentecostal teaching are: Development Associates, SALT (Sundoulous African Leadership Training), Intercessors For Uganda, Acamai Global Workplace Fellowship and Destiny Consult. These provide workshops, long courses, CPDs and even master programmes. At Destiny Consult the Executive Director and founder Dorothy Kisaka[29] explained that they always invite famous Pentecostals as guest speakers to their trainings, as for example the first lady Janet Museveni, the past Commissioner General of Uganda Revenue Authority, Allen Kagina, ex Health Minister Christine Ondoa and the then deputy Inspector General of Government (*IGG*) designate, George Bamugemereire. Those speakers share with the participants 'desirable leadership traits, etiquette and service-based leadership among others'. In an interview Dorothy Kisaka said:

> I see Destiny Consult as a major contributor to transforming Uganda, and transforming the lives of Ugandans. I believe Destiny Consult can transform the thinking of Ugandans, the thinking that drives the actions, that drives what we do. We can bring a transformation to how we dispose of garbage, to how we see the curriculum for children, to . . .

we have so many different professionals that come to us, that we can influence every sphere of Ugandan life. I want to align what we receive from the word [biblical text, God's teaching] to affect the world view on everything, including on family life, and money, time management, and economic issues. If a person's world view is not affected by the 'word' then their view of the world is not a force for good. Christians shall do what the bible teaches and we need to translate the "word", we need to know the word so that we can steward our nation.[30]

Influencing the leaders of tomorrow, according to Pentecostal dispensations, is part of the military strategy of moralisation and purification of the public. But also, displaying power through relevant connections, for example through pastors displaying strict relations with the Museveni family and the ruling party, businessmen and successful and recognisable society members, through famous congregants or sermon givers, are all strategies of affirmation of victory and continuous advancement of the holy forces on the corrupted and polluted public space. While it is not clear yet whether this battle will be successful (in Pentecostal terms), there are and will remain clear and far-reaching implications for the Ugandan political and social spheres. These implications deserve further academic attention. Ugandan Pentecostalism offers a realm of political creativity in which Christian citizens can have agency to forge not only their own futures, but those of others.

## Conclusion

This chapter recounts a specific story in terms of the impact that Pentecostal-charismatic Christianity in contemporary Uganda is having on the public and political spheres and on the way, at an individual level, it is shaping new interpretations and expectations of the (Christian) role that citizens should play to shape and re-appropriate their own future.

Against a climax of ontological insecurity, these religious communities seem to offer not only the security of the Holy Spirit, protection and a reassuring moral order, but also directions towards a more prosperous future. This is an ontological passage that allows citizens to move away from a sense of 'impotence and dissatisfaction' to a sense of possibility, agency and hope in positive change. With the framing of a new *Homo Civicus*, a responsible and moral citizen, Pentecostalism provides new possibilities for reconnecting the individual to the national project and feeling a part of and a belonging to the political community. This has implications in understanding ideas of citizenship and public action in contemporary African contexts where neoliberal interventions and prolonged state failures have eroded a sense of public participation and the engagement of individuals with the state.

Nonetheless this reaffirmed sense of belonging to a polity comes after working on the self, to become ethically sound Pentecostal subjects, and therefore there is a concurrent exclusionary process that removes non-moral citizens from the national project. Actively excluding and opposing actors,[31] like LGBTI communities, from the construction of nationhood because they do not conform to the overall teleological project implicit to a specific religious understanding is something quite different from the general inclusive interpretation of democratic citizenship.

While in Pentecostal-charismatic communities this is not in opposition with their own understanding of progress, empowerment and nationhood, this clashes with other more widely shared and secular, or religious but not Pentecostal, perceptions that also shaped the origins of the postcolonial African state. There are therefore implications not only for those who are excluded, but also for actors, local, national and international, whose worldview is avowedly different.

## Notes

1 In Uganda, online replies and comments to newspaper articles are picked up and discussed by very popular radio programmes many of whom are owned by the same newspapers. Therefore, those virtual debates have a longer lifespan and impact than their presence in blogs and online discussion fora (Bompani & Terreni Brown 2015).
2 Although it has been argued that access to internet is filtered through variables as wealth, ownership of smartphones and computers, access to coffee-shops and being based in urban environments, nonetheless research shows that there are 11.9 million internet users in Uganda, a 34% penetration rate, and that mobile phone access is of 62% ('How Africa Tweets' 2016). Furthermore, in East Africa universal access funds are being used to extend modern Information and Communication Technology (ICT) services to rural and remote areas (ibid).
3 Particularly important in an extremely 'young' country where children below 18 years constitute 55% of the population while Youths (persons between 18 and 30 years) constitutes 23% of the entire population (according to the 2014 Census; Uganda Bureau of Statistics, available at: www.ubos.org/2016/03/24/census-2014-final-results/).
4 Fieldwork observations, Kampala, 2012–2014.
5 Ibid., but also from online comments and debates.
6 For the case of Uganda and the impact of rapid social changes brought to society by neoliberal reforms, please see Wiegratz (2016), Wiegratz (2010) and Bompani (2017 forthcoming).
7 From fieldwork and an analysis of media and mass media, it is apparent that the hope that international development interventions from the West could bring Uganda out of poverty and underperformance is starting to erode. For many Ugandan church leaders Christians must confront the social and economic hardships facing the nation, and stop looking to foreign donors (fieldwork notes, 2012–2014, Kampala).
8 Historically the Ugandan public sphere was dominated by the Anglican and the Catholic church (see for example Gifford 1998; Ward 2005). In the past two decades, this sphere of influence has been altered by the growing public influence of PCCs and their connection with key public position and politics (see for example Bompani & Terreni Brown 2015).
9 A ministry in its origins started to defeat corruption in the country, now a hub to supervise 'immoral' and 'sinful' public attitudes.
10 He was excommunicated by Pope Benedict XVI when he entered politics in 2009. His predecessor in the Ministry was James Nsaba Buturo, a publically well-known Pentecostal-charismatic.

11 The same growth of Pentecostal-charismatic Christianity in Uganda can be partially explained through their developmental work in support of morally framed HIV/AIDS prevention and treatment work. In fact, due to increased international development funding towards Faith-Based Organisations (FBOs) from the 90s onwards, PCCs found a way to flourish in contemporary Uganda. For further analysis on this topic see Cooper (2015); Patterson (2011); Boyd (2015) and Valois (unpublished PhD thesis).
12 The school was senior secondary St. Peters S.S.S Nsambya in Kampala.
13 In 2011 there were 276 radios registered in Uganda; amongst these ones 37 were registered as religious radios while all of them were featuring religiously framed debates and hosting religious leaders in programmes at some point (SPRA research project, Centre of African Studies, the University of Edinburgh, 2012–2014).
14 Leverhulme Trust funded research project 'Sexuality, Politics and Religion in Africa' (SPRA), Centre of African Studies, the University of Edinburgh, 2012–2014.
15 Defined as any dress with a hemline that rose "5.08 centimetres above the upper edge of the patella" (Tamale 2016).
16 Fieldwork observations, Kampala, 2012–2014.
17 Interview with George, congregation member, Covenant Nation Church, Kampala, 23 May 2013.
18 Online debates in Ugandan Pentecostal-charismatics fora, 2015–2016, personal observation.
19 Fieldwork observation, Kampala, 2012–2014.
20 Covenant Nation Church pastor, 17 February 2013, Kampala.
21 For example, Gregory Deacon highlighted how this was usually put in contrast with perceptions of Islam as representing collective notions of global homogeneity in which the individual is subsumed and submits (Deacon 2015).
22 Pastor Stephen Asiimwe, Covenant Nation Church, Kampala, 16 June 2013.
23 Pastor Calvin, Watoto Central, Kampala, 11 May 2013.
24 Interview with Jacob, Life Line Ministries, aged 27, Kampala, 1 February 2013, Kampala.
25 Interview with Sarah, Watoto, 30 November 2012, Kampala.
26 Interview with reporter and online editor of *The Independent* magazine, 24 May 2013, Kampala.
27 Interview with one of the directors, *Red Pepper*, 10 June 2013, Kampala.
28 Patience R. Museveni, 24 March 2013, Kampala.
29 Dorothy Kisaka is also a lawyer and, at the time of the interview, a Commissioner at the Electoral Commission, as well as occasionally pastoring at the Deliverance Church at Makerere University.
30 Interview with Dorothy Kisaka, June 2013, Kampala.
31 Certain PC churches stated that they would re-integrate LGBTI people after repentance and following a right path for reintegration; many churches excluded any kind of dialogue and openness towards LGBTI people perceived as forever-corrupted and polluted evil agents that will remain extremely dangerous to the religious community. There are also a very few and non-vocal PCCs that do not discriminate same-sex minorities; but those remain an extremely limited minority and they do not promote this stance publically.

# References

Bompani, B. 2016. 'For God and for My Country: Pentecostal-charismatic Churches and the Framing of a New Political Discourse in Uganda'. In E. Chitando & A. van Klinken (Eds.) *Public Religion and the Politics of Homosexuality in Africa*. Surrey: Routledge: 19–34.

Bompani, B. 2017. forthcoming. 'Religious Economies: Pentecostal-charismatic Churches and the Framing of a New Moral Order in the Neo-Liberal Ugandan State'. In J. Wiegratz, G. Martiniello & E. Greco (Eds.) *Uganda: The Political Economy of State and Capital After 1986*. London: ZedBooks.

Bompani, B. & Terreni Brown, S. 2015. 'A "Religious Revolution?" Print Media, Sexuality and Religious Discourse in Uganda'. *Journal of Eastern African Studies*, 9(1): 110–126.

Boyd, L. 2015. *Preaching Prevention: Born-Again Christianity and the Moral Politics of AIDS in Uganda*. Athens, OH: Ohio University Press.

Coleman, S. 2004. 'The Charismatic Gift'. *The Journal of the Royal Anthropological Institute*, 10(2): 421–442.

Comaroff, J. 2009. 'The Politics of Conviction: Faith on the Neo-Liberal Frontier'. *Social Analysis*, 53(1): 17–38.

Comaroff, J. & Comaroff, J. 2000. 'Occult Economies and the Violence of Abstraction: Notes From the South African Postcolony'. *American Ethnologist*, 26(2): 279–303.

Cooper, M. 2015. 'The Theology of Emergency: Welfare Reform, US Foreign Aid and the Faith-Based Initiative'. *Theory, Culture and Society*, 32(2): 53–77.

Corten, A. & Fratani, R. 2001. *Between Babel and Pentecost: Transnational Pentecostalism in Africa and Latin America*. Bloomington: Indiana University Press.

*The Daily Monitor*. 'Lokodo Accuses Rights Activists of Abetting Immorality'. 29 April 2015. Available at: www.monitor.co.ug/News/National/Lokodo-accuses-rights-activists-of-abetting-immorality/688334-2700400-1bvawtz/index.html

Deacon, G. 2015. 'Kenya, a Nation Born-Again'. *Penteco Studies: An Interdisciplinary Journal for Research on the Pentecostal and Charismatic Movements*, 14(2): 219–240. doi:10.1558/ptcs.v14i2.25966

Decker, A. C. 2014. *Idi Amin's Shadow: Women, Gender and Militarism in Uganda*. Athens, OH: Ohio University Press.

Freston, P. 2004. *Evangelicals and Politics in Asia, Africa and Latin America*. Cambridge: Cambridge University Press.

Gifford, P. 1998. *African Christianity: Its Public Role*. Indianapolis: Indiana University Press.

'How Africa Tweets'. Portland PR Limited. 2016. Available at: www.howafricatweets.com/

Kobusingye, O. 2010. *The Correct Line: Uganda Under Museveni*. Milton Keynes: AuthorHouse.

Marshall-Fratani, R. 2009. *Political Spiritualties: The Pentecostal Revolution in Nigeria*. Chicago: University of Chicago Press.

Martin, D. 2002. *Pentecostalism: The World Their Parish*. Oxford: Blackwell.

Maxwell, D. 1998. 'Delivered From the Spirit of Poverty'. *Journal of Religion in Africa*, 28(3): 350–373.

Meyer, B. 1998. 'Make a Complete Break With the Past: Memory and Post-Colonial Modernity in Ghanaian Pentecostal Discourse'. *Journal of Religion in Africa*, 28(3): 16–49.

*New Vision*. 'Uganda Bans Miniskirts'. 18 February 2014. Available at: www.newvision.co.ug/new_vision/news/1337826/uganda-bans-miniskirts-pornography

O'Neill, K. L. 2010. *City of God: Christian Citizenship in Postwar Guatemala*. Berkeley: University of California Press.

Osha, S. 2014. *African Postcolonial Modernity: Informal Subjectivities and the Democratic Consensus*. New York: Palgrave MacMillan.

Patterson, A. S. 2011. *The Church and AIDS in Africa: The Politics of Ambiguity.* Boulder: Lynne Rienner.

Peterson, D. R. 2012. *Ethnic Patriotism and the East African Revival: A History of Dissent.* Cambridge: Cambridge University Press.

Ranger, T. (Ed.) 2006. *Evangelical Christianity and Democracy in Africa.* Oxford: Oxford University Press.

Robbins, J. 1998. 'On Reading "World News": Apocalyptic Narrative, Negative Nationalism and Transnational Christianity in Papua New Guinea Society'. *Social Analysis,* 42(2): 103–130.

Robbins, J. 2013. 'Why Is There No Political Theology Among the Urapmin? On Diarchy, Sects as Big as Society and the Diversity of Pentecostal Politics'. In M. Tomlinson & D. McDougall (Eds.) *Christian Politics in Oceania.* New York: Berghahn Books: 198–210.

Sadgrove, J., Vanderbeck, R. M., Andersson, J., Valentine, G. & Ward, K. 2012. 'Morality Plays and Money Matters: Towards a Situated Understanding of the Politics of Homosexuality in Uganda. *The Journal of Modern African Studies,* 50(1): 103–129.

Tamale, S. 2016. ' "Profile: Keep Your Eyes off My Thighs": A Feminist Analysis of Uganda's "Miniskirt Law" '. *Feminist Africa,* 21: 83–90.

Ter Haar, G. & Ellis, S. 2006. *Worlds of Power: Religious Thought and Political Practice in Africa.* New York: Oxford University Press.

*UgChristianNews.* 'Janet Museveni on a Fact-Finding Mission in the Sex Education Curriculum'. 22 July 2016. Available at: http://ugchristiannews.com/education-minister-janet-museveni-on-a-fact-finding-mission-in-the-sexual-education-curriculum/

Valois, C. 2015. 'Public Rebirth: Pentecostal-charismatic Christianity, Sexuality, Public Health & Nation Building in Uganda'. unpublished PhD thesis, Edinburgh: The University of Edinburgh.

Valois, C. 2016. 'Scandal Makers: Competition in the Religious Market Among Pentecostal-charismatic Churches'. In E. Chitando & A. van Klinken (Eds.) *Christianity and Controversies Over Homosexuality in Africa.* Surrey: Routledge: 38–50.

Ward, K. 2005. 'Eating and Sharing: Church and State in Uganda'. *Journal of Anglican Studies,* 3(1): 99–119.

Ward, K. & Wild-Wood, E. (Eds.) 2012. *The East African Revival: History and Legacies.* London: Ashgate.

Wariboko, N. 2014. *Nigerian Pentecostalism: Rochester Studies in African History and the Diaspora.* Rochester, NY: Rochester University Press.

Wiegratz, J. 2010. 'Fake Capitalism? The Dynamics of Neoliberal Moral Restructuring and Pseudo-Development: The Case of Uganda'. *Review of African Political Economy,* 37(124): 123–137.

Wiegratz, J. 2016. *Neoliberal Moral Economy Capitalism, Socio-Cultural Change and Fraud in Uganda.* London: Rowman & Littlefield International.

# 2 Vox Dei, Vox Populi

Pentecostal citizenship and political participation in Nigeria since 1999

*Asonzeh Ukah*

Religion, rather than economics or politics, presents vastly compelling and complexly layered terrains for the study of change in contemporary Africa.[1] In the last five years, the pervasive 'Africa Rising' narrative, championed by some members of Africa's political elite and their Western partners and reinforced, largely, by Western media outlets, postulates that Africa is rapidly transforming from an ostensible dark continent of wars, diseases and poverty to one of hope and economic empowerment. Based on a set of statistics of growth in international trade and gross domestic product (see Pillay 2015), the 'Africa Rising' narrative focuses on the export of natural resources and growth of the consumerist middle class as signs of hope and aspiration for the continent (Beresford 2016; Taylor 2016). The unstated assumption of this narrative is that the economy is the bedrock of Africa's transformation.

However, it may be argued that the most profound vector of change in Africa in the past 150 years, has been religion, not economics or politics. Notably, no continent has virtually abandoned its indigenous religious cultures and epistemological systems of producing and organising knowledge as Africa has done, in as short a time. In 1900, roughly 5% of Africans were Christian; in 2010, nearly 53% of a population of 1.1 billion Africans is Christian. (Jacobsen 2011:157–160). According to Douglas Jacobsen (2011:163), "Never before has Christianity expanded so quickly in any region of the world. . . . More than half the countries in Sub-Saharan Africa now have Christian majorities". Two primary sources of religious conversions in Africa are evangelism and population growth; Christians have been very active – and in some instances, aggressive – in recruiting non-Christians, and "Christian mothers having lots and lots of Christian children" (Jacobsen 2011:165). In 1900, Catholics made up about 50% of Africa's seven million Christians; Orthodox Church membership had about 25%; the remaining 25% going to protestant congregations, with Pentecostal Christians and members of African Independent Churches (AICs), almost, nonexistent. The situation is very different in 2016 when Pentecostal Christians constitute between 10–13% of African Christians while the AICs are approximately 30% of African Christians; sub-Saharan Africa is projected to have the largest Christian population growth between 2010 and 2050 (see: Pew

Research Center 2011:9; 54–55; 2015:61; 63). This changing religious profile of Africa has great consequences and ramifications for politics, society and the economy as this chapter will argue.

The success of Pentecostal-charismatic Christianity that is spreading in Africa since the 1970s, more than any other religious group before or after it, promises to revolutionise the continent. The promises of hope in the heart of Pentecostal ideology and activism have (mis)led some scholars to characterise the dizzying waves of conversion and social effervescence in a country like Nigeria as a "revolution" (Gaiya 2002; Burgess 2008; Marshall 2009). While the revolutionary potential of African Pentecostalism in its person-centred theology is not in doubt (see Yong 2010; Wariboko 2014), the capacity to practically, concretely and positively transform society is what demands critical assessment. Again, for many reasons, Nigeria offers a unique case study of the complex dynamics of Pentecostal conversions and political engagement. A distinctive factor is its huge and multifarious Christian population; of the more than 80 million Christians in Nigeria, between 10 and 15% – that is, 8–12 million Christians – is Pentecostal. With an equally large population of non-Christians in Nigeria, particularly, Muslims, the social and political environments offer opportunities for active engagement and often aggressive competition for resources and social presence for all groups. If Pentecostalism is a 'revolution' in the narrative practices of ways of being religious and Nigerian, then, it is possible to describe in what ways Pentecostal political activism has altered and transformed – positively or otherwise – the political practice and behaviour, aside from introducing a new language of political praxis. Although Sam Krinsky (2006:8), rightly, observes that "little is known about what effects, both real and potential, Pentecostalism is having on African lives and societies", a decade and a half of active political engagement of Nigerian Pentecostals in high political positions indicate palpable patterns and paradigms.

## Political and economic shockwaves: 1970–1998

From the 1970s, Nigerian 'born-again' movements evolved as a hegemonic project competing for conversions, public visibility and space, but also a vision of how to restructure and develop the postcolonial state. Pentecostal political ideology analysed the state and promised a "grand ruptural movement" (Peel 2016:198). Offering a vision for the future and a "program of thoroughgoing modernization" (Krinsky 2006:10), Pentecostal political theology identified causes of underdevelopment as well as sources of social and economic malaise, in the nation-state. Judeo-Christian scripture offered leaders of the movement a platform for reflection and hope: "When the righteous are in authority, the people rejoice; but when a wicked man rules, the people groan" (Prov. 29: 2, NKJV). The oil-boom era of the mid-1970s was a critical period of Pentecostal incursion into the political arena. The military government, under Olusegun Obasanjo, and its efforts to stage the Second World Black and African Festival of Arts and Culture in 1977

(FESTAC '77) ushered in a Pentecostal political critique of state public policy as designed and directed towards the worship of the devil. Officially, FESTAC '77 was designed to promote the country's newfound oil wealth, showcase indigenous traditions, theatre and cultures; demonstrate the developmental capacity of the nation as well as make "Nigeria the locus for production of knowledge on issues relevant to the black and African world" (Falola & Heaton 2008:194). According to the Pentecostal discourse at the time, spearheaded by a few educated leaders mainly from the southwestern Nigeria, the cause and curse of underdevelopment in the country were the government's "showcasing of idolatrous culture in the name of national pride" (Peel 2016:199; Ukah 2008:119–120). Pentecostal practice and public behaviour during this period were about the conversion of the individual believer and steering of the nation towards 'proper' worship of God. The principal public enemy, for the Pentecostal community, was indigenous religions, reviled as idolatry or the worship of the devil. Many components of Nigerian civil society at the time scrutinised the FESTAC '77 events based on mismanagement of public resources, poorly executed public works, corruption and lack of accountability by public officers. However, the Pentecostal community focused, not on any of these elements, but on framing the event as a disguise for the worship of the devil.

Pentecostal public theology underwent a sharp change in the following decade with the introduction of austerity measures precipitated by two unexpected events. The first was the crash of oil prices in 1979, after a period of high oil prices occasioned by the 1973 Yom Kippur War and the 1976 Iranian Revolution. "When petroleum prices dropped between 1976 and 1979, and again during the oil glut years of the early 1980s, the Nigerian economy suffered greatly" (Falola & Heaton 2008:183). In 1986, the military presidency of Ibrahim Babangida instituted the infamous Structural Adjustment Programme, designed by the International Monetary Fund (IMF) and the World Bank to rein in state expenditure, deregulate the economy and downsize public service. The harsh economic environment of the late 1980s, with massive graduate unemployment, stimulated a rapid growth or expansion of Pentecostal churches and ministries through young university-educated individuals who laid claim to different types of spiritual gifts such as healing and deliverance, performance of miracles of wealth and success, and prophetic utterances and guidance. Nigeria's National Mass Communication Policy of 1990 which, effectively, liberalised the media industry is of import, too, since it greatly enhanced the public advertisement and dissemination of religious events, some of which were held in public arenas, like stadia and university campuses. During the late 1980s and early 1990s, there was a clear shift of focus in theology and practice from personal sanctification and ascetic self-discipline – being 'born-again' – to material markers of salvation through this-worldly accumulation and consumption. The oppressive and coercive military dictatorships of Ibrahim Babangida (1985–1993) and Sani Abacha (1993–1998) foreclosed active political engagements by the citizens and civil society organisations.

Arguably, the economic crisis and military strangulation of the society were highly significant in shaping a strong Pentecostal apolitical position, until 1999.[2] Following the sudden death of Sani Abacha, on 8 June 1998, a prominent Nigerian religious leader, Enoch Adeboye, declared it a Pentecostal miracle and a "New Year", in the middle of the year, for the country. The mass jubilation that followed Abacha's death was reinforced by a claim that Adeboye had prophesied such a tidal shift in the nation's political future and fortunes, three days earlier (Ukah 2008:199–200). Adeboye, arguably, the most popular Nigerian Pentecostal leader, asseverates that the erasure of Abacha was a consequence of his prayers for a restoration of the nation's high destiny. Nigeria, the Pentecostal hubris insists, would be great again in manifesting the power of God to the rest of the world, a course that would have been impossible with Abacha alive and in power. In late 1998, Pentecostalism triumphantly promised the Nigerian public a pathway to individual and collective salvation based on righteous power that will make the nation great in the eyes of God and in the comity of nations.

## The Pentecostal messiah: Olusegun Obasanjo's second coming (1999–2007)

Following the release of Olusegun Obasanjo (b. 5 March 1937) from prison on 16 June 1998, Pentecostal apolitical stance experienced a shift towards activism. Significantly, Obasanjo was imprisoned on 28 February 1995, by the Abacha dictatorship for his alleged involvement in a phoney coup attempt. His sentence was, initially, for life but, following the intervention of Nelson Mandela, Helmut Schmidt and Jimmy Carter, commuted to 15 years. While in prison, Obasanjo claimed to have received a new spiritual experience of the 'born-again' type and ordained by God as a pastor. As a demonstration of his newfound faith, Obasanjo, a Baptist Christian, moved from one Pentecostal church to another in celebration of his survival of prison life. Mainstream Pentecostal leaders and organisations as well as the Christian Association of Nigeria (CAN) (under the leadership of Primate Sunday Mbang), collectively adopted and endorsed Obasanjo as a born-again political personality (Ojo 2010:44–48). From 1998 onwards (and following in the footsteps of the *Aladura* churches (see Ojo 2006:183), prophecies and revelations publicised by Pentecostal leaders became an important political discourse to chart a new future and fortune for the country. Additionally, such political prophecies were pathways of courting the emerging political class jostling for active engagement in the soon to be inaugurated Fourth Republic. Political entrepreneurs – like risk takers, generally – are drawn to prying into the future and so, Pentecostal political prophecy soon became veritable instruments of political permutation.[3]

Adopted by the Pentecostal community and bankrolled by the military, Obasanjo easily won the February 1999 presidential election. The relationship between Obasanjo and the Pentecostal community in Nigeria before and during his eight-year administration was a very complex and tenuous one. He was a (lapsed) Baptist Christian who was unapologetic about his moral and social conduct. His post-prison narrative about incarceration and survival of the draconian Abacha regime, inevitably, led to an increase of pious ardour. Surviving the draconian Abacha regime gave Obasanjo a renewed purpose in life; God, he reasoned, must have *saved* him for a higher destiny. In that political milieu, especially with the military eager to relinquish power to a trusted insider, Obasanjo was the most likely candidate, being a former military general from the same ethnicity as Moshood K. Abiola, the presumed winner of the annulled 1993 presidential election. The clamour, particularly from southwestern Nigeria, was that the election of 12 June 1993 and the mandate presumptively given to Abiola by the Nigerian electorate be "actualised", albeit indirectly. According to Julius Adekunle (2009:10), "electing a Yoruba in the 1999 presidential election seemed to be a reasonable compromise". Obasanjo supported the annulment of the 1993 presidential election and became a direct beneficiary. He had maintained that Abiola was not the messiah Nigeria needed.

Interpreted as the fulfilment of Pentecostal prayers and prophecies, Obasanjo's victory of 1999 was a validation of Pentecostal political activism and a test of what Pentecostal citizenship could mean or do for the nation. It meant the salvation and redirection of the nation towards achieving its lofty destiny. In essence, the divine choice of a leader has been validated through the ballot box. The euphoria following this event pointed to the symbolic, affective attachment and values as well as the legal responsibility which the Pentecostal community claimed to have for Nigeria as a country. Henceforth, Pentecostals believed that loyalty to God implies active participation in politics and the public life of society.

As a president, even when his aides tried rebranding him as "the father of the nation", Obasanjo left no one in any doubt that he was the 'born-again' Yoruba president from southwestern Nigeria. His self-advertisement as a "Christian" president created so much resentment among some Pentecostals and non-Pentecostals who felt he was neglecting to be a president for all Nigerians (irrespective of religio-ethnic affiliation) in preference to running a "Pentecostal presidency" in cohort with an emergent theocratic class (Obadare 2006). It is against this background that the utterances and activities of Tunde Bakare, another Pentecostal leader and founder of Latter Rain Assembly, in Lagos, are situated. Tunde Bakare (b. 11 November 1954),[4] former Muslim-turned-Christian, and former-lawyer-turned-pastor, made his now (in)famous prophetic proclamation that Obasanjo was not the country's "messiah". Rather, Bakare likened Obasanjo to "King Agag" with a prophetic axe dangling over his head.[5] Bakare's political prognostications raised prolonged public furore; he was arrested, detained briefly and released. His fellow Pentecostal pastors, most of whom were seeking political visibility, recognition, and easy money from political and the military classes, came heavily against him (Ojo 2008:112; 2010:14; Onuoha 2013:217). The Pentecostal Fellowship of Nigeria (PFN),[6] through its erstwhile President, Bishop Mike Okonkwo, dissociated itself from Bakare and his prophecy. However, one year into Obasanjo's second term in office, Bakare's vision started gathering popular support. On 31 January 2011, Bakare announced he would be running for office as a vice-presidential candidate to Muhammadu Buhari, on the platform of the Congress of Progressive Change political party. Buhari lost that election to Goodluck Jonathan, of the PDP, who got 58.89% of votes.

Tunde Bakare represents a distinctive Pentecostal conception of Christian citizenship in Nigeria since 1999. Among Nigeria's high-profile Pentecostal leaders, he represents a minority voice. However, he demonstrates skill and sharp intellect in articulating a strategic religious understanding of social processes and a critical political interpretation devoid of populist pressure. His penetrating insight into exploitative social and political structures and their implication for economic development and leadership deficits in Nigeria is unrivalled among his peers. His activist socio-political spirituality led him to establish the "Save Nigeria Group" (SNG) in 2010 to rescue the country, according to his publicised intentions, from the stranglehold of a cabal of political entrepreneurs bent on keeping the then medically incapacitated President Umaru Musa Yar'Adua in power. His is one strong Pentecostal voice of dissent, socially responsive and responsible citizenship that resonates across religious lines. For Bakare, Christian citizenship means both light and salt to the nation; Bible-believing Christians' salvific vision – modelled after the inspiration of the Judeo-Christian scriptures, history and experience – needs to be brought to bear on governance structures and culture. Holding civil, political and religious leaders to account for their actions (and inactions) is a critical aspect of this obligation. Leadership is a public trust that requires public accounting. Failing to perform this duty is an abnegation of responsible Christian citizenship. His SNG was able to mobilise Christians and Muslims to campaign and protest against corruption, mismanagement of national resources and (constitutional) misrule by politicians. Bakare, following Achebe's The Trouble With Nigeria (1983), understands that the key problem of Nigeria is more political, particularly leadership deficits and abuse, than economic. For Bakare, unethical or inequitable (rather than unchristian) leadership structures in Nigeria exacerbate economic exploitation and stunt the country's transformation enterprise (Warikobo 2012:47–48).

The second momentous challenge Obasanjo faced from within the Pentecostal fold came from the Reverend Kris Okotie (b. 16 June 1959).[7] Okotie, founder-pastor, Household of God Church and the presidential candidate of the Justice Party in 2003 and Fresh Democratic Party (FDP) in 2007 and 2011, was already a household name before becoming a pastor. Okotie alleged that the worrying spate of bloodletting in the country since 1999 was because of the struggle for the leadership of the country being waged between the "forces of evil within the government" and the forces of good which he and those in his group represent. These "occultic societies within government . . . have almost destroyed President Obasanjo", he alleged.[8] Okotie was insistent that Obasanjo had run out of ideas in handling the affairs of Nigeria because Obasanjo represented an older generation of politicians not in touch with contemporary realities. Okotie criticised Obasanjo, claiming that he (Obasanjo) represented the clique of oppressors "whose only ambition is to conquer the rest of civil society, capture power and continue with the circle of deceit, killings, maiming, looting of the public treasury and sharing our commonwealth within their family and amongst their cronies".[9] Okotie's ideas resonated with those of another Pentecostal leader, Chris Oyakhilome, who, in a rare interview declared:

> Today's Nigeria is the dream of yesterday's men, of our present crop of leaders. . . . Jesus said you cannot put new wine in old wine bottles. You cannot expect a new Nigeria from an older generation, so the only new Nigeria that can evolve is the new Nigeria that would be the dream of the younger generation. . . . The new one cannot be given to us by the present crop of leaders because this is an outgoing generation. Age is not on their side.[10]

Effectively, Oyakhilome was saying that the mainstream Pentecostal community was in support of a dying generation of politicians who were out of touch with the present generation of Nigerians and the vision of God for the country.

## Goodluck Jonathan: the accidental and miraculous president

Unlike Obasanjo's self-projection as a "Pentecostal messiah", Goodluck Jonathan (b. 20 November 1957) presented himself as the meek and righteous servant-president of Nigeria. For the evangelical community, especially its leadership, Obasanjo was the answered prayers of the righteous and faithful community of God, while Jonathan was the Pentecostal miracle, God's fortuitous gift to Nigeria. Arguably, the most dramatic demonstration of Pentecostal political power was during the general electioneering campaign of 2010/2011, when, in spite of the massive opposition by the Muslim north against the candidacy of Jonathan, he won a decisive victory over a formidable opponent, Muhammadu Buhari, who paired with a firebrand Pentecostal pastor, Tunde Bakare.[11] The north believed it was their "right", under a gentleman's agreement within the ruling PDP, to field the next presidential candidate to complete the second term of late president Yar'Adua. Jonathan's decision to contest the election, they argued, went against such an understanding. Notwithstanding the massive mobilisation of the northern electorate against the PDP, Jonathan won the election on his own cognisance, but benefited immensely from the power of the Pentecostal voting bloc. To bring Jonathan to power, the Pentecostals were eager to capitalise on their numbers to adequately sensitise their communities to the hope that their candidate would exercise righteous authority and implement a 'born-again' governance roadmap.

In December 2010, in the heat of electioneering campaign, President Jonathan visited the Redeemed Christian Church of God (RCCG) Camp for prayers and endorsement by Adeboye. In what emerged as the high point of a politico-religious drama, the president knelt down before Adeboye for blessings and prayers. Similar to endorsing Olusegun Obasanjo during the 1999 and 2003 presidential contests, Adeboye endorsed and actively campaigned for Jonathan and the PDP in 2010. "A kneeling president before another citizen [had] no precedent in the history of Nigeria. The image of a kneeling Jonathan before an establishment pastor graphically capture[d] the place of religion [and the power of Pentecostalism] in Nigeria's Fourth Republic" (Ukah 2014:88). To bolster this theological reading of political events, some political pastors and prophets became visible in the media with prognostications of the high destiny of the nation in God's plan. Numerous pastors believed and preached that the dire state of the nation was because of Muslim misrule of the country. In this respect, for example, Paul Adefarasin, founder-owner of House on the Rock, Lagos, in a sermon said "Nigerians used to be the most educated people in the world until the likes of Abacha and Murtala Muhammed came and scattered our educational system to slow down the South so that the North can catch up, instead of speeding up the north" (*PM News* [Lagos], 15 November 2010). From the preceding, in Nigeria Pentecostal citizenship developed, arguably, as an assertive, even aggressive, exercise against the background of the rhetoric of demonisation of Islam and Muslim domination.

## Yemi Osinbajo: waiting in the wings

Nigeria's current vice-president, Yemi Osinbajo, is a senior Pentecostal pastor in the RCCG. During the Holy Ghost Service, a popular all-night vigil service, held on 2 January 2015, the patriarch of the RCCG, Enoch Adeboye, instructed his teeming audience and fans to obtain their Permanent Voters Cards (PVC), a requisite document for voting in the coming elections.[12] He further instructed church members to bring their PVCs to church service on the first Sunday of January for prayers. During the Holy Ghost Congress convened in the sprawling, 2,000-hectares Redemption Camp, from 8–13 December 2014, Adeboye made a similar announcement from the pulpit. On that occasion, he held up his and his spouse's PVCs for his audience to see, as visual and material evidence that he intended to vote in the coming elections. By encouraging his congregation to obtain their own PVCs, Adeboye was exercising his civic responsibility – as a moral and religious gatekeeper – by ensuring that the Christian community in Nigeria participated fully in the 2015 general elections. However, by instructing Christians to bring their PVCs to church on Sunday, 4 January 2015, Adeboye was transgressing the boundaries of religious obligation or service by turning his church, effectively, into a micro-political infrastructure. Consistent with his political engagements and adventures since 1999, Adeboye was performing a strategic political power play; he was informing all political stakeholders that he had the power to sway the voting patterns and outcomes in the coming elections. Praying over PVCs was intended to invoke the Holy Spirit to guide voters to align their voting practice with the will of God. The voice and will of God inform or supersede, even trump, the decision of the electorate.

Significantly, Professor Yemi Osinbajo, a Senior Advocate of Nigeria (SAN), was the former Commissioner of Justice and Attorney General of Lagos State (1999–2007), and, largely, an unknown political figure with elective political experience, before 2015. However, his most important political credential turned out to be religious capital. He is a Christian from Lagos State and, crucially, a senior pastor of the RCCG, an organisation that the politically savvy Adeboye heads. His selection as a vice-presidential candidate was to moderate, even neutralise, the perception and construction of Buhari as a Muslim fundamentalist with sympathies for the dreaded Boko Haram insurgency. Specifically, Christians in northern and central Nigeria who have endured most of the religious violence since 1999 might have had some confidence and reassurance in the choice of a Pentecostal leader as the vice-presidential candidate to Buhari.

The political calculus that informed the choice of Pastor Osinbajo could not have been separated from the desire of the APC (All Progressives Congress) to divide the Pentecostal political market or voting bloc. Enoch Adeboye is a publicly known PDP sympathiser who calls Goodluck Jonathan "my son". While in office, Jonathan visited Adeboye's "Miracle City" on three occasions, at least. Adeboye played a significant role as Jonathan's emissary of peace and reconciliation to former president Obasanjo. To pick a pastor from the politically perceptive and economically powerful RCCG as Buhari's running mate was a shrewd and pragmatically (even religiously) informed political move to forestall the dominant PDP, which relishes the official endorsement of the church. It was also a public acknowledgement of the voting power of the Pentecostal community to shape the future of governance in Nigeria. The nomination of Osinbajo as Buhari's running mate, therefore, positioned him and the APC as the first choice of RCCG members in the 2015 election. Religion – and ethnicity – rather than ideological consideration, was the most significant variable, and, therefore, a formidable political capital of the APC in its attempt to wrest power from the PDP. The APC, like the PDP, instrumentalised religion in its pursuit of political power. For the two dominant political parties in Nigeria, religion, rather than political ideology and philosophy, is key to their exercise of political power.

## Pentecostal citizenship: the fiction, the failure and the reality

Citizenship is the status of citizens encrusted "in politico-legal rights and responsibilities and the symbolic-affective terms for group identification and shared value" (Chidester 2003:31; Taiwo 2004). There is a diversity of self-understanding and conceptions of Nigerian Pentecostal Christians relative to their dual membership of the nation and a religious community. For some Christians, their primary allegiance is to their religious community, not the nation-state. Writing about the "weight of citizenship", Nimi Wariboko (2014:226) says, "Believing that this is the accepted time to stand up and act for Nigeria, Pentecostals are engaging the plight of their country [. . .] by correlating their existential experience with the Bible and Christian tradition". Nigerian Pentecostal Christians offer two forms of citizenship: moral and political. Moral citizenship derives from the proposition that Nigeria will emerge from the ashes of corruption and deprivation by the personal conversion and holiness of individuals. According to Ruth Marshall (2009:125), Nigerian 'born-again' Christians offer "a vision of citizenship in which the moral government of the self is linked to the power to influence the conduct of others". Pentecostal moral citizenship projects a vision and responsibility for the future of the nation-state, especially as an alternative to secular, postcolonial development paradigms. This political principle of Pentecostal revival, in Nigeria, from the 1970s, it is fervently hoped, will save the country and realise its destiny.

Political citizenship, based on Proverbs 29:2,[13] is mobilising members of the Pentecostal community to take up positions of political responsibility and govern with the fear of God, exercise righteous authority and revert the downward spiral of the country such that God will accomplish his covenant with the nation and resurrect it from its present prostrate status. The Pentecostal vision of citizenship, godliness and a godly people, is averred as cardinal to the realisation of the compromised promises of the post-colony. Corruption, nepotism, fanaticism, economic mismanagement are collectively the outcome of ungodliness in the rapacious and predatory postcolonial state. The transformation of the wickedness of the human heart and conduct is the work of the Holy Spirit, who reforms and informs the "new creature" in mapping out a new vision where God is at the centre of socio-economic and political development. As the ultimate cause and curse of all the problems facing the nation-state is the devil or Satan[14]; the goal of citizenship is the production of righteousness that enhances the practice of virtue and the constitution and perpetuation of the community of believers.

Conception of Pentecostal citizenship defines the nature of agency and activism, which believers can exercise in transforming their societies. However, the inverse conception that attributes all the ills of nation to a metaphysical source directly absolves criminals, corrupt persons and organisations of any wrongdoing. The fundamental and foundational basis of both democracy and citizenship is "the people". Pentecostal citizenship dispenses with "the people", replacing it with the inscrutable will of God – as mediated and interpreted by powerful wo/men of God. This overly spiritualised conception informs and explains Pentecostal pragmatic engagement with politics and public office. The performance of economic, social and political duties and practices is informed by the conceptions and conditions of citizenship. Where Pentecostals in public office fail to execute Spirit-driven programmes and transformation, the devil, rather than the individual, readily takes the blame. The failure of the Obasanjo and Jonathan administrations, cumulatively 13 of the 16 years of democracy in Nigeria's Fourth Republic, to transform and improve the socio-economic and political conditions of citizens and 'heal' the nation is attributed to the devil's intent on thwarting and sabotaging the efforts of believers and the destiny of the nation.[15]

This thinking gives the devil too much power over believers. As a form of externalisation of blame, it also reinforces the lack of self-appraisal among the Nigerian Pentecostal community. It is comforting to corrupt politicians and public bureaucrats. As Ojo (2010:47) points out, the failure of Pentecostal adventure into national politics stems from its inability "to understand the complexities of the socioeconomic and political factors pertaining to governance, they still hold on to the belief that governance could be better if Christians were in the position of power, a myopic perception which negates the everyday reality on ground".

However, a critical issue that Nigerian Pentecostal leaders have elided, which needs addressing, is the practice of citizenship within the church and its contentious relationship with the larger society, as exemplified by the undemocratic organisational character of Pentecostal institutions in Nigeria.[16] Pentecostal churches are governed like fiefdoms of their founders and general overseers. The wo/man of God or prophet/ess is completely in charge of doctrine, administration and fiscal control, and not accountable to members of the church, or ecclesiastic organisations, like the PFN and CAN, autonomous auditing agencies or a governmental agency (Ukah 2015). Given the dynamics of opacity in Nigerian Pentecostalism, their activities and practices in democratic governance only perpetuate a culture of obtuse accountability and absence of transparency. Holding leadership responsible and insisting on public accountability are foundational elements and duties of citizenship. When Pentecostal leaders are unaccountable to their congregants for their actions and conduct, the membership is unable to demand and hold political leadership to account for its policies and stewardship.

Believing that they are only to account to God for their actions and the large sums of money they collect from members – and the voice of God must represent the voice of the people – it is paradoxical, even hypocritical, for them to claim to inculcate the virtue and practice of public accountability and political citizenship among their followers. Consequently, when Christians fail to question or scrutinise their pastors' actions and excesses, they invariably carry the learned behaviour over to their political (mis)rulers. It is hard, therefore, to envisage how these (undemocratic, authoritarian, even despotic) institutions, their powerful owners and leadership can foster enduring practices of responsible and accountable citizenship (legal, social, political) in a religiously plural and complex society like Nigeria; especially, as the key conundrum of Pentecostal citizenship practices in Nigeria shows marked disjunctions between the vision of moral citizenship and the practice of political citizenship, at local (church, municipal and sub-national), national and international levels.

## Notes

1 Part of the fieldwork for this study in Nigeria in 2016 was done under the Nagel Institute for the Study of World Christianity project on "Religious Innovation and Competition: Their Impact in Contemporary Africa", sub-project, "Miracle Cities: The Economy of Prayer Camps and the Entrepreneurial Spirit of Religion in Africa" (ID: 2016-SS350), funded by the John Templeton Foundation. The author thanks all those who in various ways helped during fieldwork. Thanks also go to the editors, anonymous reviewers and Professor Jude Akudinobi who read early drafts and offered comments. The usual caveat holds.
2 At the beginning of the Pentecostal resurgence in Africa, politics and political activism were not important priorities for born-again believers, organisations and their leaders. There are many reasons for this, some of which are: i) theological emphasis on salvation in a next life or afterlife, ii) overriding concern with conversion drives rather than socio-economic/political transformation, iii) contestation with mission churches over theological purity, iv) their initial minority status, v) lack of informed political intelligence or knowledge.
3 See, for example, Femi Adesina, "2015 Polls: Prophecies that Hit the Crossbar". *The Sun* (Lagos), 17 April 2015. available at: http://sunnewsonline.com/new/2015-polls-prophecies-that-hit-the-crossbar/
4 Tunde Bakare studied law at the University of Lagos, where he graduated in 1980 and was called to the bar in 1981. He established his own legal firm in 1984 and in 1988 was called into full time Pentecostal ministry. He was born into a Muslim family but converted into Christianity. He later joined the Redeemed Christian Church of God (RCCG) and became a pastor in charge of one of the experimental model parishes of the RCCG. On 1 April 1989, he broke away from the RCCG and founded his own church, the Latter Rain Assembly, in Lagos. Among his reasons for leaving the RCCG was that the leader of the church, Enoch Adeboye, was being elevated to the pedestal of a deity.
5 1Samuel 15:32ff.
6 The Pentecostal Fellowship of Nigeria is a loose association of a large number of Pentecostal and charismatic churches and para-churches that was established in 1991. Although there are other smaller associational bodies of Pentecostal and charismatic churches and organisation, the PFN is the nationally recognised representative body of Pentecostal churches and organisations in Nigeria; it is one of the five associations that make up the Christian Association of Nigeria. Membership is open to churches and organisations who subscribe to mainstream Pentecostal beliefs and practices. Since 1999, the PFN has played prominent and controversial role in public life and politics of the country by its overt support for some politicians (Olusegun Obasanjo and Goodluck Jonathan, for example) and political programmes in the country. (www.pfn.org.ng/membership/)
7 Born Christopher Oghenebrorie Okotie, he modified his name to Kris Okotie during his days as a pop musician.
8 "Obasanjo Can't Rule this Country Again – Okotie". *Vanguard* (Lagos). 14 February 2006. available at: www.vanguardngr.com/articles/2002/politics/february06/130226/p113022006.html (accessed 14 February 2006).
9 "2007: Okotie vs the Military Heavy weights". *Daily Sun* (Lagos). 26 August 2006, p. 29.
10 Chris Oyakhilome, Interview, *National Standard* (Abuja), vol. 1, no. 7, January 2005, p. 22.
11 Fielding a Pentecostal leader, who was also a public agitator or crusader, was both recognition of Pentecostalism as a public force and religion and also to split the evangelical voting bloc.
12 The PCV is the official document that authenticates a citizen as a registered voter.

13 "When the righteous are in authority, the people rejoice; But when a wicked man rules, the people groan" (NKJV).
14 For many Nigerian Pentecostals, Islam is a religion of Satan designed to subvert the will of God for his people.
15 Some Christians defend Obasanjo from any charge of underperformance by citing the Sharia controversies that dogged his first term in office. Similarly, some defend Jonathan's administration by citing the Boko Haram insurgency. Apart from these two factors – Sharia re-implementation and Boko Haram insurgency – both administrations were grossly corrupt and inept in dealing with social and economic problems (Adebanwi 2012). Apart from the tokenistic gestures to satisfy the Pentecostal constituency, there was nothing consistently "Christian" or "Pentecostal" about these administrations.
16 According to Matthews Ojo (2010: 44), "Pentecostal and Charismatic movements [in Nigeria] have started to raise some doubts about their own originality and intentions, basically, because of the contradictions inherent in their posture towards politics and materialism".

# References

Achebe, C. 1983. *The Trouble With Nigeria*. Enugu: Fourth Dimension Publishing.
Adebanwi, W. 2012. *Authority Stealing: Anti-Corruption War and Democratic Politics in Post-Military Nigeria*. Durham: Carolina Academic Press.
Adekunle, J. O. 2009. 'Introduction: Religion and Politics in Transition'. In J. O. Adekunle (Ed.) *Religion in Politics: Secularism and National Integration in Modern Nigeria*. Trenton, NJ: Africa World Press: 3–17.
Beresford, A. 2016. 'Africa Rising?' *Review of African Political Economy*, 43/147: 1–7.
Burgess, R. 2008. *Nigeria's Christian Revolution: The Civil War Revival and Its Pentecostal Progeny (1967–2006)*. Cumbra: Paternoster.
Chidester, D. 2003. 'Global Citizenship, Cultural Citizenship World Religions in Religion Education'. In R. Jackson (Ed.) *International Perspectives on Citizenship, Education and Religious Diversity*. London: Routledge Falmer: 28–45.
Falola, T. & Heaton, M. M. 2008. *A History of Nigeria*. Cambridge: Cambridge University Press.
Gaiya, M. 2002. 'The Pentecostal Revolution in Nigeria'. Occasional Paper, Centre of African Studies, University of Copenhagen.
Jacobsen, D. 2011. *The World's Christians: Who They Are, Where They Are, and How They Got There*. West Sussex, UK: Wiley-Blackwell Publishers.
Krinsky, S. 2006. 'In Search of New Beginnings: Pentecostalism, Development, and the Burden of History in Yoruba Thought'. Senior Thesis, Brown University.
Marshall, R. 2009. *Political Spiritualities: The Pentecostal Revolution in Nigeria*. Chicago: University of Chicago Press.
Obadare, E. O. 2006. 'Pentecostal Presidency? The Lagos-Ibadan "Theocratic Class" & The Muslim "Other"'. *Review of African Political Economy*, 13(110): 667–678.
Ojo, M. A. 2006. *The End-Time Army: Charismatic Movements in Modern Nigeria*. Trenton, NJ: Africa World Press.
Ojo, M. A. 2008. 'Pentecostalism, Public Accountability and Governance in Nigeria'. *Ogbomoso Journal of Theology*, XII/1: 112.
Ojo, M. A. 2010. *Of Saints and Sinners: Pentecostalism and the Paradox of Social Transformation in Modern Nigeria*. Ife: OAU Press Limited.

Onuoha, G. 2013. ' "Exist" and "Inclusion": The Changing Paradigm of Pentecostal Expression in the Nigerian Public Space'. In I. Becci, M. Burchardt & J. Casanova (Eds.) *Topographies of Faith: Religion in Urban Spaces*. Leiden: Brill: 207–225.

Peel, J. D. Y. 2016. *Christianity, Islam, and Oriṣa Religion: Three Traditions in Comparison and Interaction*. Oakland, CA: California University Press.

Pew Research Center. 2011. *Global Christianity: A Report on the Size and Distribution of the World's Christian Population*. Washington, DC: Pew Research Center's Forum on Religion and Public Life.

Pew Research Centre. 2015. *The Future of World Religions: Population Growth Projections, 201–2050*. Washington, DC: Pew Research Center's Forum on Religion and Public Life.

Pillay, D. 2015. 'The Global Economic Crisis and the Africa Rising Narrative'. *African Development*, XL(3): 59–75.

Taiwo, O. 2004. 'Of Citizens and Citizenship'. In O. Akiba (Ed.) *Constitutionalism and Society in Africa*. Aldershot, UK: Ashgate: 55–78.

Taylor, I. 2016. 'Dependency Redux: Why Africa Is Not Rising'. *Review of African Political Economy*, 43(147): 8–25.

Ukah, A. 2008. *A New Paradigm of Pentecostal Power: The Redeemed Christian Church of God in Nigeria*. Asmara, NJ: Africa World Press/Red Sea Press.

Ukah, A. 2014. 'The Midwife or the Handmaid? Religion in Political Advertising in Nigeria'. In J. Küpper, K. W. Hempfer & E. Fischer-Lichte (Eds.) *Religion and Society in the 21st Century*. Berlin: De Gruyter Publishers: 87–114.

Ukah, A. 2015. 'Obeying Caesar to Obey God: The Dilemmas of Registering of Religious Organisations in Nigeria'. In P. Coertzen, M. C. Green & L. Hansen (Eds.) *Law and Religion in Africa: The Quest for the Common Good in Pluralistic Societies*. Stellenbosch: Sun MeDIA Publications: 309–329.

Wariboko, N. 2012. 'Pentecostal Paradigms of National Economic Prosperity in Africa'. In K. Attanasi & A. Yong (Eds.) *Pentecostalism and Prosperity: The Socio-Economics of the Global Charismatic Movement*. New York: Palgrave Macmillan: 35–59.

Wariboko, N. 2014. *Nigerian Pentecostalism*. Rochester: University of Rochester Press.

Yong, A. 2010. *In the Days of Caesar: Pentecostalism and Political Theology*. Grand Rapids, MI: Wm. B. Eerdmans Publishing Co.

# 3 Election prophecies and political stability in Ghana

*Emmanuel Sackey*

In recent years we can observe the emergence of so called *election prophecies* in the Ghanaian political landscape. By election prophecies I refer to the pre-election declarations in the public sphere, pertaining to the outcome of national elections, by religious clerics who attribute their revelations to the will of God. This phenomenon is perceived to have become pronounced during the second round of the 2000 presidential elections.[1] To a significant extent, the return to democratic dispensation in 1992 (Gyimah-Boadi 2001; Addo 1997), partly contributed towards freedom of religious clerics to channel their prophetic ministration onto the political terrain. Even though a few traditional spiritualists and Moslem clerics also engage in the practice, Pentecostal-charismatic pastors remain the most prominent. This chapter examines the recent upsurge of election prophecies in Ghana, and its potential implication for political stability. Ghana has been touted among the most politically stable countries in Africa (Van Gyambo 2015; Boafo-Arthur 2008) yet the prospects of violent post-election conflict have remained a major national concern in every election year.

Since the return to multiparty politics in 1992, there have been six general elections out of which the outcome of three, (the 1992, 2008 and 2012) brought some tensions. Whereas contestations over the results of the 1992 presidential elections led to a boycott of the parliamentary elections by the NPP, the results of the 2012 presidential election were contested at the Supreme Court.[2] Even though there have been extensive studies on the connection between religion and political conflicts in Africa, only a few (Deacon 2015; Deacon & Lynch 2013; Vullers 2011) have paid attention to the phenomenon of election prophecies, and the extent to which it impacts post-election conflict in the continent. This chapter has responded to two key questions, namely why do clerics of the Pentecostal-charismatic denomination tend to engage in the practice, whereas those belonging to the *mainline* churches do not? And more importantly, to what extent could election prophecies impact on post-election conflict in Ghana? The chapter is based on the outcome of a qualitative study conducted between 2013 and 2016 that involved content analysis of 21 election prophecies that were broadcasted on radio, TV, newspapers as well as the internet. The content analysis of the prophecies was complemented with an extensive literature review as well as personal interviews with the spiritual leader of the Prophets of the Spiritual Churches Council, a Pastor of the Refreshing Hour International Church and the Chairman of the National Peace Council (a former National Head of the Methodist Church).[3] The core argument is that the recent upsurge in election prophecies has the potential to exacerbate pre-existing mistrust against the National Electoral Commission and fuel the religious dimensions of identity politics and thereby impact negatively on the political stability of the country. In this chapter reference to charismatic churches primarily refers to the neo-Pentecostal groups that emerged in the late 1970s and the early 1980s in Ghana as part of the global Pentecostal revival movement.

## Charismatic Christianity and politics in Ghana

Various studies have offered significant insight pertaining to the relationship between religion and politics in Africa (Deacon 2015; Brubaker 2015; Wariboko 2014; Marshall 2009; Basedau et al. 2011; Stewart 2009, Ranger 2008; Ellis & Ter Haar 2007, 1998). With regards to the role of Christianity and democratisation in Africa, Ranger (2008) has categorised the contributions of Christian churches into three phases, namely: the Church contribution to the anti-colonial struggle up to the 1960s; agitations against one-party and military regimes in the post-independence era until the 1980s; and, the Church involvement in contemporary democratic dispensation that began from the early 1990s till present. Ranger observed that whereas mainline denominations and African Independent Churches (AICs) played the most prominent role in the first and second phases, the contemporary era has witnessed the influence of the Pentecostal-charismatic denominations. To a significant extent, the proposition of Ranger can be said to be applicable to the case of Ghana. For example the studies of Pobee (1991) and Addo (1997) have shown how the AICs supported the struggle for political independence. In the view of Pobee (1991), the Afrocentric theology of the AICs served as an inspiration for Nkrumah's Convention People Party (CPP) and other pro-independence activists.

The second phase which Ranger outlined as the period of church agitations against one-party states and military regimes also fits the Ghanaian case. Pobee (1991) observed that Ghana's second military government (1972–1978) was opposed by the mainline churches, even though General Acheampong partly succeeded in co-opting several Pentecostal and African independent churches to support his *Union Government* (UNIGOV) proposal, which was widely seen as an undemocratic attempt to hold onto political power. But the Christian Council of Ghana and the Catholic Bishops Conference were part of the civil society alliance that resisted the regime.[4] Throughout the era of PNDC regime (1981–1992), which replaced the Acheampong Supreme Military Council, through a military coup, the Catholic Bishops, and the Christian Council remained a critic of the regime's alleged human right abuses (Gyampo 2015; Gyimah-Boadi 1996).[5] The two ecumenical bodies were also part of the pro-democracy civil society groups which agitated for the return to constitutional rule in 1992 (Gyampo 2015). Since then the democratic dispensation has provided an enabling environment for a vibrant civil society (Whitfield 2003). In the case of Ghana, this marked the origin of what Ranger (2008) outlined as the third (contemporary) phase of the influence of Christianity on democratisation in Africa.

Pobee (1991) observed that historically, the SMC era remain significant in understanding the evolution of the interaction between religion and politics in Ghana. In furtherance of the objective to perpetuate his hold on political power, General Acheampong baited several Christian churches aligned to the African Independent and Pentecostal-charismatic denominations. Pobee wrote that in January 1979, ahead of the national referendum on the UNIGOV proposal, Prophetess Elizabeth Clare of the Summit Lighthouse, a non-denominational Christian Faith based in the USA, was invited by the government for public lectures. In a series of presentations, the Prophetess openly supported the regime by declaring that UNIGOV was God's plan for Ghana. According to Pobee, Prophet Clare "redefined the Christian doctrine of Trinity in terms of the Union Government; UNIGOV was to be accepted because it demonstrated the Christian doctrine of the trinity. The Armed Forces represent God the Father; the Professional Bodies and the Students represent the son; the workers of Ghana represent the Holy Spirit" (Pobee 1991:96–97). According to Pobee, Prophetess Claire was fiercely contested by the Christian Council and the Ghana Fellowship of Evangelicals, for exploiting Christian dogma to support political ideology of the military regime.

This historical account indicates that the phenomenon of involvement of prophets in Ghanaian politics was prevalent prior to the return to democratic governance in 1992. The contemporary election prophecies became more pronounced during the 2000 general elections when Pastor Emmanuel Kwaku Aprako, the founder of the King Jesus Evangelistic Flames Ministry, a Charismatic Christian Church in Accra, made a prophetic declaration on the outcome of the elections.[6] Since then the phenomenon has become a trend every election year.[7] It became more intense and frequent during the 2008, 2012 elections and the 2016 elections.

## The salience of the prophetic ministry in the neo-Pentecostal-charismatic denomination

According to the statistical projections of the 2010 Population Census, Christians constituted 71% of the Ghana's population (Ghana Statistical Service 2013). Ghanaians who claimed to belong to Pentecostal-charismatic denomination are 28.3% of the population and constituted the majority, followed by the Protestants (18.4%) and 13.1% Catholics. The popularity of the neo-Pentecostal charismatic movement has been attributed to several factors, particularly the use of the electronic media (Asamoah-Gyadu 2005; Hackett 1998) as well as the emphasis on the gift of the Holy Spirit, which encompass a theology of prosperity. Emphasis on healing, speaking in tongues, the adoption of modern musical repertoires in their worship, the appropriation of elements of beliefs and rituals perceived to be compatible with traditional African cosmology, deliverance and prophecy remain among the factors considered to account for the prominence of the denomination (Quayesi-Amakye 2015; Gifford 2015, 2004; Asamoah-Gyadu 2005).

In his account of the evolution of neo-Pentecostal-charismatic Christianity in Ghana, Gifford (2004) outlined four distinct phases. According to Gifford, whereas the first wave (late 1970s) and the second wave (early to mid-1980s) were respectively characterised by a focus on faith and prosperity message and teaching of the Gospel, the third wave paid attention to Miracles. Following the miraculous wave in the late 1980s was the prophetic era, which in the view of Gifford became more prominent in the mid-1990s.[8] It is arguable that in addition to the other aforementioned factors, the neo-institutional tendency for organisations to respond to pressures from their external environment (Krucken & Drori 2009; DiMaggio & Powell 1983; Meyer & Rowan 1977) also contributed to the diffusion, persistence and popularity of the prophetic ministry.

As pertains in other African states, being a neo-Pentecostal-charismatic in Ghana implies seeking the interventions of the *Holy Spirit* in all aspects of one's life (Deacon 2015; Wariboko 2014; Marshall 2009; Gifford 2004). Under the current democratic dispensation it also implies seeking the intervention of God in the affairs of the state. Thus, even though Ghana is a secular state, Pentecostal-charismatic Christian citizens believe that God still intervenes in the election of political leaders. It is this belief that prompted clerics such as Rev. Owusu Bempah of the Glorious Word Power Ministries, Prophet Emmanuel Badu Kobi of the Glorious Wave Ministries, Bishop Salifu Amoako of the National Prophetic and Apostolic Churches Council (NPACC) and other charismatic clerics to engage in election prophecies.

The major explanation offered by these clerics for their engagement in election prophecies is theological. They cite verses from both the Old and New Testament of the Christian Bible. Most of the verses from the Old Testament tell stories of the biblical Jews who lived under a theocracy (Rev. Isaac Owusu Bempah, 07 January 2016, Metro TV, Accra). The narratives indicate how *Yahweh* as the *God of Israel* used the biblical prophets such as Jeremiah, Isaiah and Samuel to speak to the Jews, on matters of public affairs.[9] If the Old Testament provides instances of prophetic declaration of Yahweh's choice of political leaders in ancient Israel, the New Testament provides a more explicit theological explanation of the prophetic ministry. The favourite verses in the New Testament are often cited from the book of Corinthians and Ephesians (Prophet Agyemang Prempeh, 5 January 2016, Metro TV, Accra). The fourth chapter of Ephesians (Eph 4: 7–16) for instance mentions prophecy among the five-fold Christian ministries, the others being Apostleship, Evangelism, Teachings and Pastoring. The book of Corinthians (Bible league 2000, 1 Cor 14:3; 1 Cor 12:10) on the other hand, clarifies that the purpose of prophecy is to edify, to exalt and to comfort.

Unlike the Charismatic churches, the mainline denominations do not emphasise the gift of prophecy even though they acknowledge it as part of Christianity. A renowned cleric and former head of the Methodist Church and the chairman of the National Peace Council, for instance explained mainline churches' position in the following terms:

> We do not discourage it but we do not give prominence to it because for us prophecy is not just when somebody is doing so under ecstasy. Prophecy is declaring the Word of God so it doesn't have to be that, I am prophesying. The ancient prophets were people who spoke the word of God and they declared the counsel of God. So we have no qualms about prophecies but in the Methodist Church we do not give prominence to prophecy.[10]

In the view of Rev. Asante, the mainline churches discourage election prophecies because, from their perspective, the multiparty system is inherently divisive, hence when religious clerics make prophetic declarations that favour a particular political party it divides the people. The Methodist church like other mainline denominations therefore discourages election prophecies. Rev. Asante emphasised that:

> Because as far as we are concerned it does not help anybody. After all, my vote is a secret thing and something that is secret, what value do we gain by prophesying about it. Prophecy must edify us; prophecy must really push us forward. Prophecy that is going to create confusion, prophecy that is going to divide us is something that we should not encourage . . . Even if God should reveal something to me in respect of the coming election that A or B is going to win, I am not going to come out with it; I will pray about it in my closet. There are certain things that are intended for you to pray about; not for public consumption. For as soon as it comes out you create confusion.[11]

In accordance with the Charismatic theology, the prophetic ministry is a *divine mandate* meant to fulfil the will of God in both the physical and spiritual affairs of the nation. Thus, even though Ghana remains a secular state (Quarshigah 1999:597), some of the Charismatic Prophets perceive themselves to be fulfilling their prophetic mandate, as custodian of the national interest, in accordance with the will of the God. As social scientists, determining the ontological accuracy and ethical evaluation of these theological explanations is beyond our jurisdiction. We however have a relative competence for critical examination of the potential socio-political implications of the phenomenon.

## The sacralisation of politics and the upsurge of election prophecies

It has been noted that the tendency of Pentecostal-charismatics to seek spiritual remedies for earthly problems, is embedded in the indigenous worldview

(Wariboko 2014; Asamoah-Gyadu 2005). Following Wariboko, Studebaker (2016) maintained that the Pentecostal political theology emphasises the *Holy Spirit* transformation of believers into Christians citizens, who are not aliens to the world and thus under obligation to be concerned with the political and socio-economic realities of the world that serves as a transit to the kingdom of God. As Christian citizens, this conviction can be said to inspire Pentecostal-charismatics' criticism against underdevelopment, perceived corruption and human right abuses by African political elites, and their quest to influence national politics (Deacon 2015; Marshall 2009).

Since Ghana's return to democratic governance in 1992, charismatic churches have been organising special prayers for peace. It has also become a trend for political aspirants and party activists to seek spiritual fortification to enhance their electoral fortunes. In the run up to the 2012 election, both the incumbent National Democratic Congress (NDC) and the opposition New Patriotic Party (NPP) held various *charismatic styled* prayer crusades to solicit divine intervention for electoral success. These events occurred alongside numerous contradictory prophecies from several pastors. Emphasis on three of these prophecies will provide a useful illustration. In the run up to the 2008 elections, the then opposition presidential candidate of the National Democratic Congress (NDC), the late Prof. Atta Mills, made a spiritual pilgrimage to Prophet T. B. Joshua's Synagogue Church of Nations (SCOAN) in Lagos, Nigeria, for spiritual blessings meant to enhance his election.[12] Following the victory of the NDC, it became a public knowledge that Prophet T. B. Joshua had accurately predicted the outcome of the elections after having prayed for the late president. In a video that was widely circulated on the internet and other social media platforms, the former president could be seen giving a testimony that, the famous Nigerian pastor did not only accurately prophesy the outcome of the polls but also predicted that election would go into a run off. Indeed, the election did enter a second round following the inability of any of the parties to obtain the required majority. This made the Nigerian pastor more popular in Ghana.

In the run up to the 2012 elections, among the numerous prophecies, was one given by the president of the NPACC, Bishop Elisha Salifu Amoako. The leader of the prophetic council publicly declared that, by courtesy of a divine revelation from the *Holy Spirit* the council had foreseen the winner (Joy FM Myjoyonline.com, 22 September 2012).[13] According to the Bishop, not only had his group foreseen the outcome of the elections but also they had officially written to congratulate the foreseen winner. The prophecy and its accompanying gesture are equally interesting. Even though the prophetic Council did not publicly declare the identity of the foreseen candidate or party, Bishop Amoako stated that, the foreseen winner accepted the congratulatory letter of the prophetic council, ahead of the elections.

The third interesting case was the revelations of the Rev. Isaac Owusu Bempah, the founder and General Overseer of Accra based Glorious Word Power International Ministries, in relation to the outcome of the 2012 elections. In a series of TV and radio appearances, Rev. Bempah confidently prophesied that the Nana Akuffo Addo, the presidential candidate of the NPP, had been chosen by God to lead the country. Out of the numerous election prophecies, Rev. Bempah's also stand out for various reasons, particularly on its potential implication for national security and political stability. The uniqueness of Rev. Bempah's revelations was that, the Electoral Commission was incriminated as part of the prophecy. He publicly declared that, if his prophecies were not fulfilled, then the Electoral Commission had fraudulently manipulated the verdict.[14]

Another element of Rev. Bempah's prophecies was a consistent disclosure about an impending violent post-election conflict, which he insisted was likely to occur as a result of a dispute over the results of the election. Contrary to Rev. Bempah's prophecies, the 2012 presidential election subsequently ended with a 50.70 as against 47.74% in favour of the NDC (Ephson 2014:3). Even though no major violent political conflict occurred as prophesied, the outcome of the polls was contested at the Superior Court of Justice, which ultimately validated the results through a 5–4 majority decision in September 2013 (BBC 29 August 2013). It is imperative to emphasise that since 1992, when the NPP boycotted the parliamentary elections and published the *stolen verdict* (New Patriotic Party 1993), the mistrust of the Electoral Commission has persisted. Even though there was no clear evidence to prove that the NPP rejection of the results of the 2012 presidential elections was influenced by any pre-election prophecies, the phenomenon, the discussion of the phenomenon was prominent in the public sphere.

The prophetic trend was also widespread ahead of the 2016 elections when media networks in the country were engulfed with various election prophecies, both in favour and against the two major political parties. The contradictory nature of the prophecies have made many observers question the credibility of the acclaimed prophets. Some of these prophecies continued to be laced with visions of imminent post-election violent conflicts. In one of such prophecies, Rev. Bempah publicly declared that certain politicians were planning to assassinate Nana Akuffo Addo, the presidential candidate of NPP. According to the pastor, the assassination might occur when the NPP launch their campaign in the Volta Region, which has remained the stronghold (voting base) of the NDC (Ephson 2014). The security implication of this prophecy prompted the Ghana Police Service to invite Rev. Bempah for interrogation.[15]

In a pluralistic religious environment characterised by inter-denominational and intra-denominational competition for followers, the upsurge of election prophecies could be considered as a mechanism through which the pastors seek public attention in order to attract new members and maintain current adherents. By emphasising the acclaimed gift of the *Holy Spirit*, the prophetic ministries distinct themselves from the mainline churches, as well as from other charismatic churches, to carve a *niche* on which they could thrive in the context of inter-denominational and intra-denominational competition for adherents (Gifford 2004; Asamoah-Gyadu 2005). The proponents of the theory of religious economics for instance argued that a diverse religious environment or market often emerges in context of state deregulation. Based on these premises, it is assumed that, in a pluralistic religious environment, inter-denominational and intra-denominational competition for adherents are more likely to occur (Starke & Finke 2000; Iannaccone 1998). To thrive in the context of competition, religious organisations are perceived to lay emphasis on specific spiritual beliefs, and rituals or practices that make them unique, and thereby carve a *niche* for themselves.[16]

This perspective is compatible with previous studies on the Pentecostal-charismatic movement (De Witte 2011; Sackey 2006; Gifford 2004; Asamoah-Gyadu 2005) which indicate that the Charismatic churches adapted particular religious preferences compatible with the spiritual needs of the local populace in order to enhance their attraction. As a rational choice framework, the model could be criticised for its "economic imperialism" (Witham 2010), and therefore for analysing what might otherwise be genuine spiritual motivations in purely economic terms. Nonetheless, it is offers a relevant alternative insight for the understanding of the phenomenon.

## Implications for political stability

As part of Ghanaian civil society, the ecumenical Christian Bodies contributed towards the evolution of democratic governance, through the contestation of autocratic tendencies of incumbent governments, and promotion of peaceful elections (Gyampo 2015; Dovlo 2006;Gyimah-Boadi 2001). However the prophetic trends of the Pentecostal-charismatic clerics have the potential to undermine the contribution of Christianity towards the consolidation of democracy in the country. Against a background of mistrust towards the National Electoral Commission, the attribution of the failure of prophecy to the fraudulent manipulations of the Commission has the potential to exacerbate post-election conflict, irrespective of the genuineness of the prophecy. In a highly religious context where the belief in the supernatural remain very intense (Asamoah-Gyadu 2005; Pobee 1991) it is possible for politicians to reject the outcome of elections that go contrary to the declarations of their prophets while relying on popular support and religious justification. Even though there is no evidence to show that the contestations of previous elections results were motivated by prophecies, the religious posturing of Ghanaian politicians makes such a development possible.[17]

The possibility of *prophetically* instigated political conflict is given further impetus by previous studies that showed the involvement of religious clerics in some of the military coups attempted in the 1970s (Pobee 1991). As posited by Finke and Harris (2012:54), when religious groups get aligned to political groups, this increase the capacity of religion to mobilise for political conflict. The data analysis for instance showed a sharp division between those Prophets whose revelations favoured the NDC and those that favoured the NPP. Out of the 21 election prophecies analysed, six predicted win for the NDC, 12 for the NPP and one for the Progressive People's Party (PPP).

Prophet Agyemang Prempeh of the Springs of Joy Ministries and Prophet Emmanuel Kofi Enim of the Word Victory Chapel for instance prophesized in favour of the NDC, whereas Rev. Owusu Bempah's, Odifour Kwabena Tawiah of the Church of Rabbi and Envagelist Kwaku Aprako predicted a win for the NPP.[18]

The alignment of the leading Pentecostal-charismatic clerics to the various political parties (Gifford 2004) is an evidence of such overlapping boundary, which makes *prophetically* instigated contestations of an electoral outcome in Ghana possible. This possibility could also be enhanced by the religious diversity and the prevalence of inter-denominational and intra-denominational competition for adherents (Gifford 2004). Even though the churches as collective entities do not openly declare their affiliation to political parties, some leading clerics do publicly endorse certain parties, while others subtly do the same through prophetic declarations purported to have come from God. Gifford (2004) for instance mentioned that, during the 2000 election campaign Bishop Charles Agyin Asare, the founder of Accra based World Miracle Church, openly endorsed the late President Mills, who was then the presidential candidate of the NDC, whereas pastors like Pastor Mensah Otabil of the International Central Gospel Church (ICGC) subtly endorsed the NPP.

In view of the ethnic diversity of the membership of these churches, and the difficulty of proving the political affiliation of an entire congregation, it would be contentious to state that a church is aligned to a party because the founder or leader of the church endorses a particular party. It is however arguable that pastors, especially the Pentecostal-charismatic clerics, have a significant degree of influence over their members. The entire congregation of the Rev. Bempah's Glorious Word Power Ministries for instance welcomed the newly elected President Nana Akuffo Addo who went to the Church Sunday Service to thank the pastor and the entire church for supporting him spiritually (for the December 2016 elections) for a successful election (Citi FM Online, 19 March 2017).

In a context where individuals and organisations thrive on political patronage the prophetic endorsement of political parties makes the clerics and their churches predisposed to political cooptation (Joshua 2016; Gyimah-Boadi 2001; Hackett & Rosalind 2001; Pobee 1991), and thereby casts doubt on their credibility and legitimacy as mediators of conflict. As observed by Vullers (2011) and Gifford (2004), in the early 2000s similar involvement of charismatic clerics, including Ghana's Bishop Charles Agyin Asare, in the endorsement of fraudulent declaration of Laurent Gbagbo as the president of Ivory Coast contributed to the Ivorian conflict.

## Conclusion

Previous studies on the neo-Pentecostal charismatic clerics' involvement in African elections, such as in Kenya's 2007 and 2013 elections (Deacon 2015), and Ivorian elections in the early 2000s (Vullers 2011), have shown that the activities of the Pentecostal-charismatic churches have the potential to induce an enabling environment for peaceful elections as well as the propensity to instigate a post-election conflict. In the case of Ghana, to improve transparency and enhance the credibility of the electoral system, the state allocated GH¢146,211,972 for biometric voter registration and verification in 2012, GH¢21,228,757.00 in 2013 and GH¢139,477,235.00 in 2014 (Ministry of Finance 2015:7). It is logical to posit that, despite the underdeveloped nature of the economy, these financial allocations from the state were considered necessary for strengthening the institutional and technological capacity of the Electoral Commission, in order to enhance public confidence regarding the credibility of the electoral system.

While it is possible for the Electoral Commission to compromise its credibility through institutional weaknesses, the peculiar nature and dynamics of the recent election prophecies also poses a unique challenge to the credibility of the electoral system. I have argued that this prospective challenge cannot only be resolved through institutional reforms and technological innovations alone. The proposition is that the quest to understand the connection between religion and post-election conflict in Africa should also pay attention to the spiritual beliefs of the competing parties, and the prophetic trends of the religious groups to which the parties may have overlapping boundaries. It also implies that such studies should also pay attention to the extent to which politicians and political parties appropriate or make political use of the spirituality of voters. Even though religious denominations, such as Pentecostal-charismatic Christianity, have the potential to contribute towards political transformation in Africa, their role can be either funcational or dysfuncational to the consolidation of democratic governance.

## Notes

1 Gilbert Abeiku Aggrey, Interview on Metro TV, Accra, 5 January 2016.
2 Since 1996, both the presidential and the parliamentary elections have been held on the same day.
3 There are about five main Christian Ecumenical Councils in Ghana, namely; the Christian Council of Ghana (CCG); the Catholic Bishops Conference (CBC); the Ghana Pentecostal and Charismatic Churches Council (GPCC); the National Association of Charismatic Churches and Christian Churches (NACCC); and the Council of Spiritual Churches. The CCG is primarily made up of mainline protestant churches whereas the CBC remains the Ecumenical body of the Catholic Church in Ghana. The GPCC and the NACCC are umbrella bodies for the Pentecostal and Charismatic Churches, whilst the Spiritual Churches Council serves a pseudo-ecumenical body of the Independent Ghanaian Churches popularly refers to as spiritual churches.
4 The proposed UNIGOV political reforms were rejected in a referendum on 30 March 1978. It was a non-party political system that would have comprised the military, the police, representatives of professional bodies and civil society organisations.
5 The PNDC refers to the Provisional National Defence Council, the military regime headed by Former President Jerry Jon Rawlings that ruled Ghana between 1981 and 1992. Rawlings had previously headed another military government, the AFRC (Armed Forces Revolutionary Council) which overthrew the SMC

and handed over to a constitutionally elected government (the People National Party) in 1979 (Ocquaye 1980).
6 Gilbert Abeiku Aggrey, a popular Ghanaian broadcaster posited that the phenomenon existed prior to the return to the democratic dispensation in 1992 but appeared to be popular and widespread thereafter, due to the liberalisation of the media. The ace broadcaster stated on Accra based Metro TV, *Good Evening Ghana* programme, that the election prophecy in 2000 was among the first to attract significant media attention under current democratic dispensation (Metro TV, 5 January 2016).
7 The church was located in Madina, a suburb of Accra and became prominent in the early 2000s as a result of healing, deliverance and prophetic claim of its founder, especially for the use of anointed Lemons and *koko* (a local porridge usually taken for breakfast) in curing all kind of health problems (Personal Interview, Pastor/Theologian, Refreshing Hour Ministries, Accra, 23 May 2015). The church attracted significant congregants from various socio-economic backgrounds.
8 According to Gifford, whereas the first and second waves were epitomised by the emergence of Archbishop Duncan William's Christian Action Faith Ministries (CAFM) and Pastor Otabil's International Central Gospel Church (ICGC), the miraculous wave was epitomised by the emergence of Bishop Charles Agyin Asare's World Miracle's Church in the 1980s. Gifford identified Prophet Salifu Amoako's Alive Chapel among the ministries that laid much emphasis on the prophetic ministry in the mid-1990s.
9 Rev. Isaac Owusu Bempah, and Prophet Agyemang Prempeh cited these biblical on different episodes of the *Good Evening Ghana* programme on Accra based Metro TV hosted by Paul Adom Otchere, in January 2016.
10 Interview with Rev. Prof. Emmanuel Asante, Methodist Church/Chairman, National Peace Council, July 2016, Accra.
11 *Ibid*.
12 A video of Prof. Atta Mills encounter with the Nigeria Popular Charismatic Prophet T. B Joshua in the church is available at: www.youtube.com/watch?v=VifKmCFBXac (accessed 14 May 2015).
13 It was not only charismatic Christian pastors who were at the centre of these election prophecies. Spiritualists aligned to African Traditional Religion and a few of Islamic clerics were also involved in the phenomenon. Notable among the African traditional priests were the famous Nana Kwaku Bonsam and Naa Tia Salifu Shiraz. Sheikh Mallam Musa, an Islamic cleric, also came out with some prophetic declarations
14 Prior to the 2012 elections, Archbishop Duncan Williams of the Christian Action Faith Ministries, a prominent pioneer of the charismatic movement, admonished his colleagues that the gift of prophecy should not be hijacked for political purposes. He reminded Ghanaians of the violent political conflict in neighbouring Cote D'ivoire, where the charismatic churches manipulated religious and ethnic sentiments in favour of the then incumbent President Gbagbo (Vüllers 2011).
15 While a certain degree of state regulation of the religious landscape remains a potential option, any such attempt has implications on religious freedom (Fox & Flores 2012; Finke & Harris 2012) and likely to face some resistance from civil society as occurred under military rule in the 1980s (Hackett 1998).
16 In the view of one the pastors interviewed, Ghana is a secular state, not a theocracy, as such even though he is a Pentecostal-charismatic theologian he does not see the need for election prophecies. He also argued that media contributes to exacerbate tensions in the country because a significant proportion of media practitioners are not professionally trained, and tend to focus on *sensationalism* and *parochial* journalism. He also stressed that a large number of pastors in the Pentecostal-charismatic denomination are not professionally trained in any

credible Theological Institutions (Rev. Justice Arthur, Pastor Refreshing Hour International Ministries, Accra, 17 May 2015).
17 During the 2000 election campaign the NPP adapted Cindy Thompson's (a local Gospel musician) famous *Ewuarde Kasa* (God Will Speak) Gospel song (Gifford 2004). In 2008 Prof. Mills voyaged to T. B. Joshua's Synagogue Church of Nations (SCOAN) for a prophecy and *anointing* for a successful elections) whereas the NPP candidate Nana Akuffo (also a lawyer) made a religious pilgrimage to Jerusalem for Prayers towards a successful election. The NPP slogan for the 2008 election was the "the Battle is the Lord's", and adaptation from 2 Chronicles 20:15 of the Christian Bible.
18 In 2012, Nana Kwaku Bonsam, a famous traditional priest contested the election prophecies of Rev. Bempah. This led to a confrontation (via the media) and a challenge for a spiritual contest to show which of the two has genuine spiritual powers (Peace FM online, 21 February 2013).

## References

Addo, O. E. 1997. *Kwame Nkrumah: A Case Study of Religion and Politics in Ghana*. Lanham, MD: University Press of America.

Asamoah-Gyadu, K. 2005. *African Charismatics: Current Developments Within Independent Indigenous Pentecostalism in Ghana*. Studies of Religion in Africa Series. Leiden: Brill.

Basedau, M., G. Strüver, J. Vüllers & T. Wegenast. 2011. 'Do Religious Factors Impact Armed Conflict? Empirical Evidence From Sub-Saharan Africa'. Working Paper No 168. German Institute of Global and Area Studies (GIGA) Research Program on Violence and Security. Available at: www.giga-hamburg.de/working papers (accessed 26 February 2015).

BBC Africa Online. 2013. 'Ghana Supreme Court Upholds John Mahama's Win'. 29 August 2013. Available at: www.bbc.com/news/world-africa-23878458 (accessed 4 August 2016).

Boafo-Arthur, K. 2008. Democracy and stability in West Africa: the Ghanaian experience. Nordiska Afrikainstitutet: Department of Peace and Conflict Research. Uppsala: Uppsala University.

Brubaker, R. 2015. 'Religious Dimensions of Political Conflict and Violence'. *Sociological Theory*, 33(1): 1–19.

De Smedt, J. 2009. ' "No Raila, No Peace!" Big Man Politics and Election Violence at the Kibera Grassroots'. *African Affairs*, 108(433): 581–598.

De Witte, M. 2011. 'Touched by the Spirit: Converting the Senses in Ghanaian Charismatic Church'. *Ethnos: Journal of Anthropology*, 76(94): 510–533.

Deacon, G. 2015. 'Driving the Devil Out: Kenya Born Again Elections'. *Journal of Religion in Africa*, 45: 200–220.

Deacon, G. & G. Lynch. 2013. 'Allowing Satan in? Toward a Political Economy of Pentecostalism in Kenya'. *Journal of Religion in Africa*, 43(2): 108–130.

DiMaggio, P. J. & W. Powell. 1983. 'The Iron Cage Revisited" Institutional Isomorphism and Collective Rationality in Organizational Fields'. *American Sociological Review*, 48(2): 147–160.

Dovlo, E. 2006. 'Religion and the Politics of Fourth Republican Elections in Ghana (1992, 1996)'. *Ghana Bulletin of Theology*, 1: 3–19.

Ellis, S. & G. Ter Haar. 1998. 'Religion and Politics in Sub-Saharan Africa'. *The Journal of Modern African Studies*, 36(2): 175–201.

Ellis, S. & G. Ter Haar. 2007. 'Religion and Politics: Taking African Epistemologies Seriously'. *Journal of Modern African Studies*, 45(3): 385–401.
Ephson, B. 2014. *2012 and 2016 Elections*. Accra: Allied Press.
Finke, R., & J. Harris. 2012. Wars and Rumours of Wars: Explaining Religiously Motivated Violence. In J. Fox & D. Flores (Eds) Religion, Politics, Society and the State. New York: Oxford University Press: 53–71
Fox, J., & D. Flores. 2012. Religious Freedom in Constitutions and Law: A Study in Discrepancies. In J. Fox (Ed) Religion, Politics, Society, and the State. New York: Oxford University Press: 27–52.
Ghana Statistical Service. 2013. '2010 Population and Housing Census: National Analytical Report'. Available at: www.statsghana.gov.gh/docfiles/2010phc/National_Analytical_Report.pdf
Gifford, P. 2004. *Ghana's New Christianity*. London: Hurst and Co Publishers.
Gifford, P. 2015. *Christianity, Development and Modernity in Africa*. London: Hurst and Co. Publishers.
Gyimah-Boadi, E. 1996. 'Civil Society in Africa'. *Journal of Democracy*. 7(2): 118–132.
Gyimah-Boadi, E. 2001. 'Peaceful Turnover in Ghana'. *Journal of Democracy*, 12(2): 103–117.
Hackett, R. 1998. 'Charismatic/Pentecostal Appropriation of Media Technologies in Nigeria and Ghana'. *Journal of Religion in Africa*, 28: 258–277.
Hackett, R. & J. Rosalind 2001. 'Prophets, "False Prophets," and the African State: Emergent Issues of Religious Freedom and Conflict'. *Nova Religion: The Journal of Alternative and Emergent Religions*, 4(2): 187–212.
Iannaccone, L. R. 1998. 'Introduction to the Economics of Religion'. *Journal of Economic Literature*, XXXVI: 1465–1496.
Joshua, M. 2016. 'Co-optation Reconsidered: Authoritarian Regime Legitimation Strategies in the Jordanian Arab Spring'. *Middle East Law and Governance*, 8(1): 32–56.
Krucken, G. & G. Drori. 2009. World Society: A Theory and Research Program in Context. In G. Krucken & G. Drori (Eds) World Society: The Writings of John Meyer. Oxford: Oxford University Press: 3–35.
Marshall, R. 2009. *Political Spiritualties: The Pentecostal Revolution in Nigeria*. Chicago: University of Chicago University Press.
Metro TV. 2016. 'Assessing the Role of Prophecies in the 2016 Elections'. Broadcasted on 5 January 2016 Edition of Good Evening Ghana Program, Hosted Paul Adom Okyere With Prophet Agyemang Prempeh of the Springs of Joy Ministries and Broadcaster Gilbert Abeiku Aggrey as guests. Available at: www.youtube.com/watch?v=aXAKnFcZ2mA (accessed 14 November 2017).
Metro TV. 2016. 'Assessing the Role of Prophecies in the 2016 Elections'. Broadcasted on 5 January 2016 Edition of Good Evening Ghana Program, Hosted Paul Adom Okyere With Rev. Isaac Owusu Bempah of the Glorious Word Ministries as guest. Available at: www.youtube.com/watch?v=aXAKnFcZ2mA (accessed 14 November 2017).
Meyer, J. W. & B. Rowan. 1977. 'Institutionalized Organizations: Formal Structure as Myth and Ceremony'. *American Journal of Sociology*, 83(2): 340–363.
Ministry of Finance Government of Ghana. 2015. 'Medium Term Expenditure Framework (MTEF) for 2015–2017'. Programme Based Budget Estimates for the Electoral Commission. Available at: www.mofep.gov.gh/sites/default/files/budget/2015/MDAs/Budget-Estimates-008-EC.pdf

New Patriotic Party. 1993. *The Stolen Verdict: Ghana, November 1992 Presidential Election: Report of the New Patriotic Party*. Accra: New Patriotic Party.

*New York Times*. 2000. '235 Sect Members Reported in Suicide by Fire in Uganda'. Available at: www.nytimes.com/2000/03/19/world/235-sect-members-reported-in-suicide-by-fire-in-uganda.html (accessed 13 November 2016).

Ocquaye, M. 1980. *Politics in Ghana: 1972–1979*. Accra: Tornado Publishers.

Pobee, S. J. 1991. *Religion and Politics in Ghana*. Accra: Asempa Publishers.

Quarshigah, E. 1999. 'Legislating Religious Liberty: The Ghanaian Experience'. *Brigham Young University Law Review*, 2: 589–607. Available at: http://digitalcommons.law.byu.edu/lawreview/vol1999/iss2/6 (accessed 7 November 2016).

Quayesi-Amakye, J. 2015. 'Prophetic Practices of Contemporary Pentecostalism in Ghana'. *Canadian Journal of Pentecostal Charismatic Christianity*, 6: 43–69.

Ramsbotham, O. 2005. 'The Analysis of Protracted Social Conflict: A Tribute to Edward Azar'. *Review of International Studies*, 31(1): 109–126. Available at: www.jstor.org/stable/40072074 (accessed 7 March 2017).

Ramsbotham, O., T. Woodhouse & H. Miall. 2011. *Contemporary Conflict Resolution: The Prevention, Management and Transformation of Deadly Conflicts*. Cambridge: Polity Press.

Ranger, T. (Ed) 2008. *Evangelical Christianity and Democracy in Africa*. Oxford: Oxford University Press.

Sackey, M. B. 2006. *New Directions in Gender and Religion: The Changing Status of Women in African Independent Churches*. Oxford: Lexington Books.

Stark, R. & R. Finke. 2000. *Acts of Faith: Explaining the Human Side of Religion*. Berkeley, CA: University of California Press.

Stewart, F. 2009. 'Religion Versus Ethnicity as a Source of Mobilization: Are There Differences?' MICROCON Research Working Paper 18, Brighton. Available at: www.microconflict.eu/publications/RWP18_FS.pdf (accessed 13 March 2015).

Studebaker, S. 2016. *A Pentecostal Political Theology for American Renewal*. New York: Palgrave.

van Gyampo, R. E. 2015. 'The Church and Ghana's Drive Towards Democratic Consolidation and Maturity'. *Journal of Political Sciences and Public Affairs*, 3(2): 1–7.

Vüllers, J. 2011. 'Fighting for a Kingdom of God? The Role of Religion in the Ivorian Crisis'. A working paper of the German Institute of Global and Area Studies (GIGA) Violence and program Security No 178. Available at: www.giga-hamburg.de/de/system/files/publication/wp178_Vullers.pdf (accessed 12 May 2015).

Wariboko, N. 2014. *The Charismatic City and Public Resurgence of Religion: A Pentecostal Social Ethics of Cosmopolitan Urban Life*. New York: Palgrave Macmillan.

Whitfield, L. 2003. 'Civil Society as Idea and Civil Society as Process: The Case of Ghana.' Oxford Development Studies. 31(3): 379–400.

Witham, L. 2010. *Markets Place of the Gods: How Economics Explain Religion*. Oxford, New York: Oxford University Press.

# 4 Democratic backsliding, religious institutions and the constitution of citizenship in sub-Saharan Africa

*Elizabeth Sheridan Sperber*

In recent decades, several major socio-demographic and political-economic trends have transformed sub-Saharan African societies. In this chapter, I focus on the intersection of two of these trends, namely the ongoing struggle for more democratic political systems and the rapid growth of Christianity, especially Charismatic and Pentecostal Christianity – the fastest growing religious groups on the subcontinent (Lugo & Cooperman 2010). By examining the reciprocal relations between these two trends, I aim to shed new light on the significance of Christianity in African politics, and its increasingly contested nature.

Specifically, I draw on original qualitative research conducted in the officially Christian state of Zambia between 2011 and 2016 to explore variation in the conception and enactment of 'Christian citizenship' across denominations and over time. As I detail below, I adopt an inclusive definition of citizenship focused on individuals' voluntary participation in activities intended to influence social, economic or political norms and institutions (Citizenship Development Research Center [C-DRC] 2011:4). As such, I conceptualise *Christian citizenship* in terms of i) the use of explicitly Christian *values or beliefs* to influence social, economic or political norms and institutions, and ii) the role of *faith-based institutions* in the mobilisation and expression of citizens' preferences over social, economic or political outcomes.

The recent transformation of Africa's religious landscape is difficult to overstate. Over the last 60 years, the percent of Christians in sub-Saharan Africa has more than doubled, with Pentecostal and Charismatic forms of Christianity growing fastest (Lugo & Cooperman 2010). Members of these groups emphasise the gifts of the Holy Spirit, including prophesy, exorcism, supernatural or divine healing, and speaking in tongues, among others. They also emphasise literal interpretation of the Bible, narrative theology and witness, community-based evangelism, and demonise tribal or traditional religion (Meyer 2004; religious terminology is further defined in the following section).

The rapid growth of these movements within Christianity has also been accompanied by a rise in the 'politicisation' of religion, meaning that political coalitions are increasingly organised around religious identity and institutions, or that access to political or economic benefits is perceived to depend upon religious identity (Fearon 1999). The Pew Forum (2010), for instance, juxtaposes the importance of Pentecostals in the public sphere today with other major socio-political trends in Africa's recent history:

> While nationalist movements drove African politics during the era of decolonization in the 1950s and 1960s, and mainline church leaders were deeply involved in the continent's efforts at democratization in the 1980s and early 1990s (Gifford 1995), Pentecostals have become increasingly important political actors in the last 15 years.
> (Lugo & Cooperman 2010)

An important and growing body of research on Pentecostal and Charismatic Christianity has advanced understanding about the connections between the rise of these groups in sub-Saharan Africa and the effects of neoliberalism and globalisation (Marshall 1998, 2009; Comaroff & Comaroff 2008; Comaroff 2012; McGovern 2012). This literature emphasizes that:

> Pentecostal movements do not merely question, from below, the tenets of liberal modernist knowing and being. They aim, also, to counter the signature institutional arrangements that have nurtured the modernist world view . . . [which] presume a clear separation between a secular neutral public domain and the realm of private commitment, interest and belief. . . . Born-again faiths have tended to challenge that divide in various ways, seeking to reshape the received order of things, challenging the 'impartiality' of state law, the legitimacy of secular government, and the perceived moral vacuity of public institutions.
> (Comaroff 2012:47)

Less understood, however, is the relationship between the historic Catholic and mainline Protestant churches at the forefront of many African struggles for democratisation, and the rise of new and often competing forms of Christianity in the public sphere. A main contribution of this chapter is to excavate connections between these two overlapping 'moments' in African Christianity and politics, and to draw out the roles that different Christian institutions have played in the (re-)definition of Christian citizenship. In doing so, this chapter also illuminates the important yet understudied role of meso-level Christian institutions, such as mainline Protestant umbrella bodies and coalitions of Evangelical and Pentecostal churches, in the *constitution* of new modes of Christian citizenship, i.e, religiously inflected political engagement.

Below, I clarify my use of key religious terms in this chapter, and then review the roles that various Christian institutions played in 'third wave' democratisation in the region. In light of this history, the analytical advantages of inclusive conceptualisations of citizenship are clear. This is especially relevant for scholars of religion and politics in Africa, where (religious) associational life has helped to constitute new political systems and identities. Building on this history and conceptual discussion of religious associational life in African politics, I then examine why and how Christian umbrella bodies occupied powerful political positions in many African states by the end of the Cold War. Given that these institutions often saw themselves as 'watchdogs' of new democratising governments, I argue that they unwittingly incentivised politicians to cultivate a competing modes of Christian community building and citizenship to counter criticism from the older 'activist' churches. The final section illustrates this argument – and teases out its stakes for Christian citizenship on the continent through qualitative analysis of original data from Zambia.

## Religious terminology

This chapter focuses attention on the roles of older mission churches, I therefore reserve use of the term Charismatic to refer to members of Charismatic Renewal movements *within* the Catholic and mainline Protestant churches. Unless otherwise noted, I follow the Pew Forum and others who use the term Pentecostal to refer to members of both older 'mainline' Pentecostal churches, such as the Assemblies of God, and newer 'third wave' churches, which others in this volume refer to as Pentecostal-charismatic. Admittedly, all of these categories rely on ideal types, that blur and even overlap. Nevertheless, they are useful in research (such as my own) because they align with the categories that demographers and other quantitative scholars employ. For instance, the World Christian Database reveals that today, approximately one in 12 of the 480 million Christians residing in sub-Saharan Africa identifies as Pentecostal, and another one in 12 identify as Charismatic Catholics. Millions more claim membership in Charismatic subgroups of mainline Protestant and older Evangelical churches (Johnson, & Zurlo 2015; Lugo & Cooperman 2010).

Although the terms Evangelical, Charismatic and Pentecostal are often used interchangeably in common parlance, I follow Freston (2004), Bebbington (1989) and others in using the term "Evangelical" (with a capital e) to refer to older missionary churches, such as the Baptists, Lutherans and Methodists, which embrace many similar tenants as other born-again sects, but which were well-established on the continent decades before Pentecostal and Charismatic movements exploded demographically. Notably, Evangelicals are often contrasted with Pentecostals and Charismatics, because they do not believe that the gifts of the Holy Spirit (e.g., speaking in tongues, exorcism) can be experienced today. When used with a lowercase e, the terms evangelical and evangelical(ism) refer to efforts to spread the Christian gospel.

## Constructing citizenship amidst struggles for democratisation

Beginning in the late 1980s, a stunning wave of political transformation swept the African subcontinent: between 1989 and 1994, *more than half* of all major sub-Saharan states transitioned from single party to multiparty electoral regimes (Bratton & van de Walle 1997). In at least half of these states, domestic Catholic and Protestant churches played key roles, providing mobilising frames, social and informational networks, and material support needed to facilitate transition (Toft, Philpot & Shah 2011:96; Gifford 1995, 1998; Ranger 2008).

In every African country where churches played major roles facilitating post-Cold War political transitions, they wielded their influence largely *through collective bodies* that aimed not only to mobilise pro-democratic citizens, but also to influence conceptions of national belonging, civic rights and legitimate governance. As I detail below, these collective bodies often embodied the "norms of community cooperation, structures of voluntary association, and networks of public communication" that typically define civil society (Bratton 1994:2). While these structures vary organisationally across denominations, their ability to aggregate and direct their influence through collective, often hierarchical bodies helped to facilitate and defend their political involvement. Catholics, for example, refer to their numerous and well-staffed organisations as 'Episcopal Conferences', while mainline Protestants have created umbrella bodies at the national level that mirror the World Council of Churches, each with its own unique name. These structures help them collect and disseminate information and mobilise collective action.

It is in this context that the analytical advantages of more recent, "inclusive" definitions of citizenship become clear. As noted in the introduction, this approach conceptualises citizenship broadly in terms of individuals' capacity to participate in society in ways that influence political, economic, social and cultural institutions, including but not limited to formal political rights (C-DRC 2011:4; also see Gaventa 2002:2; Nyamu-Musembi 2002; Cornwall 2006). Importantly, such a definition shifts emphasis away from *de jure* rights, and towards *de facto* experiences of associational life. Even when regimes severely constrain political participation, for instance, citizenship practices manifest in concerted attempts to revise "exclusionary practices and bring about change" (Kabeer 2005:22). Although such practices are not always geared towards the ideal typical secular democratic mode of citizenship that Western-educated scholars sometimes "project" onto other societies (Kasfir 2013), these practices are nevertheless constitutive experiences connecting individual agency to institutional change (or defence of stasis).

Such an inclusive definition of citizenship is particularly useful for scholars of religion and politics. If you imagine a Venn diagram with one sphere that represents religious practice and belonging, and another that represents national identity and citizenship, it is clear that Christian citizenship, meaning participation in the public sphere framed by specific Christian values or facilitated by specific faith-based institutions, lies in the overlapping portion of the spheres. In doing so, we can see clearly that practices associated with belonging in (different) Christian religious institutions are increasingly inseparable from and *constitutive of* (different) citizenship practices. While this might not have surprised scholars of colonial governance, it is a far cry from the visions held by African nationalists less than 50 years ago.

Of course, this does not mean that all individuals engaging in what I am designating as 'Christian citizenship' share interests, preferences or even religious convictions. There are important questions about the substance of citizens' ideas and actions, as well as the organisational structures and institutional capacity of specific Christian institutions that they distinguish different forms or 'modes' of Christian citizenship. The next section traces the recent history of how an important, older modes of Christian citizenship not only came to exist, but came to occupy a particularly privileged socio-political position by the end of the Cold War, as well as the political pushback that this power incentivised in some "democratising" African countries.

## The role of collective religious institutions

The important role of the older churches and their groups of lay believers and activists arose largely as an unintended consequence of intense state repression and prohibitions on civil society during the 1980s (Bayart 1986; Phiri 1999). Whether it was thanks to their transnational ties, claims to spiritual authority or deep roots within local societies, major Christian institutions emerged from the 1980s as some of the most resilient and respected civil society institutions on the continent (*Ibid*; Gifford 1995; Toft, Philpott & Shah 2011). For instance, the fact that religious institutions such as the Kenyan Catholic Justice and Peace Commission (CJPC) and the National Council of the Churches of Kenya (NCCK) could justify their calls for democratisation on the basis of both their members' preferences *and* their devotion to a pro-poor, pro-democratic Christian social doctrine likely imbued these bodies with unique forms of authority (Gathuo 2004; Throup 2015).

Whatever the cause, church-state relations unfolded similarly in numerous other African states, such as Benin, Ghana, Malawi, Namibia, South Africa and Zambia. In Ghana, for instance, the mainline Protestant umbrella body, the Christian Council of Ghana, united with the Catholic Bishops' Conference to "radically challenge" the provisional autocratic government (Aboagye-Mensah 1993). Coalitions like this continuously "demonstrated a firm commitment to getting involved and making suggestions [about political transition] with a view to ensuring that there would be no manipulation, to any group's advantage, of the process expected to lead to a democratic Fourth Republic" (Gifford 1995:263). Therefore, by publicly challenging the legitimacy of nondemocratic rule, and simultaneously providing networks to disseminate information and mobilise action, well-trained, paid religious leadership to coordinate and articulate pro-democracy sentiment, and relatively secure space for organisation, these bodies played major roles in African political transitions in the early 1990s. Further, these Christian institutions often helped to transform church members into self-identified members of an aspirational, egalitarian, liberal polity that recognised the secular liberal state as a means to a faith-based end: greater protection for the poor and marginalised, and less abuse of power (*Ibid*; see Meyer 2004:13; Bediako 2007; I return to this below).

*Powerful positions*

In this effort, church bodies and coalitions benefited from relatively high levels of institutionalisation (e.g., bureaucratic capacity and established rules for leadership succession), as well as their structural position in society. Figure 4.1 depicts this position in a simplified form. It is clear from this depiction how the position of meso-level religious collective religious institutions can exert influence over the flow of information and other resources (e.g., social services) between state and community members, members' opinion-formation and expression, and relations between African citizens and government officials, on the one hand, and international power-brokers, on the other (e.g., the Vatican or World Council of Churches).

Broadly speaking, to the extent that any religious institution functions as an ecumenical arbiter of citizens' socio-political attitudes and behaviours, and international sources of power and prestige, they constitute noteworthy political actors. This is true regardless of the specific religious faith or country in question. But there are certain features of sub-Saharan political institutions, on the one hand, and specific attributes of the Christian mission churches in Africa, on the other, that give these churches an even greater potential for political influence in the region. Many African states

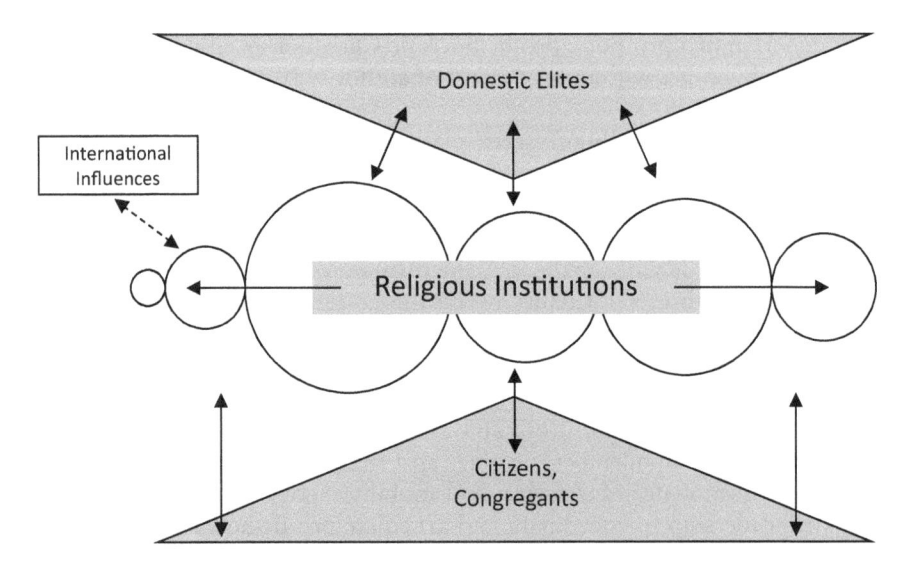

*Figure 4.1* Simplified illustration of influences at the meso-level

have been influenced, for example, by regional trends including: i) relatively recent colonial underdevelopment and related histories of politicised ethnicity (Mamdani 1996); ii) Cold War interventions that sometimes left lasting effects through civil conflict (Reno 1999); iii) socio-economic crises – and neoliberal 'solutions' – that undermined state legitimacy and prior civic and social institutions (van de Walle 2001; Comaroff 2012); iv) rapid urbanisation; and v) disproportionately large youth population (Sommers 2010; Sy 2017). These trends matter because they contribute to persistently low levels of institutionalisation across many sub-Saharan African states, which struggle to exert control over sparsely populated territories (Herbst 2014; Rakner & van de Walle 2009).

By contrast, many of the older, established Christian churches are highly institutionalised, with thousands of "points of presence" across African countries, even in extremely rural areas. The Catholic, mainline Protestant churches, and older Evangelical churches also benefit from the fact that they have clear training requirements for church leaders, which contributes to high levels of human capital (education) within their organisations. Additionally, these older churches operate with relatively centralised, hierarchical leadership structures that may promote the efficient division of labour and dissemination of information. In particular, the Catholic Church's hierarchal organisation makes it considerably easier for the church to "speak with one voice" in public affairs. Access to international volunteers and material support also strengthens the established churches and their mother bodies. For all of these reasons, Christian umbrella organisations, especially among the Catholic and mainline Protestant churches, and, to a lesser extent, older Evangelical churches, appear ideally positioned to model and facilitate Christian citizenship (i.e. the expression of agency intended to affect political, economic or social institutions that is rooted in Christian beliefs and/or mobilised through faith-based institutions). Indeed, as noted above, these churches have, to varying degrees, provided platforms for their members to enact citizenship.

However, Sperber (2016) documents that the success of older, established churches in promoting a version of Christian citizenship in the late 1980s and 1990s that accepted the core tenets of the liberal democratic state had a reciprocal influence on politicians in many African states after multiparty transitions. In these states, politicians simultaneously faced heightened political competition and pressures from the 'watchdog' mainline churches, and were often also engaged in the adoption of painful and unpopular structural adjustment policies. Under these conditions, politicians were significantly more likely to seek to *promote* of *alternative* forms of Christian citizenship for political gain. The new Christian citizen, for instance, would be so wedded to the totalizing impulse to collapse boundaries between formerly 'secular' and 'sacred' realms of life that they would tolerate antidemocratic reform packaged as policy change required to demonstrate national devotion to God. The reciprocal influence of religious movements and political incentives to intervene in the religious sphere are best illustrated through the specific history of individual cases. In the following section I introduce the case of Zambia, and then describe how this process unfolded drawing on an inductive analysis of religious leaders' reflections on the construction of Christian citizenship(s) in Zambia in the post-Cold War period.

## Zambian 'mother bodies' and the making of Christian citizenship

### Democratic backsliding

Zambia is a particularly illuminating case when it comes both to the role of Christianity in African politics, as well as the fundamental struggle for democratisation. Held up as an exemplary transition to multipartyism in 1991, the country witnessed major democratic reversals by 1996. To ensure a second electoral victory, born-again president, Frederick Chiluba, and members of his Movement for Multiparty Democracy (MMD) party, disregarded key tenets of democratic governance. Hence, a Freedom House report described Zambia's 1996 elections as "neither free nor fair", and noted:

> State resources and state media were mobilized extensively to support Chiluba and the ruling MMD [party]. Serious irregularities plagued election preparations. Voters' lists were incomplete or otherwise suspect; independent monitors estimated that more than two million people were effectively disenfranchised. The election was conducted under a new June 1996 constitution shaped to bar the election of Kaunda, the most credible opposition candidate. Most opposition parties boycotted the polls, and the MMD also renewed its parliamentary dominance. International observer groups that did monitor the polls, along with independent domestic monitors and opposition parties, declared the process and the results to be fraudulent.
> (Freedom House 1999)

Chiluba's party retained power for 20 years before being narrowly ousted from the Presidency in 2011 by Michael Sata's Patriotic Front (PF) party, which was essentially a splinter party led by a former MMD cabinet minister. In 2016 Zambia held its most turbulent elections in a generation, replete with major restrictions on the press, significant election-related violence and allegations of election fraud that have yet to receive in-depth investigation. On all of these grounds, Zambia constitutes both an important and emblematic case of the ongoing struggle for democratisation on the continent (Phiri 2008; Elone 2010).

### Christianity and Zambian politics

Zambia is also an important case to study from the perspective of religion and politics in the discipline of comparative political science. This is because widely influential studies of identity and politics in Zambia have focused on ethnic and linguistic divides, and left major questions about religion and politics in the country unasked (Posner 2005; Baldwin 2014). This is surprising, since Zambia's older, established churches played a central role in the 1991 transition, and continue to play critical leadership roles in the quest for accountable and transparent governance, pro-poor social policies and environmental protection (Gifford 1998; Cheyeka 2008; Sperber 2016).

Moreover, my own work (Sperber 2016) indicates that the prominent role of pro-democratic, established churches in Zambia – a country that is roughly 85% Christian – increased incentives for Zambia's ruling elite to cultivate of Pentecostal constituencies. To do so, the party disproportionately targeted valuable state resources, such as lucrative tax breaks, development funds, urban land plots and media license, to a burgeoning population of Zambian-run Pentecostal churches. The MMD also used rhetoric, government appointments and symbolic politics to enhance the social standing of Pentecostals, and to grow their churches. Most notably, this manifested in Chiluba's public and then constitutional declaration of Zambia as a Christian nation:

> On behalf of the nation, I have now entered into a covenant with the living God [. . .] I submit the Government and the entire nation of Zambia to the Lordship of Jesus Christ. I further declare that Zambia is a Christian Nation that will seek to be governed by the righteous principles of the Word of God.
> (*The Times of Zambia*, 20 February, 1994)

The mainline Protestant and Catholic mother bodies strenuously opposed this declaration. It was unchristian, they argued, to adopt a rhetorically exclusionary (if also legislatively toothless) position. The MMD succeeded in both maintaining protections for religious freedom and amending the constitution to declare Zambia an officially "Christian nation" (Gifford 1998; Phiri 2008; Cheyeka 2008).

In what follows, I draw on the words of major religious leaders in Zambia, as well as primary source documents from church mother bodies, to explore how the coexistence of this earlier mode of Christian citizenship relates to a newer, competing visions of Christian citizenship, which seek to collapse distinctions between the secular and the sacred in the public realm.

## Reflections of religious leaders

### *Catholic approaches to the formation of Christian citizens*

Since transition in 1991, established church leaders have routinely met with government officials. They made their discomfort with the government known through private conversations, public statements, pastoral letters (read aloud to all church members), and press releases. With respect to the Catholic Church, the power and perseverance of determined pro-poor, pro-democracy activism has manifested in numerous ways over time.

As a programme officer at Caritas explained in 2013, the Catholic Church "has in no way lessened its efforts to encourage the formation of a critical, active, and organized citizenry". Similarly, a leader of the Law Association of Zambia, a prominent progressive NGO, described the Catholic Church as "Zambia's second government".[1]

An illustrative example of the Zambian Catholic Church's grass-roots activism is the ambitious effort to establish Justice and Peace Teams (JPTs) in every parish throughout the country. Caritas Zambia – one of the seven departments of the Catholic Secretariat in Zambia – was responsible for this effort. The primary goal of the JPTs was to raise awareness about and to establish groups capable of advancing rights that include the rights to transparent and accountable governance, safe working environments, adequate social services and living wages (especially where foreign firms are concerned), among other rights.

The formation of JPTs is a prime example of the ways in which the Catholic Church can use its well-trained personnel, extensive resources and transnational infrastructure to promote democratic accountability in the far reaches of the country. For instance, in 2011, Eugene Kabalika, then-national Justice and Peace Division Program Manager at Caritas (current Executive Director of Caritas Zambia), described the effort:

> The hope is that throughout the country we shall have Justice and Peace teams who are able to respond – *respond* – to the needs of their communities. The specific mandate that is given to us comes from the bishops, and let me say right through from the Pope. The mission is the same throughout all of Africa, [and] the mission is to promote and defend human rights, and to make people know about human rights. So that is specific to the commission. The commission does that in different ways of promoting, defending, and also making people aware of their human rights. It could be issues around community justice, . . . issues around political awareness and justice, . . . [or] issues of the environment. It could be various issues.
>
> My goal is that these small teams we have, dotted around the country, would one day be able to respond to these challenges that we face. Because each community at each locality has its own different challenges; they are not all the same. Of course, they are influenced by international and national engagement that the government sometimes puts [creates], itself. For example, right now, [there is] a lot of collaboration with China. This comes with its own challenges, like how China treats the workers, so that is another dynamic. But that is now foreign influence into the community, so how do these Justice and Peace members respond to that in their community? How do they hold government accountable if members of their communities are exploited, or any other economic issues influence them? . . . It is hoped that they will be able to take action, and some of them have been able to take action.[2]

Working through Caritas, the Catholic Church therefore called for grassroots activism to promote good governance. Caritas organised citizens in localities that the state often cannot reach without working through local ethnic associations or other religious leaders. The Church supplied personnel,[3] and other resources, such as information and modest programmatic funding. And, in the spirit of democratic mobilisation, Caritas's training materials for JPTs strongly encourage JPT members to include members of other religious groups in their local organising.

This is consistent with the broader mission and structure of Caritas Zambia, which is "to foster and promote human dignity through programmes that endeavor to uplift the poor and marginalized from their situation and also to confront structures that deprive and oppress the weak" (Mulafulafu 2013). This mission is further reflected in numerous other ambitious, multi-year efforts that Caritas facilitates, such as a parliamentary scorecard project intended to promote accountability and transparency in government, and the formation of the Christian Churches Monitoring Group (CCMG), which has monitored several elections in Zambia.

More recently, in a 2016 interview with the Secretary General of the Zambian Episcopal Conference (of which Caritas is a part), Father Cleophas Lungu affirmed this emphasis on citizen "formation" and the active participation of church members as major priorities for the church. "One of the things the Bishops wanted to see is the Bishops speaking less and less, and the people – especially the laity, the lay faithful, the members of the church – speaking out" on such issues as electoral violence and gender based violence. These concerns, he noted, are concerns not only of the Bishops, after all, but "of the entire body of Christ, the *people*".[4]

## Mainline Protestant influences

Along similar lines, the Secretary General of the mainline Council of Churches in Zambia (CCZ), Rev. Susan Matale, emphasised the urgency of the social justice objectives that mainline Protestant churches implicitly accept as their Christian duty. For instance, she described the churches' commitment to push Zambia's government towards pro-poor, environmentally conscious policies:

> Our theme is very simple: Zambia is not a poor country. That's why we participate in programs about extractive industries [involved with Zambia's mineral deposits]. . . . We are concerned about environmental degradation, displacement of people, the wanton destruction of natural resources for the sake of mining activities. And also we are concerned that the huge proceeds generated from mining are not benefitting the people. The people get poorer, and yet the price of copper on the exchange is very high! . . . [And] at the same time, we've seen that politicians and a very *few* people get richer every day. Their lives improve *every day*. Yet, on the other side, the gaps are just widening.[5]

In a severely poverty-impacted country like Zambia, it is unsurprising that economic wellbeing is a concern for religious and civil society actors. But it is important to grasp the degree to which influential leaders, such as Rev. Matale, frame their obligation to promote equity as a *Christian goal*, insofar as inequity and poverty are "wrong" and social justice is "right". For instance, Rev. Matale extrapolated on the churches' involvement with "poverty issues":

> We don't want to go to church and talk about how good God is, when half the congregation has not had a meal! That is why we get involved. And the government many times will say, "go back to the pulpit and preach! You are sidestepping your roll! You belong in the churches!" And we say "we will preach on the streets if we have to. We will remind you, we will make your lives *uncomfortable* until you do the right thing".[6]

Here, poverty alleviation is framed as a Christian goal in at least two regards. First, individuals cannot live out their God-given potential when they are inhibited by extreme poverty, which makes poverty an obstacle that the Church has an interest in addressing. Second, Christian morality should drive citizens to attempt to constrain the abuse of power. But here, as in the case of Catholic social justice programmes, the ends (the conception of a socially just world), is fundamentally secular: it does *not* insist on Christianising that world in order for it to be just.

Lastly, reflecting on the differences between Pentecostal churches and member churches within CCZ, Matale related questions about structural differences between Pentecostal and mainline Protestant churches to their implied visions of Christian citizenship:

> [Another] big thing is that those Pentecostal churches belong to individuals. They belong to him [the pastor] and his wife, and his family. But for us, we are institutional: It is not about *me*, it is about the *institution*. When I go, the institution remains. . . . [With] these other churches, it depends on the leadership. And the leader can be there forever, making money and collecting tithes. . . .
>
> So the differences are there, they are there like day and night. On the other side, it's very easy for them [Pentecostals] to praise politicians because they want them [politicians] to come to their churches. . . . [But] we know that the government, because it has our basket – our cake – it has to be shared equitably among the people.[7]

As we would expect, this mainline vision of Christian citizenship deemphasizes the personal relationship with God, both among church leaders and members. In its place, the emphasis is on the role of enduring institutions, which purposefully minimise the significance of the individual and maximise the significance of the social objectives that members believe God wants Christians to promote, i.e., good governance and equitable distribution of resources.

### Unique challenges for the Evangelical fellowship of Zambia

By contrast, when asked to ruminate on some of the main similarities and differences among Pentecostal and other churches, Rev. Pukuta Mwanza, Executive Director of the Evangelical Fellowship of Zambia, began by stressing the very different relationship that Evangelical and Pentecostal churches have had with respect to social justice, or what he terms "holistic ministry". Put simply, Zambian Evangelicals were not in the business of providing social services historically, which makes them "laggards," in Mwanza's eyes.[8] Mwanza is intent on encouraging EFZ member churches to provide more social services and, perhaps to a lesser extent, advocacy on social justice issues, such as the need for access to healthcare, food and water. On this point, Mwanza identified the need to train pastors about the importance of holistic ministry:

> It continues to be a major problem – not a major problem, but challenge to increase the churches' understanding about the holistic mission. . . . Our biggest desire is that individual pastors at the community are able to internalize that vision – they have that wider perspective to ministry. At a recent [church] elders' meeting, it was announced that 5% of the tithe goes to widows, orphans, and vulnerable children. One of the elders, and engineer, said "but pastor, you'll be turning the work of the church into the work of an NGO!" Which meant that for a long time the general understanding was that helping the poor, helping the needy, these were not the work of the church, they were the work of NGOs. That has to be transformed.[9]

The problem, Rev. Mwanza continued, is that EFZ faces structural handicaps when it comes to the promotion of a more holistic ministry. First, Mwanza contrasted EFZ member churches' organisational structure with the Catholics and mainline Protestants:

> Our friends the Catholics are very different from us, . . . because they are very hierarchical and very, very systematic. They flow through a very definite line of communication, which is very different from us. And even though they say "the three church mother bodies," the Evangelicals are the more complex because of the diversity. We are dealing with thousands of different churches, and some of them are just one congregation, maybe they've got 2000 people. . . . So when you have thousands of these different churches, to mobilize them to rally behind one objective is very difficult.[10]

Second, Mwanza articulated disappointment that EFZ member churches have not had more support from international churches. Again, he contrasted this with the Catholic and mainline Protestant churches that have extensive international training programmes for their leadership, transnational NGOs and volunteer programmes, and broader opportunities for external material support (e.g., through partnerships with major development agencies). Reflecting on the 1990s and 2000s when EFZ member churches grew significantly, he noted that American churches should have played a more active role, even if it was "not necessarily money, but . . . even just prayer support or sharing information and strategies: How do you go about this, and so on. Because most of what we were doing was job-on training, learning as you go". The asymmetry of institutional strength and know-how across mother bodies clearly affects their capacity to serve, unify and mobilise their member churches.

Third, Mwanza delicately alluded to the challenge that some Pentecostal churches face when they accept support from the government. While having a born-again Christian president "helped to, for lack of a better word, to 'market' or 'promote' the church," and also came with new forms of material support for church growth, this support was not without complications. There are "two sides to the coin" of government support, Mwanza explained, noting that politicians' desire for political survival can lead them to "tamper with certain policies, including components of the constitution". When these politicians perceive a church to be very strong, and "able to say 'no to this, no to that,' who would give money to an institution that will not support you for whatever you [politicians] want to do? . . . The natural thing is to avoid supporting those churches, so that their strong advocacy role is not enhanced by government contributions". This can have a chilling effect on the willingness of some pastors – particularly pastors who run relatively small churches – to speak against antidemocratic reform, even if they wanted to.

Perhaps the most notable feature of these interviews, however, was the *absence* of support for the more "totalizing" Christian worldview that Comaroff (2012), Meyers (2004) and others have described. This was also true in over the course of multiple interviews with Bishop David Masupa, the founder and leader of Independent Churches of Zambia (ICOZ), a smaller and politically controversial competitor mother body for Pentecostal-charismatic churches in Zambia. Of course, the absence of evidence is not the same thing as evidence of absence, and I am not arguing that such a totalising Christian worldview is not present in Zambia. On the contrary, popular media and political discourse attest to its prevalence. Yet, it is plausible that the long-term effect of Zambia's strong competing vision of Christian citizenship – the pro-democracy and pro-poor activist vision associated with third wave democratisation struggles – has a moderating effect on Evangelical and Pentecostal leadership in the country over time. This is a topic ripe for further research.

## Conclusion

This chapter has sought to advance understanding about the evolution of Christian citizenship in Africa by returning to an earlier moment in the history of religion and politics in the continent. Specifically, I examined the relationship between the historic Catholic and mainline Protestant institutions that helped lead struggles for democratisation, and the rise of new and competing modes of Christian citizenship on the continent. Older conceptions of Christian citizenship are distinguished by their broadly secular policy objectives, and defence of the liberal attempt to separate church and state. By contrast, an emergent alternative to this approach posits a form of Christian citizenship intent on collapsing distinctions between church and state, sacred and profane (Comaroff 2012:45–48).

By analysing the historical trajectories of these two competing models of Christian citizenship in the Zambian case, the chapter illuminated previously understudied connections between (mainline) Christian political mobilisation associated with third wave democratisation (and ongoing struggles against democratic backsliding), and the more recent rise of Pentecostalism within African public spheres. Additionally, the chapter's focus on collective Christian institutions – such as umbrella or 'mother bodies' as well as broader religious coalitions – shed light on similarities and differences in the objectives and challenges facing Pentecostal, mainline Protestant, Catholic and other Christian institutions. These institutions have played pivotal roles in recent African history, and will continue to exert influence over the (re-)definition of Christian citizenship on the continent for years to come.

## Notes

1 Author interview, 9 June, 2011, Lusaka.
2 Author interview, Eugene Kabalika, 27 July, 2011, Lusaka.
3 Caritas reportedly employs over 100 paid staff members and 50 volunteers in Lusaka, alone. Available at: www.caritas.org/where-we-are/africa/zambia/
4 Author interview, Eugene Kabalika, 27 July, 2011, Lusaka.
5 Author interview, Rev. Susan Matale, 18 August, 2016, Lusaka.
6 *Ibid*.
7 *Ibid*.
8 Author interview, 17 August, 2013, Lusaka.
9 Author interview, Rev. Pukuta Mwanza, 17 August, 2013.
10 *Ibid*.

## References

Aboagye Mensah, R. K. 1993. 'Mission and Democracy in Africa: The Problem of Ethnocentrism'. *International Bulletin of Missionary Research*, 17(2): 130.
Baldwin, K. 2014. 'When Politicians Cede Control of Resources: Land, Cheifs, and Coalition-Building in Africa'. *Comparative Politics*. 46(3): 253–271.
Bayart, J. F. 1986. 'Civil Society in Africa'. In P. Chabal (Ed.) *Political Domination in Africa: Reflections on the Limits of Power*. Cambridge: Cambridge University Press: 109–125.
Bebbington, D. W. 1989. 'Evangelical Christianity and the Enlightenment'. *Crux*, 25(4): 29–36.
Bediako, K. 2007. 'Christian Witness in the Public Sphere: Some Lessons and Residual Challenges From the Recent Political History of Ghana'. In Sanneh, L. and J. Carpenter (Eds *The Changing Face of Christianity: Africa, the West, and the World*. Oxford Scholarship Online: 117–132.

Bratton, M. 1994. *Civil Society and Political Transition in Africa*. Boston, MA: Institute for Development Research: 51–82.

Bratton, M. & Van de Walle, N. 1997. 'Neopatrimonial Regimes and Political Transitions in Africa'. *World Politics*, 46(4): 453–489.

Cheyeka, A. M. 2008. 'Towards a History of the Charismatic Churches in Post-Colonial Zambia'. In J. B. Gewald, M. Hinfelaar & G. Macola (Eds.) *One Zambia, Many Histories*. Leiden: Brill: 144–163.

Citizenship Development Research Center (C-DRC). 2011. 'Blurring the Boundaries Citizen Action Across States and Societies: A Summary of Findings From a Decade of Collaborative Research on Citizen Engagement'. DRC Citizenship, Participation and Accountability. available at: www.drc-citizenship.org/system/assets/1052734700/original/1052734700-cdrc.2011-blurring.pdf

Comaroff, J. 2012. 'Pentecostalism, Populism and the New Politics of Affect'. In D. Freeman (Ed.) *Pentecostalism and Development: Churches, NGOs and Social Change in Africa*. Basingstoke: Palgrave Macmillan: 41–66.

Comaroff, J. & Comaroff, J. L. (Eds.) 2008. *Law and Disorder in the Postcolony*. Chicago: University of Chicago Press.

Cornwall, A. 2006. 'Historical Perspectives on Participation in Development'. *Commonwealth & Comparative Politics*, 44(1): 62–83.

Elone, J. 2010. 'Backlash Against Democracy: The Regulation of Civil Society in Africa'. *Democracy and Society*, 7(2): 13–16.

Fearon, J. D. 1999. 'What Is Identity (As We Now Use the Word)'. Unpublished manuscript, Stanford University, Stanford, CA.

Freedom House. 1999. 'Freedom in the World: Zambia'. Available at: https://freedomhouse.org/report/freedom-world/1999/zambia

Freston, P. 2004. *Evangelicals and Politics in Asia, Africa and Latin America*. Cambridge University Press.

Gathuo, A. W. 2004. 'A Country in Democratic Transition: Kenyan Churches in Civil Society'. Ph.D. University of Mass, Boston.

Gaventa, J. 2002. 'Exploring Citizenship, Participation and Accountability'. *IDS Bulletin*, 33(2): 1–14. Available at: http://onlinelibrary.wiley.com/doi/10.1111/j.1759-5436.2002.tb00020.x/full

Gifford, P. (Ed.) 1995. *The Christian Churches and the Democratisation of Africa* (Vol. 12). Leiden: Brill.

Gifford, P. 1998. *African Christianity: Its Public Role*. Bloomington: Indiana University Press.

.Herbst, J. 2014. *States and Power in Africa: Comparative Lessons in Authority and Control*. Princeton, NJ: Princeton University Press.

Johnson, T. M. & Zurlo, G. A. 2015. *World Christian Database*. Boston, MA: Brill.

Kabeer, N. 2005. *Inclusive Citizenship: Meanings and Expressions* (Vol. 1). London: Zed Books.

Kasfir, N. 2013. *Civil Society and Democracy in Africa: Critical Perspectives*. London: Routledge.

Lugo, L. & Cooperman, A. 2010. *Tolerance and Tension: Islam and Christianity in Sub-Saharan Africa*. Washington, DC: Pew Research Center.

Mamdani, M. 1996. *Citizen and Subject: Contemporary Africa and the Legacy of Late Colonialism*. Princeton, NJ: Princeton University Press.

Marshall, R. 2009. *Political Spiritualities: The Pentecostal Revolution in Nigeria*. Chicago: University of Chicago Press.

Marshall-Fratani, R. 1998. 'Mediating the Global and Local in Nigerian Pentecostalism'. *Journal of Religion in Africa*, 28(3): 278–315.

McGovern, M. 2012. 'Turning the Clock Back or Breaking With the Past? Charismatic Temporality and Elite Politics in Cote d'Ivoire and the United States'. *Cultural Anthropology*, 27(2): 239–260.

Meyer, B. 2004. 'Christianity in Africa: From African Independent to Pentecostal-charismatic Churches'. *Annual: Review of Anthropology*, 33: 447–474.

Mulafulafu, S. 2013. *Caritas Zambia Parliamentary Core Card Project: Measuring the Performance of Legislators*. Lusaka: Caritas Zambia.

Musembi, C. N. 2002. 'Towards an Actor-Oriented Perspective on Human Rights'. IDS Working Paper 169. Vancouver. Available at: www.drc-citizenship.org/system/assets/1052734370/original/1052734370-nyamu-musembi.2002-towards.pdf

Phiri, I. 1999. 'Why African Churches Preach Politics: The Case of Zambia'. *Journal of Church and State*: 41: 323–347.

Phiri, I. 2008. 'President Frederick Chiluba and Zambia: Evangelicals and Democracy in a "Christian Nation"'. In T. Ranger (Ed.) *Evangelical Christianity and Democracy in Africa*. Oxford: Oxford University Press: 95–130.

Posner, D. *Institutions and Ethnic Politics in Africa*. Cambridge University Press, 2005.

Rakner, L. & Van de Walle, N. 2009. 'Opposition Weakness in Africa'. *Journal of Democracy*, 20(3): 108–121.

Ranger, T. O. 2008. *Evangelical Christianity and Democracy in Africa*. Oxford: Oxford University Press.

Reno, W. 1999. *Warlord Politics and African States*. Boulder: Lynne Rienner.

Sommers, M. 2010. 'Urban Youth in Africa'. *Environment and Urbanization*, 22(2): 317–332.

Sperber, E. S. 2016. 'Deus Ex Machina? The Political Roots of Religious Change in Sub-Saharan Africa'. Unpublished PhD. New York: Columbia University.

Sy, Amadou (Ed.) 2017. *Foresight Africa: Top Priorities for the Continent in 2017*. Washington, DC: Brookings Institution. Available at:www.brookings.edu/wp-content/uploads/2017/01/global_20170109_foresight_africa.pdf

Throup, D. 2015. 'Politics, religious engagement, and extremism in Kenya'. In Cooke, J. & R. Downie (Eds) *Religious Authority and the State in Africa*. Washington D.C., Center for Strategic and International Studies with Rowman and Littlefield: 29–48.

Toft, M. D., Philpott, D. & Shah, T. S. 2011. *God's Century: Resurgent Religion and Global Politics*. New York: W. W Norton & Company.

Van de Walle, N. 2001. *African Economies and the Politics of Permanent Crisis, 1979–1999*. Cambridge: Cambridge University Press.

# Part 2
# Regenerating society
Economies and the public sphere

# 5 Heavenly commonwealth and earthly good

## Contemporary African Pentecostal-charismatic discourses on responsible citizenship

*J. Kwabena Asamoah-Gyadu*

In this chapter, I examine the meaning of citizenship with its implications for prosperity, privilege and responsibility in an African Christian context. Writing the introduction to a recent Charter on *Religious Freedom and Citizenship* in Africa, Yale University based Gambian professor of World Christianity, Lamin Sanneh, refers to the fact that the religious institutions in Africa lack both the resources and physical assets to substantially transform the conditions of living for its citizens.[1] In spite of this as he notes, their enduring presence and increasing influence means "religious institutions represent an important source of hope in a time of great uncertainty" (Sanneh 2012:2–3). I will argue in this chapter that Sanneh's submission here is very true of the new forms of religious movements that seem to be reshaping Christian spirituality in Africa, the Pentecostals. The religious and sociocultural contexts within which these reflections take place are important for at least three reasons. First, Africa has within the last half-century developed as a major heartland of Christianity. Second, religious leaders have had to give considerable attention to matters pertaining to the relationship between church and state because of the political instability and the endemic morale sagging corruption that keeps undermining public trust and confidence in governance. Third, this discussion is conducted within the context of contemporary African Pentecostal-charismatic Christianity, arguably the most significant religious development on the continent in the postcolonial era.

I will work with a definition of Pentecostalism as any Christian movement that affirms, values and consciously promotes the experience of the Holy Spirit as normative to Christian life, worship and expression. For Pentecostalism as a whole an emphasis on the experience of the Holy Spirit could be considered a common defining denominator. Historically, classical Pentecostal churches represented by the Assemblies of God have been better known around the world. Their key theological themes have traditionally included belief in Jesus Christ as saviour, baptiser with the Holy Spirit, healer and as the King who is soon to judge the world. The strong holiness and eschatological themes of classical Pentecostalism meant that there was much warning in their hermeneutics about the dangers of pleasure and material things. In classical Pentecostal preaching, heaven is their home, the world could be a dangerous place and its material things in particular are presented as prime obstacles in one's aspirations to enter God's kingdom (Anderson 2004; Asamoah-Gyadu 2015).

There are different types of Pentecostals but in this chapter, we take on notions of citizenship within contemporary Pentecostalism or Pentecostal-charismatic Christianity. The rise of contemporary Pentecostal-charismatic Christianity from the second half of the twentieth century led to a shift in emphasis from an eschatological message focusing on heaven and hell to one that challenges the faithful to pursue and gain wealth. For the avoidance of doubt the main characteristics of the new Pentecostals include: a charismatic and well-educated leadership, a membership of upwardly mobile youth, urban-centered mega-size congregations, an extensive appropriation of modern media technologies, a powerful sense of internationalism and prosperity preaching (Asamoah-Gyadu 2015:15–29). They have now have virtually become the *religious mainstream* as far as Christian presence on the continent is concerned. Increasingly, especially with advent of the prosperity gospel, the empowering presence of the Holy Spirit is also said to be evident in the material side of life and this I will argue has implications for citizenship. In keeping with the social and religious location of my knowledge and experience, most of my examples come from Ghana but this would be fairly representative of various developments outside the country.

## Pentecostalism and citizenship

Citizenship, in the context of this study, is the status of a person recognised under custom or law as the legal member of a community or sovereign state. Pentecostal-charismatic Christianity is associated with a view of citizenship that focuses very much on divine prosperity in both its spiritual and material senses. In Pentecostalism, the idiom of prosperity goes beyond material wealth to embrace "spiritual renewal of the relationship with God in Christ through the power of the Holy Spirit, the rebuilding of all forms of brokenness, the provision of health, the reversal of economic desolation, and the political and social wellbeing of individuals and communities" (Kalu 2008:213). Prosperity is synonymous with human flourishing. Pentecostal-charismatics have embraced a spiritual understanding of citizenship that has implications for human life on earth and also beyond our earthly existence. Related in particular to Christian citizenship in this life is Pentecostal-charismatic Christianity's theology of spiritual and material prosperity or human flourishing that is supposed to be a prime indicator of heavenly citizenship in this world. What are the implications of the belief that Christians, as citizens of heaven on earth, are expected to prosper or flourish in this world and what are the responsibilities associated with this worldview?

Human flourishing is a major theme in Miroslav Volf's book *A Public Faith*. In my judgement this idea is no different from the sort of prosperity sought for in Pentecostal-charismatic Christianity. Every human gift is an expression of love, Volf writes, and at the heart of our hoped-for future, which is a gift from a God of love is the flourishing of individuals, communities and our whole globe (Volf 2011:56). The theological premise of this understanding of human flourishing or prosperity as outlined by Volf is his contention that "a secular quest for the meaning of life is very likely to fail, and that the viable candidates for the meaning of life are all religiously based" (Volf 2011:65). This note on the religious foundations of human flourishing by Volf is particularly instructive for the African context. Here, no distinctions are made between the sacred and secular spheres of life. This worldview of the inseparability between sacred and secular realities has found some resonance with the Pentecostal worldview of reality. The biblical text often quoted by Pentecostal-charismatics to support this connection between divinity and humanity in the quest for our wellbeing is the word of Jesus in the gospel of John:

> The thief comes only to steal and kill and destroy. I came that you may have life, and have it abundantly.
> (John 10:10)

Added to this is another cardinal text of the prosperity gospel quoted from the first epistle of John and that reads as follows:

> Beloved, I pray that all may go well with you and that you may be in good health, just as it is well with your soul.
> (III John 2)

Taken together these biblical texts talk about human flourishing or prosperity that has its source in divine providence. Pentecostal hermeneutics take a literal approach to biblical texts of this nature and works hard at not only "claiming" their actualisation through authoritative prayers but also uses motivational messages of empowerment to encourage people to work towards their realisation. Some prosperity preachers take a simplistic approach to these promises of God, but increasingly there is a growing cohort of African Pentecostal pastors who combine the spiritual principles behind these promises with practical suggestions on how citizens must take their destinies into their own hands and work hard at what they do to achieve the required divine blessings. Pastor Mensa Otabil of Ghana's International Central Gospel Church (ICGC) is an example of this new breed of prosperity preachers. In one sermon transmitted over the radio, he told his youthful congregation: "you do not even have windows, and you expect God to open doors for you". "Doors" in this context referred to bigger opportunities that young people seek and the pastor's point was that those who desire those bigger opportunities must first learn to use "windows", which was a figure of speech meaning, "learn how to use the computer"! In other words, those young people who wanted to go far in life were being encouraged to take information communication technology seriously.

## Contemporary Pentecostalism and its dominion worldview

In discussing the relationship between human flourishing or prosperity and citizenship in this chapter, I do refer generally to Pentecostal discourses of prosperity as accessed from their media resources. These resources include book publishing, television and radio ministries and other such new media as the Internet, Facebook and Twitter. We will not discuss all these resources in full but the point is that there is an extensive engagement with Africa's upwardly mobile youth by their media-savvy Pentecostal-charismatic pastors. My reflections are illustrated from the sermons of ICGC's Pastor Otabil, a leading voice in Pentecostal-charismatic Christianity. ICGC is a mega-size Pentecostal-charismatic church that was founded in the early 1980s. In a period of 30 years, ICGC now has branches in other African countries, Europe and North America.[2] What makes such a figure significant is that a number of charismatic pastors like Otabil have built huge media ministries and wield much influence as international speakers within both Christian and secular contexts. His *Living Word* ministry on television and radio, which is also streamed live on the Internet, attracts quite a following beyond ICGC. The voice of a charismatic leader like Mensa Otabil is important to our understanding of Christian citizenship for a number of reasons. First, he represents those who focus on a prosperity that calls for a different approach to human flourishing beyond the exercise of mere faith and the use of authoritative words. Second, the translation of Christian spirituality into practical everyday action through the application of certain practical principles is paramount in his preaching. Third, in the application of the prosperity message, Christians are required to take their civic responsibility seriously.

The sort of Pentecostal-charismatic Christianity that Pastor Otabil represents has within the last half-century grown to become one of the largest streams of Christianity in the world (Synan, Yong, Asamoah-Gyadu 2016). Much of Pentecostal-charismatic Christianity's prosperity or dominion worldview was inspired by North America televangelism and the idea was that Christians must be rich and do well because it is the will of God for his children to prosper. Prosperity texts are verbalised in what are termed "confessions" or "declarations", especially during corporate prayer in the strong belief that they will come true for those who exercise strong faith in the "power of the word". The prosperity gospel shares the spirit of what Volf describes as the focus of "prophetic religion" and that is, "being an instrument of God for the sake of human flourishing, in this life" (Volf 2011:5). The prosperity gospel is about God's children, the "citizens of heaven", doing materially and spiritually well in this world evidenced by good health and wealth.

The theology of positives, success and prosperity fits very much into the atmosphere of globalisation in the world today. Given the numbers of young university students, graduates and professionals that these new churches attract, it would be very safe to argue that the leadership of the contemporary Pentecostal movement is shaping the lives and spirituality of those to whom the future of the continent of Africa belongs, at least in terms of leadership and governance. He may not thought of it that way, but prosperity preachers would love Volf's statement, "God wants to empower us to succeed" (Volf 2011:26). Prosperity preachers have developed a religious menu that refuses to idolise suffering (Kalu 2008:214). Pastor Mensa Otabil's Nigerian counterparts like Pastor Enoch Adeboye of the Redeemed Christian Church of God and David Oyedepo of the Living Faith Church Worldwide have become so influential that their religious services are patronised by politicians and public office holders (Ukah 2008:201–207).

That the official popular name of Bishop Oyedepo's church is "Winners' Chapel" says much about the sort of theological orientation that the new charismatic churches seek to bring into Christian spirituality. The expression "dominion" also features in their discourses as an umbrella term signifying a certain divine privilege, if not right to "dominate" world systems through the application of the practical principles of prosperity. Thus, one of Mensa Otabil's books is titled *The Dominion Mandate* and David Oyedepo has one titled *Walking in Dominion* (Otabil 2013; Oyedepo 2006). Prosperity occurs through the application of certain formulaic principles including naming-and-claiming things in the name of Jesus Christ or faithfully fulfilling one's tithing obligations (Gifford 1998). God gave Adam and Eve a "dominion mandate", it is thought, and current generations must seize on it to make a difference to their world. Paul Gifford has noted for example that Pastor Otabil's practical orientation to prosperity is easily discerned through his writings, which invariably, are transcribed sermons (Gifford 2004:113–139). His work *Enjoying the Blessings of Abraham* (1992), Gifford notes, brings him up as fairly standard faith preacher. However, there is much more to the understanding of Pastor Otabil in terms of prosperity than the simplistic approach taken by other preachers. His other work, the *Four Laws of Productivity* (1991) takes things further by demonstrating his concern for "effort and productivity" in human flourishing. He has another work titled *Beyond the Rivers of Ethiopia: God's Purpose for the Black Race* (1992) that according to Gifford underscores his practical approach to prosperity. This is a book that "finds Blacks in many crucial parts of the Bible, and is written to instill pride in them, since he thinks they are still inclined to regard themselves as inferior to whites" (Gifford 2004:113). There are other charismatic preachers who take a practical and popular liberationist approach to prosperity and this would include Pastor Matthew Ashimolowo of the Kingsway International Christian Center in London.

The new cohort of charismatic pastors are designated as charismatic "motivational speakers" because they seek to raise a new type of Christian citizen that focuses on applying management principles from biblical perspectives in building lives and communities. Unlike the old classical Pentecostal message that kept human aspirations permanently focused on making it to heaven through a strong holiness ethic and self-denial, the new type of Pentecostal-charismatic citizen aspires to do well in this life. The charismatic churches attract a lot of university students and young professionals. These constitute the future of African society. They are encouraged to engage their talents and abilities constructively in the building of their countries. Charismatic pastors speak at corporate business retreats and young peoples' conventions motivating them towards hard work and responsible citizenship. Pastor Otabil leads a team of Christian leaders in the organisation of annual "Festival of Ideas" in Ghana. This is a highly patronised programme that brings together young business executives and university graduates who are challenged speakers to set their minds to work by dreaming big and standing firm in the power of the Spirit to see their ambitions bear fruit for the service of humanity. The inspirational ministries we are talking about here touch on all the social and economic institutions including politics, economics, marriages and business management. As an example of this new form of motivational preaching aimed at creating a new citizen through charismatic Christianity, let us consider a sermon titled *Your Vote* preached by Pastor Otabil within the period of democratic elections in Ghana.

## *Your Vote*

Ghana went to the polls in December 2016 to elect a new President and close to three hundred parliamentarians to represent different constituencies around the country. Ghana's political temperature usually soars during the electioneering campaigns and 2016 was no different. In the midst of calls for prayers towards peaceful elections, Pastor Mensa Otabil decided to preach a sermon titled *Your Vote*, the first such election-related sermon by a Pentecostal-charismatic preacher. Pastor Otabil started this sermon by noting that he wanted to bring what he called "biblical perspectives" to what Christians should be doing during elections. He chose two biblical passages as his anchor texts. The first Bible passage came from Proverbs 1:10–15, and deals with warnings against casting one's lot with a gang of bandits. Verse 14 of the chapter states "cast your lot among us" and as he explained the picture was one of voting for a cause, although in this case it was a course of action that Christians would not endorse. The second passage came from Acts 1:21–26 which has to do with casting lots to select a successor to Judas. They voted on two people, Matthias and Barsabbas or Justus and Matthias won the election.

In what appeared to be a well-researched script, Pastor Otabil started with the etymology of the word "vote" and explained that according to its Latin roots, *votum* implied a promise or a vow made within the context of sacrifice in expectation of some salvific favour from the gods. The ancient Romans gave offerings at their shrines in return for divine favours, he noted. "A vote is like an offering", Pastor Otabil continued and "when we give to God, he gives it back to us in blessings". In the same way when we give politicians our vote we must expect them to deliver on their promises. "A vote is sacred", he explained, and therefore it is a way of entering into a covenant with the one for whom one votes. In a modern democracy, Pastor Otabil preached, citizens possess the right to vote and voting connotes endorsing an idea or system of governance. This was done in expectation that those we vote for would serve our interests: "voting means giving support to an idea in expectation that the idea will benefit you; something beneficial must come out of one's vote" he explained. For a Christian who must vote, there is a dilemma because, he noted, we live in the world as dual citizens – we are citizens of heaven and citizens of the earth at the same time. Pastor Otabil noted: "Christians are citizens of heaven but living on earth" and so when we pray "Thy kingdom come" we are affirming this fact. This "dual citizenship," according to Otabil, is a challenge to the Christian because it is not easy to please God and please human beings at the same time.

Pastor Mensa Otabil gives three main reasons for voting. First "your vote" is your sovereign will and when one votes he or she cedes that sovereignty to those in government. "Your vote is about surrendering your sovereignty to the President and it is a very serious action because no citizen can govern legitimately without the collective votes of those who go to the polls" he noted:

> On December 7, 2016, we will surrender our sovereignty as citizens to certain persons through voting for them and in doing that each citizen must ask himself or herself: "does the person I am voting for deserve my sovereignty?"

Second, according Pastor Otabil, we vote as a "sacred responsibility of citizenship". He explained how we must go beyond advertisements to interrogate political party proposals closely to ensure that they serve the best interest of the nation. He cautioned that it was irresponsible to put one's vote on "autopilot," meaning, citizens must never vote simply because they were affiliates of a particular political party or are related to someone seeking election into parliament. "Be free to change your mind if those you have voted for in the past have not delivered on their proposals" he advised. Third, Pastor Otabil noted that "our quality of life is determined by the results of our votes and therefore we should never allow any politician to take our votes for granted". "Vote for your beliefs and values", he advised and as a Christian your values must consist of truth, honesty and integrity. "Do not vote with selfish interests in mind", rather he noted, "vote for the best interest of the country".

Pastor Otabil's sermon was relevant. In many countries the loss of elections has not been taken lightly. Incumbent governments have sought to manipulate the systems of governance in order to perpetuate their regime leading to some of the bitterest conflicts that have occurred in countries like the Ivory Coast, Liberia and more recently the Gambia, all in West Africa. The connection Pastor Otabil makes between voting and a person's quality of life in also instructive. In African politics it is common practice for politicians to dole out little monies and gifts to especially poverty-stricken communities in subtle and blatant attempts to "buy" their votes. Such people and communities are then neglected once the political office has been secured (Gifford 1995, 1998; Ranger 2008). "Given their endurance and . . . increasing influence, religious institutions represent an important source of hope in a time of great uncertainty" (Sanneh 2012:3). Certainly the new charismatic motivational speakers fulfill such a role. Pastor Otabil cautions here about citizens not falling for such vote-buying deceptions because, as he notes, those temporal gifts do not determine what quality of life one would have in future. It is your vote that counts!

## Citizenship, kingdom and responsibility

In the Christian context then, citizenship means more than belonging to a nation. It encompasses belongingness both to Christ and to a community of believers. Citizenship for the Christian is heavenly but it must be translated for earthly good. Christians are referred to as "citizens" of heaven, a biblical description that as we have seen, has implications not just for our life with God after transitioning this physical existence but also brings with it responsibility towards society and neighbourhood. Citizenship thus relates to the legal right of a person to belong to a particular country or people group (Sanneh 2012). There are different ways of acquiring such a right of belonging. Citizenship could for example be acquired by birth or by being adopted into a particular family that already possesses such a right of belonging. In a world of conflict, civil wars, political instability, religious persecution and poverty, migration has soured considerably. Applying this to a Christian context the framers of the *Accra Charter of Religious Freedom and Citizenship* write:

> We are deeply convinced that faith gives its noblest expression in settings where all are free to serve the common good . . . where government secures the peace and good order taught by all the world's great faiths, and where government affords its citizens the right to live freely and recognizes their power to hold it accountable.
> (Sanneh 2012:7)

I have shown elsewhere that salvation in Pentecostal-charismatic thought begins with the born-again experience continues with the Baptism of the Holy Spirit manifesting in speaking in tongues but then usually moves on quickly to encompass the idea of material prosperity (Asamoah-Gyadu 2005: chapter 5). Pentecostal-charismatics love the patriarchal narratives in which God's blessing is manifested most concretely in human prosperity and wellbeing; long life, wealth, shalom or peace, fruitfulness in both agriculture and human reproduction. The promises of blessing to the patriarchs as Wright points out are thus a reassertion of God's original intentions for all humanity (Wright 2006:209). One way in which the patriarchal and exilic narratives are applied in Pentecostal-charismatic discourses is to see the "bondage" in which Israel found herself as being akin to the manner in which sin or worldly values hold people in bondage.

The story of the Prodigal Son in Luke 15 is a powerful illustration of how through divine intervention a person could be restored to dignity when he returns home from wild living in an alien land. In an alien land far away from home the gentleman lost his dignity. His life hit rock bottom to the point where he would even crave for food offered to pigs but could not get it. It was at that point that he comes to his senses, decides to do something about the situation, and actually puts his intention into action by returning home. Here he receives some form of welcome and restoration in defiance of the wishes of his elder brother to whom he had become an alien through loss of citizenship. It was important for the gentleman to be received back into community through an elaborate process of restoration as described by his father instructing his slaves:

> "Quickly, bring out a robe – the best one – and put it on him; put a ring on his finger and sandals on his feet. And get the fatted calf and kill it, and let us eat and celebrate; for this son of mine was dead and is alive again; he was lost and is found!" And they began to celebrate.
> (Luke 15:22–24)

In Pentecostal-charismatic discourses then the word citizenship has often been applied to at least two situations: firstly it is applied situations in which a person confesses Jesus Christ as Lord and therefore becomes a Christian. This is what is called the 'born-again experience'. Secondly a Christian is described as a "citizen of heaven" but who is expected to live a life of material success in this life. In other words, Christian citizenship could have both an existential and an eschatological means. In this life the Pentecostal citizen is encouraged to fight back, refuse to accept defeat, want, failure, pessimism and negativity (Kalu 2008:214). In order to achieve the Christian citizen is expected to engage with the socio-economic and political orders of their societies. The framers of *The Accra Charter of Religious Freedom* summarise the dual nature of Christian citizenship succinctly as follows:

> we recognize that governments and societies are provisional arrangements, for by faith we live in our countries while we look "forward to the city which has foundations, whose builder and maker is God" (Hebrews 11:9–10). As Christians we feel a particular burden to put forward a positive vision of how we worship the living God and point the way to God's reign, while giving due regard and respect to the governments under which all people, of all faiths, live together as fellow citizens, and so honor our rulers without ceasing to serve and to fear God.
> (I Peter 2:16–17) (Sanneh 2012:7)

These are the two senses in which Pastor Otabil used the expression citizen in his sermon *Your Vote*. The practicality of the message would have been relevant to non-Christians too but his primary audience was the Christian community of ICGC. We acquire the citizenship of heaven when we accept Jesus Christ as Lord and when we live in hope that one day when we pass on in death, we will join other citizens who live in heaven with God. The thought of Christian citizenship as life with God after physical death is outlined very powerfully by Paul in the following words to the Philippians: "But our citizenship is in heaven, and it is from there that we are expecting a saviour, the Lord Jesus Chirist" (Philippians 3:20). What the Savior will do when he arrives from heaven is "transform the body of our humiliation that it may be conformed to the body of his glory" and this he will accomplish "by the power that also enables him to make all things subject to himself" (Philippians 3:21).

The ancestors of the Christian faith lived their lives on earth with the ultimate goal of being with God in glory (Hebrews 11:13–16). Paying attention to the demands of this worldly existence is important but as far as the Christian life is concerned, citizenship requires more than just being a legal member of a particular group of people. Christians are called to live as "aliens" in the world because the values of this world in many respects are diametrically opposed to the values of the eternal kingdom into which ultimately, God expects to receive his children. In the words of Jesus, his people are in the world but they are not of it, which means, Christians live in this world as citizens of heaven. Pastor Otabil's sermon *Your Vote* attempts to bridge the gap between socio-political responsibility and Christian commitment as far as citizenship is concerned. "God did not create you with failure in mind but with success" Otabil would preach. His however is a different pathway to success from that offered by the simple naming-and-claiming approach associated with certain Word of Faith churches. For Otabil, "success is reached through confidence, pride, determination, motivation, discipline, application, courage – and by skills and techniques" and it is through these that the new African citizen is made (Brouwer, Gifford & Rose 1996:172).

Citizenship as we have noted relates to legal belongingness. People are citizens of particular domains and these domains have rulers, authorities or what we encounter in the Bible and traditional societies as kings. The English word "kingdom" is made up of two expressions and they are first, king which refers to the person who exercises authority and second, domain, which refers to the sphere of geographical control. Kingdom therefore refers to the domain over which a particular king exercises authority. Those who live within a king's domain are expected to live in obedience to his authority and of course the sovereign also has responsibility towards his citizens. Thus when Jesus taught his disciples to pray to God saying "Thy kingdom come", he was teaching them to desire the establishment of the authority of God in the lives of his people. The word could have eschatological implications by referring to being with God after leaving this earth in death but most importantly, Christian citizenship means living life under the sovereignty of God.

The coming of the kingdom of God marks the establishment of his *shalom*, peace, with its implications for harmony, tranquillity, health, wholeness, communal peace and divine grace in all things. The point in *Your Vote* was to make the point that the Kingdom of God was not simply to be understood in its eschatological sense but also in terms of human responsibility in making political choices that would help in nation building. This is an important one especially when considered against the backdrop of the fact that early Pentecostal movements had taken an extreme eschatological position to Christian citizenship. The reinterpretation of the Kingdom of God in Pentecostal-charismatic discourses of salvation marked a departure from what was preached in early classical Pentecostalism. The earliest Pentecostals expected Jesus Christ to arrive in their lifetime and so the material world, especially wealth, was approached with suspicion as potentially obstructive to genuine spirituality. Contemporary Pentecostal-charismatic theologies of prosperity and dominion work with an understanding of soteriology that is very "this-worldly" and practical in its theological orientation. This constitutes a move from an approach in which the Christian was thought to see things like politics as mundane and so were not encouraged to take active part in party politics to one in which secular politics is expected to be redeemed through Christian influence. There has been a dramatic shift in that position with many leading African political leaders not only campaigning on their Christian orientation but also church leaders now frequently hold special prayer services for their members in government.

The next line, following the statement "thy kingdom come" in the Lord's Prayer actually explains the meaning of kingdom even better when it says, "thy will be done on earth as it is in heaven". According to Pastor Otabil the Christian during voting must allow God to direct his or her will. In democratic systems of governance he noted, the president may not be one appointed by God as we have in the Old Testament but at least God recognises human choices. There is therefore a direct relationship between responsible Christian citizenship and human prosperity or flourishing. If God's will is done on earth then both personal and social realities will be transformed. In place of "kingdom" Paul often used "citizenship" in order to connect with his Greco-Roman audience. To the Philippians who were proud of their status as a Roman colony, as we have noted, Paul reminds them that their true citizenship is in heaven. Those who are mindful of their heavenly citizenship then live out their lives on this earth characterised by heavenly values. The proclamation of the kingdom, as Brenda Colijn notes, is the announcement of God's lordship over creation. It is more than the reign of God in the hearts of believers, she writes, the proclamation is "an authoritative summons to obedience" (Colijn 2010:72).

## Translating heavenly citizenship into earthly use

If Christian citizenship is more than merely belonging to a people or nation by birth, adoption or naturalisation, then what are the responsibilities that go with it? In many senses becoming a Christian also involves "swearing" an oath to owe allegiance to Jesus Christ as God's ultimate revelation to the world. Thus, a citizen of heaven is one who owes allegiance to Jesus Christ as Lord and lives in this world guided by the values of Christ. This is what Peter attempts to communicate to the Christians who had scattered under persecution when he writes to them:

> Beloved, I urge you as aliens and exiles to abstain from the desires of the flesh that wage war against the soul. Conduct yourselves honorably among the Gentiles, so that though they malign you as evil doers, they may see your honorable deeds and glory God when he comes to judge.
> (I Peter 2:11–12)

Christian citizenship then, as Peter explains here, has implications for personal morality and civic responsibility. Moral purity based on the fact that Christians are called into a life of holiness is critical to Christian citizenship. It is critical because Christians are supposed to be exemplary as far as personal lifestyles are concerned and this has implications for how people serve as private citizens and public servants. In a context like sub-Saharan Africa where Christianity has been growing by leaps and bounds, some have questioned the depth of spirituality that is professed in the churches. This is on account of the fact that corruption remains endemic even in places where Christians are in leadership. Pastor Otabil's challenge to citizens not to compromise their political votes for temporary benefits such as gifts from politicians in thus relevant in this context and so is taking the responsibility to vote seriously. A number of Africa's politicians profess Christianity and yet some of the worst forms of abuse of office, authoritarianism and dictatorships are associated with Christian leadership. What this means is that there seems to be a gap between Christian spirituality and Christian citizenship in society and that ought not to be the case.

## Conclusion: citizenship and contemporary Pentecostal-charismatic prosperity discourses

The word citizenship, particularly its implications for living in the world, features very strongly in Pentecostal-charismatic discourses of prosperity. In the first place to become a believer or to be born-again is to make a transition from a life of bondage to sin and worldly values into a new life that opens up possibilities for the believer in the world. Steve Brouwer and others have shown how in its origins in the USA this sort of "Christian fundamentalism" as they called contemporary Pentecostalism had the ambition to turn that country into a more Christian one and the earth into a more Christian world. This is now a global form of Christianity in which the Holy Spirit embraces active engagement with the social and political world (Brouwer, Gifford & Rose 1996:31). Through the new adaptations of the faith introduced by contemporary Pentecostal-charismatics, "many Christians come to understand that they are 'entitled' through divine intervention in their lives, to material rewards on earth" (Brouwer, Gifford, & Rose 1996:28).

The task of the prosperity-preaching charismatic leader then is to "declare the full counsel of God" to the present generation (Gifford 1998:79). There is obviously a case to be made for the exploitative aspects of this hermeneutic in which the charismatic pastor or televangelist's lifestyle of opulence and extravagance has often been presented as paradigmatic of divine prosperity.

In sub-Saharan Africa many have not prospered materially as promised even after observing all the so-called principles of prosperity. In a continent where belief in supernatural causality, especially witchcraft, is still very much a part of the Christian worldview, the power of evil has been invoked to explain the shortfalls of prosperity (Onyinah 2012:170). This has led to another difficult phenomenon – the creation of healing and deliverance centres – to deal with the problems of those who explain their declining fortunes in terms of the workings of witchcraft and other negative principalities and powers. Prosperity preaching is often merciless when it comes to poverty because a number of its preachers explain these things simply in terms of lack of faith and non-fulfillment of sowing-and-reaping obligations. It has a very weak theology of pain and misfortune that leaves many Africans without adequate pastoral answers to the quagmires of life. That type of prosperity preaching can be very anti–human development and progress because it over-spiritualises real human problems.

However, in what we have seen of Pastor Otabil's preaching, there are also practical and rational aspects of this discourse that are often overlooked. One of them is that prosperity in both its spiritual and material senses often results from the shift in lifestyle that comes with the born-again experience. Testimonies abound of people who as a result of listening to the motivational prosperity preachers available through the church and its media ministries have experienced a turn around in life. The establishment of Pentecostal-charismatic universities in Ghana and Nigeria has encouraged the born-again and Spirit-filled to return to school to improve their market value and take their place as citizens of developing economies with a lot to contribute towards nation building. There are many Pentecostal Christians in African politics today and pastors drum home the fact that the duty of the Christian citizen is work towards the prosperity of "Jerusalem", that is the country to which one belongs. On the personal level, the wellbeing of the believer begins when as a result of being in Jesus Christ a person rises above morally depraving habits such as sexual promiscuity, excessive clubbing and corrupt behaviour that denies communities the full benefit of their resources. Personal resources that were previously available for wild living is now garnered for a more responsible family life leading to stable home and better education for children.

Corruption is endemic in African public life and it has been cited as the single most important reason for the existence of certain types of poverty across the continent. The Pentecostal born-again leader is the new citizen of heaven who knows that his work and life must be governed by heavenly values and therefore positively affects workplace ethics in terms of the use of time and the management of resources. This explains why I have often spoken of the new prosperity hermeneutic in terms of a dominion theology in which the believer is called to dominate his/her world first through a sense of moral correctness that is extended into whichever areas of life that one finds himself or herself: politics, education, sports, economics and other areas of both domestic and public engagement. Thus, responsible citizenship is an important relatively new area of emphasis for motivational preaching and the fact that not a few Pentecostal-charismatic pastors have taken on the responsibility of leadership from previous lives as professionals only serve to motivate their upwardly mobile following. Africa's university campuses are major hotbed of Pentecostal-charismatic activity and young people looking for models in life have found the pastors of these churches as embodying their aspirations in life as citizens of a democratic and developing Africa.

## Notes

1 *The Accra Charter of Religious Freedom and Citizenship* was put together at a Conference held in Accra, Ghana in 2011. This conference on citizenship is an initiative of the Oxford Studies in World Christianity and edited and directed by Lamin Sanneh, the D. Willis James Professor of Mission and World Christianity, the Yale Divinity School. The Charter is available for free download from the Internet at: www.oxfordstudies.org/charter.html. Signatories to the Charter came from across Africa and they include the Most Rev. Dr. John Olorunfemi Onaiyekan, then Roman Catholic Archbishop of Abuja and Prof. Mercy A. Oduyoye, one of Africa's most accomplished female theologians.
2 ICGC's main auditorium, Christ Temple, in Accra seats about 4,000 persons. With its two Sunday morning services, the main temple where Pastor Mensa Otabil serves as pastor brings together at least 8,000 people every Sunday. The church has other branches all over Ghana and beyond with several boasting of mega-size congregations of between 2,000 and 3,000 worshippers every Sunday.

## References

Anderson, A. 2004. *An Introduction to Pentecostalism*. Cambridge: Cambridge University Press.
Asamoah-Gyadu, K. J. 2005. *African Charismatics: Current Developments Within Independent Indigenous Pentecostalism in Ghana*. Leiden: E.J. Brill.
Asamoah-Gyadu, K. J. 2013. *Contemporary Pentecostal Christianity: Interpretations From an African Context*. Oxford: Regnum Books International.
Asamoah-Gyadu, K. J. 2015. *Sighs and Signs of the Spirit: Ghanaian Perspectives on Pentecostal Renewal in Africa*. Oxford: Regnum Books International.Brouwer, S., Gifford, P. & Rose, S. D. 1996. *Exporting the American Gospel: Global Christian Fundamentalism*. New York, London: Routledge.
Colijn, B. B. 2010. *Images of Salvation in the New Testament*. Downers Grove, IL: IVP Academic.
Gifford, P. (Ed.) 1995. *The Christian Churches and the Democratization of Africa*. Leiden: E.J. Brill.
Gifford, P. 1998. *African Christianity: Its Public Role*. London: Hurst and Co.
Gifford, P. 2004. *Ghana's New Christianity: Pentecostalism in a Globalizing African Economy*. Bloomington, Indianapolis: Indiana University Press.

Kalu, O. 2008. *African Pentecostalism: An Introduction.* Oxford: Oxford University Press.

Onyinah, O. 2012. *Pentecostal Exorcism: Witchcraft and Demonology in Ghana.* Dorcet, UK: Deo Publishing.

Otabil, M. 1991. *Four Laws of Productivity: God's Foundation for Living.* Tulsa, OK: Vincom Inc.

Otabil, M. 1992a. *Beyond the Rivers of Ethiopia: A Biblical Revelation on God's Purpose for the Black Race.* Accra: Altar International.

Otabil, M. 1992b. *Enjoying the Blessings of Abraham.* Accra: Altar International.

Otabil, M. 2013. *The Dominion Mandate: Finding and Fulfilling Your Purposes in Life.* Accra: Kairos Books.

Oyedepo, D. O. 2006. *Walking in Dominion.* Lagos: Dominion Publishing House.

Ranger, T. O. (Ed.) 2008. *Evangelical Christianity and Democracy in Africa.* Oxford: Oxford University Press.

Sanneh, L. (Ed.) 2012. *The Accra Charter of Religious Freedom and Citizenship.* New Haven, CT: OMSC Publications.

Synan, V., Yong, A. & Asamoah-Gyadu, J. K. (Eds.) 2016. *Global Renewal Christianity: Spirit Empowered Movements: Past, Present and Future.* Lake Mary, FL: Charisma House.

Ukah, A. 2008. *A New Paradigm of Pentecostal Power: A Study of the Redeemed Christian Church of God in Nigeria.* Asmara, NJ: Africa World Press.

Volf, M. 2011. *A Public Faith: How Followers of Christ Should Serve the Common Good.* Grand Rapids, MI: Brazos Press.

Wright, C. J. H. 2006. *The Mission of God: Unlocking the Bible's Grand Narrative.* Nottingham, UK: Intervarsity Press.

# 6 Forging economic citizens

## Financial integrity and national transformation at Watoto Church in Uganda

*Caroline Valois*

In 2012 Uganda celebrated its Golden Jubilee, commemorating 50 years of independence from British rule. Addressing the public President Museveni declared how the next 50 would culminate in an apotheosis for the Ugandan nation, transitioning into "a first world country" through the "entrepreneurial spirit" and "private initiative" of its people (Museveni 2012). Any anniversary marking the independence of an African nation justifiably includes talk of economic transformation and progress. Yet, far from being only slogans for national celebrations, throughout the past decade these topics have come to increasingly characterise the Ugandan public sphere in the form of distinct discourses of economic transformation.

More frequently Ugandan political discourse is informed by a teleological understanding of the future defined in terms of unlimited economic potential for the nation and its citizens. As this notion holds distinctly moral qualities transforming Uganda is achieved by hardworking individuals living responsible lives – a vision that often incorporates an outright biblical understanding of the world. While broader political discourses stemming from the political elite understandably emphasise economic progress the particular concept proves more reflective of the paths of financial prosperity emanating from local *born-again* or Pentecostal-charismatic churches (PCC). Within PCCs fiscal responsibility and wealth building are fundamental components of living a Christian life – and ultimately cornerstones to transforming the nation. Yet, as this chapter makes clear, this goes beyond the well-documented prosperity gospel often espoused by African PCCs – or belief that God rewards faith through material accumulation "promising reward for totally non-economic reasons . . . a belief that God will not allow his faithful to perish" (Ranger 2003:117). Rather this employs a more pragmatic strategy that includes strategic financial planning and responsibility – traits that are seen to help believers be not only *good* Christians, but *good* Ugandan citizens as well.

Although diverse in nature Ugandan PCCs share a model of citizenship that is integral to broader church strategies of transformation, wherein the economic is central. From the perspective of local churches *good* economic citizens will not only transform the lives of parishioners, but will also create the broader conditions for national prosperity by cultivating the individual fiscal habits of the Ugandan citizenry. For Ugandan PCCs, 'economic citizenship' is a central component of a broader strategy of 'Christian citizenship' defined by a sense of collective belonging to a nationwide community of born-again followers ascribing to a set of narrow moral parameters that requires active political engagement.

This chapter investigates the concept of economic citizenship promoted within prominent Pentecostal-charismatic churches in Kampala, Uganda. I contend that the structural and ideological conditions of neoliberal reform that have taken place in Uganda, aided in the emergence of the Pentecostal-charismatic movement, and speaks to the underlying ideological components of Pentecostal-charismatic belief while merging with the longstanding concept of Christian citizenship.

Within the Ugandan context economic citizenship has become a defining feature in the public sphere, working as an assemblage produced by two interconnected elements. The first component is the neoliberal underpinnings of the Ugandan state, the legacy and impact of which – since the 1990s – has resulted in the retracted role of the state as a service provider, exacerbated economic uncertainty, widening inequalities, and the promise of largely unfulfilled economic and material accumulation. The second element is the rising prominence of the moral and material theology promoted by Pentecostal-charismatic churches. In Uganda, the historical conditions of neoliberal reform helped to make Pentecostal-charismatic churches more prominent political-legal entities, capable of playing a larger role in the production of public authority, and ultimately tapping into the void left by the retracted state as a consequence of neoliberal reforms.

Drawing on 14 months of ethnographic fieldwork from 2011 to 2013 this chapter elucidates the notion of economic citizenship by analysing the case study of *Watoto Church*, one of the largest and most established PCCs in Kampala, Uganda. Offering pragmatism and planning, church sermons function as 'teaching opportunities' to educate the congregation on how to be *good* Christian citizens by displaying responsible and communal financial habits. Employing a conception of citizenship that is identity over rights-based, *Watoto* utilises an idea of imagined citizenship in an effort to "forge a common identity and collective experience for" those included in church's distinct parameters (Adejumobi 2001:79). At *Watoto* individuals are charged with becoming *good* Christian citizens through a practical blueprint offered in church discourse on *how* to reform and self-regulate behaviour. Yet, *Watoto's* lessons hold greater purpose – to transform the nation to a land of autonomy and prosperity, a land of economic plenty. The chapter concludes that the idea of citizenship should not be narrowly defined in relation to the nation-state, but rather as it correlates to the moral, political and socio-economic discourses that help to define broader notions of Ugandan citizenship.

This chapter begins by elaborating the theoretical underpinnings of economic citizenship in order to analytically ground ethnographic observations. The theoretical section is followed by an overview of the origins and structure of *Watoto Church*. An examination of weekend services at *Watoto* follows. By including the 'everyday' life at *Watoto* the church's vision for both its congregation and nation is clearly elaborated. The next section considers *Watoto's* drive to transform the individual through a pragmatic economic framework. On a practical level the case study explains the necessity of individual behavioural change to the national project. Creating good fiscal behaviour helps to establish an ideal citizenry capable of transforming the nation. As a result, a macro-examination of national progress is offered before the conclusion to help delineate the importance of economic citizenship within the broader Pentecostal-charismatic project.

## The economic citizen

A wealth of existing work on Pentecostalism highlights its emphasis on the economic. Wealth accumulation (Haynes 2012; Hunt 2000; Marshall 1991; Maxwell 1998; Meyer 1998; Ukah 2005), new articulations of the Protestant work ethic (Bialecki, Haynes & Robbins 2008; Martin 1995) and consumerism (Gifford 2004) are reoccurring themes of academic examination. In one degree or another the economic relevance of Pentecostal-charismatic churches proves a consistency of the global movement. While the economic component has been elaborated in numerous contradictory ways the significance of neoliberal patterns of restructuring remains profoundly relevant (Comaroff 2009; Meyer 2007).

From this vantage Barker (2007) suggests Pentecostalism's ability to promote behavioural norms or models of citizenship that act in synchronicity with the ideological norms of neoliberal reforms – ultimately reinforcing neoliberal capitalism. To an extent Barker's findings apply to the Ugandan context – as the ideological foundations of neoliberal capitalism are consistently evident in church discourse. Yet, the structural realities of neoliberalism prove even more fundamental. While the tendency to attribute sweeping social transformations across sub-Saharan Africa to a vaguely defined catch-all of neoliberalism is reductionist, the specific ways Pentecostal-charismatic churches developed and continue to evolve in Uganda are inextricable from underlying processes of neoliberal reform.

The retracting role of the state as a service delivery provider created new opportunities for the private sector. As a result of the sweeping deregulation that came with the neoliberal epoch the African state "relinquished significant responsibility for schooling, health, and welfare – in short, for the social reproduction of their citizens – religious organizations have willingly reclaimed this role" (Comaroff 2009:20). Overall reductions in foreign aid to the central government in conjunction with an increase in the amount of money redirected to international and domestic NGOs worked to undermine the ability of state institutions to provide services – in turn shifting the capacity to NGOs and other civil society actors (Freeman 2012:5). According to Müller "neoliberal policies and Structural Adjustment Programmes have conditioned the privatisation of health services, faith-based NGOs have rapidly taken up the delivery of these services, and thus come to play an ever more prominent role" (2014:295). In Uganda this translated into a rapid surge of Pentecostal-charismatic organisations as service delivery providers.

In Uganda the implications of the newfound social dependency and political legitimisation of Faith-Based Organisations (FBOs) are profound – sweeping across approaches to public health and sexuality. Here I suggest that these specific conditions are integral to church visions in the political, economic and moral subjectification of Pentecostal-charismatic believers – particularly as it manifests as an essential concept of Christian citizenship. In sub-Saharan Africa significant historical factors like the legacy of colonialism (Mamdani 1996) complicate arrangements of citizenship between the state and polity. In conventional Western models the relationship between citizen and state operates vertically, with civil society functioning as an intermediary (Ferguson & Gupta 2002:983) in the social reproduction of its citizens. Within these more fluid contexts where public authority is fragmented competing political entities – like churches – can be "conceptualized not as 'below the state, but as integral parts of a transnational apparatus of governmentality . . . [which] overlays and coexists with" the state (Ferguson & Gupta 2002:994).

Reflective of these more fluid arrangements the types of citizenship being alternatively defined are based far less on rights and more around forging a sense of collective identity. The juncture between PC Christianity and citizenship creates "new social relationships, modes of political participation, and understandings of personhood" by teaching believers "how to participate" in a shared national project (O'Neill 2009:334). In this arrangement congregants learn how to execute their citizenship through faith, merely than rather than alongside it, as an act of self-governance that is learned at church activities and reinforced discursively. Drawing from Foucault, O'Neill notes that amidst the retracted state and services of post-war Guatemala Pentecostal-charismatic churches envision citizenship as a technique of governance that actively encourages citizens to participate in the production of a new nation founded on principles of freedom and democracy. In this example churches introduce new modes of understanding and governing the self, "one that links morality to citizenship through what Foucault calls the 'interiorization' of governance" (O'Neill 2009:342).

While the parallels to the Ugandan case are numerous rather than freedom and democracy the end goal stresses a financially prosperous nation – one that rivals global economic hegemons like the United States. Within the broader model of Christian citizenship the emphasis on fiscal responsibility is central to *Watoto's* strategy for transforming the nation into a moral archetype for sub-Saharan Africa. At *Watoto* this is achieved by breaking with what is seen as a chaotic past – in terms of both individual's former fiscal behaviour and more generally Uganda's historical past. The idea of rupture (Engelke 2010; Freeman 2012; Marshall-Fratani 1998; McCauley 2013; van Dijk 1998) is fundamental in *Watoto's* transformative model of economic citizenship for both the individual and the nation – as attendees are encouraged to relinquish what once was in an effort to become new Christian citizens.

## The origins and Watoto perspective

*Watoto's* origins date back to 1982 when Pastor Gary Skinner, a Canadian missionary, relocated to Uganda with his wife Marilyn after travelling throughout sub-Saharan Africa. Now one of the largest and most financially solvent churches in all of East Africa, *Watoto* began modestly, operating out of the Grand Imperial Hotel in downtown Kampala under the name *Kampala Pentecostal Church* (KPC).

Relocating to Uganda at a politically tumultuous time, devastated by years of civil war and social upheaval, Skinner claims "we would see bodies in the streets in the morning, we were broken into more times than we can remember, our first two cars we lost at gunpoint, so it was very difficult days" (NTV Uganda 2012). For Skinner, or Pastor Gary as he is known among his parishioners, he aimed to start an English-speaking church in an effort to unify the nation. The focus on language highlights the church's nationalist undertones, as language lays "the bases for national consciousness" by creating unified sites to communicate and foster a sense of communal belonging (Anderson 1991:56–57). According to Skinner "sectarianism and tribalism had been cancers in the nation . . . the English language and the practice of true Pentecostalism would be a unifying factor" to the future of Uganda (Watoto Website 2012).

After two years at the Grand Imperial Hotel the congregation moved into an old cinema in downtown Kampala. According to Pastor Gary, the "building was dirty, rickety, the roof leaked so badly you had to have an umbrella when it rained . . . I said to God . . . 'Oh what a waste of a fabulous building' and I had a vision . . . I saw it as it is today . . . and God gave" us the building (Watoto Website 2012). The cinema is now *Watoto Church Central*, the headquarters of the *Watoto* Empire. Out of *Watoto Central* six weekend services are necessary to accommodate the massive *Watoto* congregation.

Along frenetic Kampala Road the renovated three-storey building is full of churchgoers participating in weekly Bible study, youth outreach or countless other events. Services are in the main auditorium, a large bright room with a second-storey balcony. The professionally lit stage houses the speaking pastor, guest speakers, the *Watoto* band and weekly musical guests, like the famous Ugandan gospel singer Judith Babirye. Rows of wooden pews are crowded together. Regardless of the numerous services – one on Saturday evening and five Sunday services – extra chairs fill empty space beside the pews to allow for additional seating. Services are recorded and available to download at the *Watoto* website and posted on *YouTube*.

In 2009 *KPC* celebrated their twenty-fifth anniversary and renamed the church *Watoto*, or 'the children' in Swahili, after their successful children's choir (New Vision 2009). Adopting the new name was meant to signify the church's focus on the future, proving "synonymous with the true meaning of what the church is meant to be . . . [an] embrace [of] the future" (Gary Skinner cited in New Vision 2009).

The choir seldom performs at church services, but "tours the world . . . [to advocate for] the 14 million African children currently orphaned by AIDS" (Watoto Website 2012). Outfitted in barkskin, Acholi beads, vibrant East African textiles and leopard print trousers, the children perform with professionalism and precision, dancing and singing in perfect synchronicity to hand drums and keyboards. The choir has gained *Watoto* international recognition. Yet, their exaggerated smiles are juxtaposed with graphic images of children in the throes of famine, violence and illness.

These images are not limited to the videos produced for the choir, but in Skinner's very language. His accounts detail dead bodies lining the streets of Kampala and discarded children, to the dilapidated state of the building they rehabilitated for *Watoto Central*. Skinner's portrayal of Uganda reinforces the transformative role *Watoto* has played in rebuilding the people and landscape to beaming smiles and restored facades. His role as 'White Saviour' is part of a discursive formation that works to reproduce material life, projecting a portrayal of "African peoples as passive and helpless" (Bell 2013:3).

In a saga of war and disease *Watoto* is the transformative protagonist. Recently the church opened a branch in the northern town of Gulu. In 2008 *Living Hope* was launched in Gulu and Kampala, the programme is "committed to transforming the lives of 1,200 women in Kampala and 900 women in Gulu. Left abandoned or widowed, the target group is HIV+ single women, returnees from abduction, and teenage mothers" (Watoto Website 2012). *Living Hope* aims to restore dignity to vulnerable and marginalised women. To generate self-sustainability women are enrolled in vocational training programmes and micro-finance loans are available for small business enterprises.

In the promotional video for *Living Hope*, Marilyn explains, "Every girl has a dream . . . but for many women in Africa their dreams have been stolen from them" (Watoto Website 2012). While Marilyn speaks, a montage of devastated women fades to black. Their dejected faces are quickly replaced with unrestrained optimism, as the ladies of *Living Hope* recount their own stories of transformation. Marilyn continues, "Poverty, war, disease, abandonment, human trafficking, child abduction, those are the things that have taken dreams from the women of Africa" (ibid.). The video universalises the life stories of *specific* women to encapsulate *all* 'African' women. Before *Watoto* the women were agentless, yet, with *Watoto's* intervention self-sustainability is attainable, an essential element in the project of national transformation.

## Church structure and organisation

While the church relies upon a team of pastors to deliver weekly sermons, Pastor Gary remains the face. Overseen by a church council to outline policy,

*Watoto* boasts an extensive clerical team for spiritual guidance, a team of deacons to draft daily procedures and a team of elders to govern church doctrine. *Watoto* maintains eight churches in Uganda alone that offer 22 weekend services.

Five churches are located in and around Kampala, *Watoto Church Central* in Downtown Kampala, *Watoto Church North* in Ntinda-Kisaasi, *Watoto Church East* in Kazinga, *Watoto Church South* in Lubowa and *Watoto Church West* in Kyengera. Beyond the capital is *Watoto Church Gulu* in Uganda's infamous 'war-ravaged' north, so often drawn upon in *Watoto* discourse and visual imagery. Two additional *Watoto* churches are a part of the larger *Watoto* Children's Villages for orphaned children. In 2012 *Watoto* launched *Watoto South Sudan* in the "world's youngest and newest nation" with Pastor Joe Ogwal (Watoto Website 2012). Church planting is a central principle at *Watoto*, to grow and multiply "bringing healing to the cities and nations" (ibid.). The year before saw the launch of *Watoto Church Cape Town*. At the opening ceremony Pastor Gary commented that:

> It has long been a dream of ours to see the Watoto model replicated across our beloved continent. We strongly believe the local church is the hope of the world, and so, true to form, the Watoto model will first be replicated with the launch of a life giving church.
> 
> (Watoto Website 2012)

In order to maintain intimacy within the vast network of branches, *Watoto* is structured into smaller groups called cells that number over 2,000. Cell leaders are equipped with a weekly leader's guide to direct fellowship. While institutionalised, fellowships are also personalised to meet the group's individual needs. The fellowship opens with a standardised question that varies weekly. Biblical text then reinforces the weekly theme to ground discussion in scripture. In the intimate setting participants are able to relate scripture to their own life experiences, while establishing a direct relationship with the church and, subsequently, God. Yet, while *Watoto* emphasises the personal it simultaneously incorporates an ethos of national reform and progress. *Watoto's* broader project employs a nationalistic and near-colonial discourse of replication, reform and transformation.

## Weekend service at Watoto Church

Before Saturday evening or Sunday services begin a short film is projected above the stage. Graphic images of local violence, poverty, failing infrastructure, illness and starvation emerge with the words "the people living in darkness have seen a great light on those living in the land of the shadow of death a light has dawned Matthew 4:16".[1]

The words fade to black as the familiar voice of Pastor Gary rises above a montage of hopeless imagery and news sound bites. The outline of Uganda develops from the darkness illuminated by a shining white light, the *light*

106  *Caroline Valois*

*unto the nations*. Pastor Gary proclaims, "I believe that the church of the Lord Jesus Christ is the hope of the world, God has shaped this great church into a powerful and significant beacon of hope in the land of Uganda, and positioned her influence in the rest of Africa and around the world".[2]

The imagery of overt poverty and illness is replaced with smiling faces, unified communities and abundance. "If humanity had a hero", the screen reads, "he is Christ".[3] An actor with long brown hair and a full beard takes shape, draped in white linen he steps into the sun's rays and is illuminated by golden light. The music quickens pace:

> The church that I see is not just theological, but it's relational . . . to the nation of Uganda and to the continent of Africa who have been empowered through it, *Watoto* is synonymous with the true meaning of what the church is meant to be.[4]

As the video ends the service begins, reinforcing many of the film's themes. Technology is a mainstay – videos resembling professionally produced advertisements play before and during sermons. The church also boasts an integrated and up-to-date website that outlines all upcoming events and makes sermon podcasts available to stream, in addition to an active *Twitter* account.

Beyond *Watoto's* technological expertise, the videos demonstrate the use of an antiquated near-colonial language the church often adopts, juxtaposing the modernity of technology with an entrenched language of colonial authority.[5] The language evokes "many of the old tropes: Africa, savage and infantilized, devastated by slavery, its women disposed and its men laid low – all awaiting the white saviour to regenerate them so that they might once more harvest their own crops" (Comaroff & Comaroff 1997:124).

In *Watoto's* vision the African populous is passive, war-torn and infantilised, in need of Divine intervention, who without its guidance are rendered hopeless, devastated, orphaned and ill. A language of conquest – bringing order to the dark wilderness – is consistent throughout church discourse. The church Skinner envisioned was one that was "alive and not wild" positioning potential converts as both passive and animalistic. The language is consistent – extending to talk of the Divine to the practical and mundane aspects of daily life, like finances.

### The fiscal Watoto

At *Watoto* economic responsibility is an integral component of Christian citizenship. A vocal advocate for fiscal accountability for its parishioners, the church holds itself to the same standard:

> Watoto Church is a Bible-based church and recognises the practise of tithes and offering by the voluntary membership. . . . Financial statements are prepared annually after a comprehensive assessment by

independent auditors. . . . The financial reports are compliant with International Financial Reporting Standards under the historical cost convention. . . . Annual audited financial statements are presented at an Annual General Meeting open to the public.

(Watoto Website 2012)

*Watoto's* financial records are available online. Financial responsibility is a perpetual theme. Church discourse encourages individual, church and national fiscal accountability. Weekly sermons discuss financial planning, overcoming poverty and tithing. Parishioners are taught to have 'financial integrity' – or "aligning your financial decisions to biblical principles . . . involving the giving and receiving of money" – in their individual lives.[6] While the sermons prove practical for any parishioners unfamiliar with fiscal budgeting, they also infantilise listeners and suggest fiscal irresponsibility. The theme illustrates the two-fold approach to faith employed at *Watoto*: the individual and the nation.

As part of a three-part series on personal, financial and sexual integrity, Pastor Gary encourages parishioners that "we have somewhere fantastic to go [as a country] . . . we've had fifty bad years . . . without a lot of integrity. But we are going to have fifty phenomenal years and it is because [you] the next generation . . . are going to rise up and be people of integrity".[7]

The statement reveals the future orientation of *Watoto* and perception of nation's potential if Pentecostal-charismatic ideology is adopted as a way of life. At *Watoto* the youth – Gusman's (2009) 'Joseph Generation' – will be the carriers of change. Skinner claims "everything we do is about raising the next generation of young Ugandan leaders, who will bring transformation to their community" (NTV Uganda 2012).

The sermon continues to explain that financial integrity does not stop with our individual bank accounts, but challenges the future of the nation. Pastor Gary's wife, Marilyn, adds "the problem with Uganda is that we have not held close, we have not held tight to a strict code of financial ethics . . . but the good news is if we become people of financial integrity it results in strength, financial strength, financial security and financial blessing".[8] Along with other factors, the perceived absence of financial integrity is a central obstacle to obtaining God's blessing and achieving national progress.

The sermon expands on the purpose of financial integrity, "God gives us money to advance his kingdom here on Earth . . . to meet our personal needs . . . and to become a conduit of help to others".[9] The key to integrity is ambiguous, to live with faith and not fear. Yet, as the sermon unfolds the instructions become practical. *Watoto* provides a concrete outline of fiscal management centred on living within your means. All parishioners are encouraged to make their own budgets – detailing the minutia of accounting, from computer budgeting software, to how and when to balance expenditures. *Watoto* is about the banality of everyday life as much as the Divine.

At *Watoto* your responsibility to the church surpasses all other responsibilities. Listing your financial obligations enables parishioners to create realistic budgets, with tithing as the first and most necessary expense, followed by taxes, savings and investments, and all other financial obligations. Marilyn affirms tithes as the foremost expense, "Our tithes are taken off before anything else, before our rent, before the school fees, before our food . . . our tithes come off".[10] Pastor Gary reiterates, "If you are not tithing you do not have financial integrity . . . if you get through this one thing it will set you up in the other areas" because integrity generates blessings.[11] A tenth of one's income is the expected tithe, while additional donations to the church are encouraged as separate offerings. Beyond tithing Pastor Gary and Marilyn extol the virtues of paying your bills, being punctual and avoiding corruption.

Individual and familial 'financial integrity' expands to national 'financial integrity' and the dangers of debt. "We will never get out of national debt, until we don't get out of personal debt . . . governments around the world are . . . going into greater debt . . . the wicked borrows and does not pay back".[12] The fluidity of jumping between the micro and macro is demonstrated in all sermons. *Watoto* organises sermons around evolving themes – 'the blessed life' quickly moves to 'the blessed nation'. Throughout the 'Financial Responsibility' sermon, Pastor Gary effortlessly jumps between the individual and national scale, reaffirming the importance of biblical morality on a personal, familial and national level. For Skinner, Uganda's national motto must be applied to our everyday lives. "Let's live our lives in such a way that whatever we do we can say, I'm doing this for God and I'm doing this for my country. If we really lived according to that motto we would change Uganda" (NTV Uganda 2012).

The transformative model – individual, family and nation – is applicable to all of the sermons at *Watoto*, and proves the church's overriding message: individual moral transformation generates a citizenry capable of changing the nation. To achieve its transformative goals requires 're-educating' parishioners with practical sermons on all aspects of daily life, including finance. Congregants draw off of the moral parameters and codes of behaviour imparted at church to "govern their conduct and the conduct of other and that these efforts at governing conduct constitute citizenship participation" (O'Neill 2009:342).

Discourse aims to 'teach' congregants *how* to live as responsible citizens, paying bills and taxes punctually, abstaining from premarital sex and extramarital affairs, raising a family, even instructing the congregation on how to go on job interviews. Yet while the path towards progress resides in the everyday, with the individual, the nation proves the ultimate goal.

## Transforming the nation

As the previous section addressed the individual is an inextricable component in church goals to transform the nation through the production of a disciplined citizenry. The project of rendering a distinct Pentecostal-charismatic citizenry points to the broader socio-economic and political impacts of neoliberal policies in Uganda since the 1990s. In many ways churches have provided a means of negotiating new uncertainties generated by the limited capacity of the state as a service provider (Comaroff & Comaroff 2003), economic stagnation and widening inequality (Pfeiffer, Gimbel-Sherr & Augusto 2007) and new material realities (Comaroff & Comaroff 2000), while attempting to make good on promises of economic and political inclusion (Deacon & Lynch 2013). In such shifting realities Pentecostal-charismatic churches not only 'do the job of the state' by providing a wealth of services from health to education, but ideologically work in harmony with fundamental neoliberal principles, such as capitalist accumulation and conspicuous consumption, while ultimately not challenging any underlying systemic factors reproducing inequalities.

Within these contexts, Pentecostal-charismatic communities provide much needed social services "along with moral frameworks regarding how social needs should be met, by recasting individual values and practices, and by reconfiguring community and social identity" (Barker 2007:417). From a structural perspective individuals and the local community take on the responsibility of the state to ensure social needs are fulfilled. Yet, church discourse operates equally as an ideology – and works to render the subjectivities of believers.

Beyond the tangible role churches play structurally they function on perhaps an even more formative level. For Barker (2007) churches provide a new means to interpret the economic volatilities of life where uncertainty has become a defining factor. Within contexts where the significant restructuring of national economies has taken place Pentecostal-charismatic churches encourage "norms and values that harmonize well with a neoliberal work ethic. . . . Fostering the personal discipline and self-confidence . . . networks of social capital . . . [and] reliability in the eyes of potential employers" (Barker 2007:422). It is here, within the structural and ideological interaction, where the relationship between fiscal citizenship and nation building becomes evident.

Pentecostal-charismatic churches aim to achieve their transformative goals by rendering and regulating a citizenry, a process that necessitates the conceptualisation of national identities that stand more in line with the Christian identity. National identity is a fluid and dynamic category (Lee 2005:100). For church leaders establishing a Christian citizenry will "usher in unprecedented prosperity, such as the world has never seen . . . our economy is founded on the corner stone of Jesus Christ, we will never be shaken. The value of our currency is pegged to the Name of the Most High God, we are forever strengthened" (Uganda Declaration 2012).

Above all churches envision congregants as "citizens of heaven [and] in heaven you have rights . . . responsibilities . . . requirements . . . rewards . . . [but] you have no rights unless you are in the kingdom" of God.[13] The acquisition and maintenance of citizenship status is based on exhibiting moral behaviour. Yet, ultimately these citizens should be self-replicating, "autonomous and calculable members of society [who are] able to be left for the most part to regulate their own behaviour" (Hindess cited in O'Neill 2009:341).

Within this configuration a distinct moral citizenry is established through the internalisation of a particular subjectivity where "the Bible is a prescription on how to live our individual lives . . . for nations".[14] As demonstrated in the previous section these subjectivities, like fiscal integrity, operate by creating a self-regulating citizenry who "vote conscientiously, invest responsibly, and work diligently, while moving about and maintaining the modern city with suitable civic pride" (Legg 2005:140).[15]

By adopting a theological veneer of development and progress Pentecostal-charismatic churches function as surrogates of the state. As noted by Appadurai (1996) "the capabilities of the nation-state to monopolise the 'moral resources of community' and command political loyalty . . . [have] steadily eroded" with heightened processes of globalisation (Appadurai cited in Marshall-Fratani 1998:279). Religion has long defined communal identity long before the formation of nation-states (Anderson 1991). A communal or national identity based on religious authority is nothing new.

Yet, within the context of neoliberal globalisation the worldwide Pentecostal-charismatic movement takes on a profound new relevance (Marshall-Fratani 1998). Offering a contesting voice to public authority, churches work to destabilise the state's monopoly in defining the parameters of citizenship and belonging. The nation-state is no longer the primary conduit in the construction of ideology and national belonging. In many regards the nation-state is not even the principal *context* where communal identity is imagined and political loyalty is conveyed (Marshall-Fratani 1998:278–279).

Nation-states, and their inhabitants, are not isolated from the outside world. Both are equally subject to external forces. In Uganda, the nation-state is not the singular determinate or context of identity and community formation. The heightened fluidity of public space to ideological constructions from alternative discursive forms has opened up space for Pentecostal-charismatic subjectification. At the heart of the Pentecostal-charismatic movement exists a "quest for absolute sovereignty" calling into question "the authority and neutrality of state law" (Comaroff 2009:20). The movement works to further blur the already arguable delineation between 'secular' realms, challenging state neutrality and market secularity, as both are appropriated as "instruments of divine purpose" (ibid.). As a result, believers are more active in the political process influencing political discourse and more significantly public policy.

At its core the Pentecostal-charismatic project proves a nationalist endeavour. While religious discourse circulated at church events and throughout the broader public sphere, through the radio, television and at public activities, helps in the creation of particular types of nationalist subjects, it simultaneously operates by defining those who are excluded from the national landscape. Those who 'belong' come to "embody the nationalist ideal and carry out nationalist projects" (Zake 2002:218), defining those who are excluded proves equally relevant. While the Ugandan case makes the growing climate of those who do 'not belong' remarkably clear, most notably for lesbian, gay, bisexual, transgender and intersex (LGBTI) Ugandans, contracting parameters of citizenship are occurring throughout sub-Saharan Africa (Chitando & van Klinken 2016).

## Conclusion

As the chapter has demonstrated notions of citizenship must not be narrowly defined in relation to the nation-state alone. Rather our understandings of citizenship should come to reflect greater complexities – including the moral, political and socio-economic understandings provided by Pentecostal-charismatic churches within the public sphere that prove equally as determinant. In Uganda and throughout sub-Saharan Africa the impact of Pentecostal-charismatic movements is far more than ideological. Church discourses increasingly inform the ways individuals spend, invest and save – how they live their lives and interact in their communities. Yet, perhaps more significantly it increasingly defines the parameters of citizenship in terms of those who belong by virtue of economic inclusion. This has profound implications beyond congregations. Throughout sub-Saharan Africa national policy and legislation increasingly reflects the moral principles of Pentecostal-charismatic churches. In Uganda alone the past decade has ushered in a wave of 'moral' legislative initiatives ranging from homosexuality to regulating women's dress. Churches negotiate and further blur the indistinct boundaries that exist between the church and state, as well as the public and private spheres throughout the African context.

## Notes

1 Participant observation conducted at *Watoto* Central January 2012.
2 Ibid.
3 Ibid.
4 Ibid.
5 It also demonstrates the competing and incongruous nature of *Watoto* discourse.
6 Participant observation conducted at *Watoto* Central March 2012.
7 Ibid.
8 Ibid.
9 Ibid.
10 Participant observation conducted at *Watoto* Central March 2012.
11 Ibid.
12 Ibid.
13 Participant observation conducted at *Watoto* Central June 2012.
14 Participant observation conducted at *Watoto* Central January 2012.
15 Regardless if individuals privately comply with PC behavioural precepts, the overall goal is to constitute the principles of individual behaviour to build the nation. Nationalist projects are always contested, "There is no singular, irreducible national narrative . . . there always exist counter claims and alternative readings" (Bell 2003:73–74).

## References

Adejumobi, A. 2001. 'Citizenship, Rights and the Problem of Internal Conflicts and Civil Wars in Africa'. *Human Rights Quarterly*, 6(2): 77–96.

Anderson, B. 1991. *Imagined Communities*. London: Verso.
Appadurai, A. 1996. *Modernity at Large: Cultural Dimensions of Globalisation*. Minneapolis: University of Minnesota.
Barker, I. 2007. 'Charismatic Economies: Pentecostalism, Economic Restructuring, and Social Reproduction'. *New Political Science*, 29(4): 407–427.
Bell, D. 2003. 'Mythscapes: Memory, Mythology and National Identity'. *The British Journal of Sociology*, 54(1): 63–81.
Bell, K. 2013. 'Raising Africa? Celebrity and the Rhetoric of the White Saviour'. *Journal of Multidisciplinary International Studies*, 10(2): 1–24.
Bialecki, J., Haynes, N. & Robbins, J. 2008. 'The Anthropology of Christianity'. *Religion Compass*, 2(6): 1139–1158.
Chitando, E. & van Klinken, A. (Eds.) 2016. *Christianity and Controversies Over Homosexuality in Contemporary Africa*. London: Routledge.
Comaroff, J. 2009. 'The Politics of Conviction: Faith on the Neo-Liberal Frontier'. *Social Analysis*, 53(1): 17–38.
Comaroff, J. & Comaroff, J. 1997. *Of Revelation and Revolution*. Chicago: University of Chicago Press.
Comaroff, J. & Comaroff, J. 2000. 'Millennial Capitalism: First Thoughts on a Second Coming'. *Public Culture*, 12(2): 291–343.
Comaroff, J. & Comaroff, J. 2003. 'Reflections on Liberalism, Policulturalism, and ID-Ology: Citizenship and Difference in South Africa'. *Identities*, 9(4): 445–474.
Deacon, G. & Lynch, G. 2013. 'Allowing Satan in? Moving Toward a Political Economy of Neo-Pentecostalism in Kenya'. *Journal of Religion in Africa*, 43(2): 108–130.
Engelke, M. 2010. 'Past Pentecostalism: Notes on Rupture, Realignment and Everyday Life in Pentecostal and African Independent Churches'. *Africa*, 80(2): 177–199.
Ferguson, J. & Gupta, A. 2002. 'Spatializing States: Toward an Ethnography of Neoliberal Governmentality'. *American Ethnologist*, 29(4): 981–1002.
Freeman, D. 2012. 'The Pentecostal Ethic and the Spirit of Development'. In D. Freeman (Ed.) *Pentecostalism and Development: Churches, NGOs and Social Change in Africa*. Basingstoke: Palgrave Macmillan.
Gifford, P. 2004. *Ghana's New Christianity: Pentecostalism in a Globalizing African Economy*. Bloomington: Indiana University Press.
Gusman, A. 2009. 'HIV/AIDS, Pentecostal Churches, and the "Joseph Generation" in Uganda'. *Africa Today*, 56(1): 67–86.
Haynes, N. 2012. 'Pentecostalism and the Morality of Money: Prosperity, Inequality, and Religious Sociality on the Zambian Cooperbelt'. *Journal of the Royal Anthropological Institute*, 18(1): 123–139.
Hunt, S. 2000. 'Winning Ways: Globalisation and the Impact of the Health and Wealth Gospel'. *Journal of Contemporary Religions*, 15(3): 331–347.
Lee, M. D. P. 2005. 'Contested Narratives: Reclaiming National Identity Through Historical Reappropriation Among Korean Minorities in China'. *Stanford Journal of East Asian Affairs*, 5(1): 100–112.
Legg, S. 2005. 'Foucault's Population Geographies: Classifications, Biopolitics and Governmental Spaces'. *Population, Space and Place*, 11: 137–156.
Mamdani, M. 1996. *Citizen and Subject: Contemporary Africa and the Legacy of Late Colonialism*. Princeton, NJ: Princeton University Press.
Marshall, R. 1991. 'Power in the Name of Jesus'. *Review of African Political Economy*, 18(52): 21–37.

Marshall-Fratani, R. 1998. 'Mediating the Global and the Local in Nigerian Pentecostalism'. *Journal of Religion in Africa*, 28(3): 278–315.
Martin, B. 1995. 'New Mutations of the Protestant Ethic Among Latin American Pentecostals'. *Religion*, 25(2): 101–117.
Maxwell, D. 1998. 'Delivered From the Spirit of Poverty'. *Journal of Religion in Africa*, 28(3): 350–373.
McCauley, J. 2013. 'Africa's New Big Man Rule: Pentecostalism and Patronage in Ghana'. *African Affairs*, 112(446): 1–21.
Meyer, B. 1998. 'Make a Complete Break With the Past: Memory and Post-Colonial Modernity in Ghanaian Pentecostal Discourse'. *Journal of Religion in Africa*, 28(3): 316–349.
Meyer, B. 2007. 'Pentecostalism and Neo-Liberal Capitalism: Faith, Prosperity and Vision in African Pentecostal-charismatic Churches'. *Journal for the Study of Religion*, 20(2): 5–28.
Müller, A. 2014. 'Transnational Moralities and Invisible Sexual Minorities'. In N. Beckman, A. Gusman & C. Shroff (Eds.) *Strings Attached: AIDS and the Rise of Transnational Connections in Africa*. Oxford: British Academy by Oxford University Press: 289–310.
Museveni, Y. 2012. 'A 50-Year Journey Since Independence (1962–2012): A Good Foundation for Socio-Economic Transformation'. The State House of Uganda: Presidential Statements. available at: www.statehouse.go.ug/media/presidential-statements/2012/10/04/50-year-journey-independence-1962-2012-good-foundation-soci
New Vision. 2009. 'KPC Renamed Watoto Church'. 12 April. available at: www.newvision.co.ug/D/9/34/677847
NTV Uganda. 2012. 'Profile Pastor Gary Skinner'. available at: www.youtube.com/watch?v=4UYhQnANP_k
O'Neill, K. 2009. 'But Our Citizenship is in Heaven: A Proposal for the Future Study of Christian Citizenship in the Global South'. *Citizenship Studies*, 13(4): 333–348.
Pfeiffer, J., Gimbel-Sherr, K. & Augusto, O. J. 2007. 'The Holy Spirit in the Household: Pentecostalism, Gender, and Neoliberalism in Mozambique'. *American Anthropologist*, 109(4): 688–700.
Ranger, T. 2003. 'Evangelical Christianity and Democracy in Africa: A Continental Comparison'. *Journal of Religion in Africa*, 33(1): 112–117.
Uganda Declaration. 2012. *Watoto Church*. Kampala: Watoto Internal Press.
Ukah, A. 2005. 'Those Who Trade With God Never Lose: The Economies of Pentecostal Activism in Nigeria'. In T. Falola (Ed.) *Christianity and Social Change in Africa: Essays in Honor of J.D.Y. Peel*. Durham: Carolina Academic Press: 253–274.
van Dijk, R. 1998. 'Pentecostalism, Cultural Memory and the State: Contested Representations of Time in Postcolonial Malawi'. In R. Werbner (Ed.) *Memory and the Postcolony: African Anthropology and the Critique of Power*. London: Zed Books: 155–181.
Watoto. 2012. 'Watoto Church'. available at: www.watotochurch.com
Zake, I. 2002. 'The Construction of National(ist) Subject: Applying the Ideas of Louis Althusser and Michel Foucault to Nationalism'. *Social Thought & Research*, 25(1–2): 217–246.

# 7 Pentecostals and developmental citizenship in Ethiopia

*Emanuele Fantini*

The image of "shining Ethiopia" (Gascon 2008) as roaring African lion amid the most dynamic emerging African economies has been recently obfuscated by the slowing down of its GDP double digit growth, and even more by an unprecedented waves of protests in Oromia and Amhara regions, pointing at the corruption of national and local elites and reclaiming more inclusive growth and development (Lefort 2016).

But indeed contemporary Ethiopia is being reshaped by deep socio-economic transformations (Pankhurst 2017) as well as spiritual transformations. Among the latter, one of the most striking is the expansion of the Pentecostal movement, the fastest growing religious group in the country, that challenges the oldest African autochthonous church, the Ethiopian Orthodox Church (EOC), as well as an historically rooted presence of Islam. National censuses have recorded the steady rise of the religious believers officially registered as Protestants: from 5.5% in 1984, to 10.2% in 1994 and up to 18.6% in 2007, when Christian Orthodox and Muslims were respectively counted as 43.5% and 33.9% of the population (Office of the Population and Housing Census Commission 1991, 2008). The most recent projections suggest that Protestants in 2011 were 21% of the population (Central Statistical Agency 2012). The official label Protestants includes mainline Evangelical and Pentecostal churches (like the Lutheran Evangelical Church *Mekane Yesus*, the largely Baptist *Kale Heywet* Church or the first autochthonous Ethiopian Pentecostal church, *Mulu Wongel*) as well as new independent or (neo)charismatic groups. Vernacularly these groups are called *Pente*[1] as one, to emphasise the charismatic turn they all currently experience. While acknowledging their plurality, I will refer to these groups as a whole as Pentecostals, since they refer to a common, although disputed, history (Haustein 2011) and they share a repertoire of theological notions, spiritual imaginaries and techniques of organisation. Moreover, the term is increasingly used as self-designation among Ethiopian Christians not belonging to the Orthodox or Catholic churches (Pew Forum on Religion and Public Life 2010). Pentecostals are swelling not only in statistics, but also in affirming their presence in public affairs and their visibility in public spaces. Such endeavours – shared by other religious groups too – have suggested the interpretation of religion as emerging "alternative civic identity" (Abbink

2011:274), contrasting the closing of political space and opportunities for other actors such as independent media, opposition parties and NGOs.

Which is the relation between the Pentecostal call for a moral regeneration of the country and the political and socio-economic transformations in contemporary Ethiopia? To address this question, I will first introduce the notion of developmental citizenship, to describe the strategy adopted by the Ethiopian ruling elite to organise the participation of the population to public affairs (politics, economy, development) according to the principles of ethnic federalism and the developmental state. Second I will retrace different trajectories delineated by Pentecostals in making sense and navigating such organising structures. These trajectories indicate how, far from offering a single and coherent alternative civic identity, Pentecostalism allows for a plurality of itineraries, imaginaries and practices, resulting in moral conflicts within and outside the movement. The Pentecostal call for moral regeneration of the country apparently echoes the Ethiopian government official discourse on good governance, development and economic transformation, contributing to nurture a widespread – also outside the Pentecostal movement – culture of aspiration to partake the development cake. However, the rigid tenets of developmental citizenship fail to fully accommodate Pentecostal logics and aspirations, thus alimenting their narratives of spiritual crisis and moral corruption.

## Developmental citizenship and religion in Ethiopia

The "spectacular developmental success in East Asia – most particularly in Japan, Korea, and Taiwan" (Zenawi 2011:167) has been the reference of late Ethiopian prime minister Meles Zenawi in adopting the developmental state as political economy model alternative to the neoliberal paradigm (Zenawi 2011). The model sets a key role for the state – and the ruling class that controls it – in actively engaging in and orienting the economic development of the country. All other actors have to steer their endeavours in line with the government official strategy and development policies, with their activity getting labelled accordingly, as for instance in the case of "developmental journalism" (Skjerdal 2011). To describe this strategy of political mobilisation and economic organisation, I will revert to the category of "developmental citizenship", as it has been adopted to analyse the relationship between economic development, citizenship and democracy in South Korea since the late 1980s. Chang describes Korean governments pursuing "developmental citizenship" by "industrialisation at a pace that create jobs and raised incomes, even if social security benefits were minimum" (Chang 2012:67). Thus South Korea focus on economic development never translated into comprehensive social citizenship rights, in spite of democratic improvements in civic and political rights (Chang 2012).

While the Ethiopian government does not explicitly refer to "developmental citizenship", similar dynamics in the relation between economic development and citizens' engagement in society can be witnessed in contemporary

Ethiopia. Here, developmental citizenship is constructed by the government and practiced by the people against two main tenets: participation to civic and political life within the ethnic federalism framework, and participation to economic life within the structures of the developmental state. Religious actors' public engagement should be understood in interaction with these two tenets too. The 1994 Ethiopian Federal Constitution institutionalises ethnicity as the main organising principle of political life, recognising the right to self-determination for all nations, nationalities and people of the country, and dividing accordingly the country into nine regional states and two districts encompassing the main cities, the capital Addis Ababa and Dire Dawa. As criteria to identify the "belonging to nations, nationalities or people" the Constitution lists the sharing of "intelligible language, common culture, similar customs, common psychological make up and predominantly contiguous territory" (art. 39). Religion is not explicitly mentioned in spite of the fact that throughout Ethiopian history religion and ethnicity have mutually informed each other (Ostebo 2008). In fact the Constitution is inspired by a secularist approach, recognising the separation of state and religion, the proscription of interference in their respective domains (art. 11), as well as the recognition of religious pluralism and freedom of religious association and expression. Political life in Ethiopia remains organised along ethnic lines and institutions – such as political parties or mass organisations targeting the youth, women and farmers – with the national government held since 1991 by the Ethiopian People Revolutionary Democratic Front (EPRDF), a coalition of regional parties each of them governing the respective regional states.

In spite of its secularist attitude, the EPRDF – and in particular the oligarchy composing of the Tigray People's Liberation Front (TPLF)'s inner circle close to former Prime Minister Meles Zenawi – is attentive in monitoring religious movements, interacting with their institutions and dialoguing with their leaders. EPRDF cautiously delimits the space for religious leaders' engagement in public affairs, restricting it to public addresses in occasion of feast days or to calls to peace and conciliation in occasion of main political events such as the national elections. This approach recalls the TPLF's experience during the armed struggle in Tigray (1975–1991) where the core of its current leadership was trained and consolidated as ruling class. A key factor in the TPLF's political and military success was the support given by a peasantry highly devoted to the Christian Orthodox Church. In order to achieve that support, the TPLF elite took a careful and sensitive approach to the religious sphere. In particular they were able to recognise the internal plurality within the Orthodox Church of Tigray and to establish a pragmatic alliance with the parts of its clergy and members more supportive of TPLF claims for regional autonomy. A similar pragmatism inspires nowadays the cautious control by the EPRDF government of the church's potential in terms of political mobilisation. Thus, while religious actors enjoy a relative freedom of association and expression compared to other civil society organisations, they still have to abide by the delimited space granted by the government. The recent tensions between the government and the Muslim community offer a meaningful example of these dynamics. In 2011 the EPRDF attempted to control the Ethiopian Islamic Affairs Supreme Council, by installing an accommodating leadership in the name of the fight against religious extremism. This attempt generated an unprecedented wave of nonviolent protests by the Islamic community that lasted for more than a year, and that were later repressed through arrests and allegations of extremism and terrorism. The unfolding of this story indicates how religious bodies are increasingly seen as challengers by the ruling coalition and how the government sanction them by deploying the same anti-terrorism narrative and coercive means as in the case of political opponents (Bach 2015).

Similar interference by the government in orienting people participation to public affairs applies to the second tenet of developmental citizenship, namely the organisation of economic life according to the model of the developmental state. Since the 1990s, the EPRDF undertook a limited programme of privatisation of public assets and enterprises, retaining monopolistic control of key sectors, like energy and telecommunication, and active involvement in others, like finance, through state owned or party affiliated enterprises. By dint of its strong control on key economic sectors, the government aims at steering the economic development of the country, with the official goal of achieving the status of "middle income country" by 2025 (FDRE 2010). This strategy aims at transforming the socio-economic fabric of the countryside towards a market-oriented agriculture, as well as at promoting industrialisation. In this perspective the articulation of two elements seems particularly relevant. The first element is the emphasis on the leadership. In carving the ideology that inspires the Ethiopian developmental state, Meles Zenawi argues that the transformation of a pre-capitalist system to a "sustainable" market economy should be ensured by the "central direction" of a "political class that has both the will and the ability to bring about the economic processes mentioned above" (Zenawi 2011). This is ensured by the practices of what has been qualified as "developmental patrimonialism", namely a situation in which rents are centralised and leaders take a long-term approach to rent maximisation. The state may retain patrimonial characteristics, but is more likely to be broadly developmental" (Vaughan & Gebremichael 2011:7). On the other side, the search for the broadest participation, with the developmental state conceived as a "hegemonic project in the Gramscian sense where key actors voluntarily adhere to its objectives and principles" since "development is an exercise that requires appropriate behaviour on the part of millions of individuals" (Zenawi 2011). Thus, at grass-roots level, the delivery of basic social services interweaves with political mobilisation, with the goal of legitimising the state's vanguard role and its control over the people and the resources of the country. The government retain control of key economic inputs, like credit, land and fertilisers, co-opting the most successful small entrepreneurs – the so called "model farmers" – into party structures (Lefort 2010). By incorporating a considerable portion of the population through party affiliation and bio-political devices such as the development armies of role models (farmers, women, youth) and by getting embodied in people's daily life and practices, the developmental state has achieved an unprecedented level of penetration within the society, but at the same time gets constantly renegotiated and diluted in everyday practices (Villanucci & Fantini 2016).

The principles of the secular state apply to the field of development too. Religious proselytism in development activities is strictly forbidden. faith-based organisations (FBOs) and the branches of the churches that promote development projects – in Ethiopia usually referred to as church development wings – should abide to the same rules applying to other NGOs and civil society organisations. All their activities are called to be in line with local authorities' plans and are implemented in partnership with them. Beneficiaries of development activities cannot be discriminated along religious lines. Furthermore, according to the 2008 Regulation on Civil Society Organisations (CSOs) the main churches' development wings and FBOs, as per other organisations receiving more than 10% of their budget from foreign sources, are no longer allowed to operate in politically contentious domains like civic and voters education, human rights advocacy or conflict resolutions.

The tenets of developmental citizenship recall how the opportunities in terms of freedom of expression and association granted by the Ethiopian Constitution to religious bodies should be analysed within the boundaries imposed by the EPRDF's stand vis-à-vis the religious factor, and more in general against its political strategy. When trying to promote and increase their involvement in public affairs, religious actors have to negotiate and to accommodate their priorities with those of a government that competes with them in orientating, controlling and disciplining peoples' lives.

## A call to renewed Pentecostal citizens

Historically, the Ethiopian Pentecostal movement has been permeated by an ascetic attitude, emphasising the separation between the spiritual and the secular, and avoiding active involvement in public affairs. This apolitical stand was reinforced by the narrative and self-representation of the movement, emphasising the memory of the persecution suffered under the military regime of the *Derg* (1974–1987) and the resulting identification of politics and public affairs as a dangerous worldly thing (Haustein 2011). In the last few years, these positions have been increasingly challenged by a theological shift promoting a holistic approach to salvation and calling on Christians to become actively involved in the public arena in order to evangelise and transform the country. This shift has been urged by the perception of moral decay affecting the country, as affirmed throughout many interviews to spiritual leaders conducted in Ethiopia between 2010 and 2015. It was also facilitated by the climate of religious freedom inaugurated with the 1995 Constitution. Thus a group of neo-charismatic churches and proactive pastors, mostly based in urban contexts, have been particularly vocal in reclaiming Pentecostals' visibility in public spaces and growing engagement in public affairs (Fantini 2013). Initially these groups acted outside the main body encompassing Evangelical and Pentecostal churches, the Evangelical Churches Fellowship of Ethiopia (ECFE). They explicitly exhorted their Christian fellows to actively engage in politics.

Such involvement is framed in general and neutral terms, avoiding any explicit stance for specific parties or candidates. Reference is usually made to the need to answer the call to serve and transform the country according to God's will, as well as to witness and to promote Christian values in public affairs. Concepts such as righteousness, leadership and transformation are mobilised to legitimate and encourage a new season of public engagement. These notions contribute to defining the ethos of the converted – honest, hardworking, trustworthy and incorruptible – applied to politics, combining ethics of service in public affairs with behavioural purity in personal life.

Similarly in the development and economic domains, there has been the attempt to revitalise existing professional associations, like the Ethiopian Christian Graduates Fellowship, or to create ad hoc ministries, groups and networks dealing with economics and development. Nowadays, almost all the main independent and neo-charismatic churches – such as Beza International Church, City of Refugee (formerly You-Go City) Church, Unic 7000, Exodus – have established their own fellowships targeting the business and professional communities.

This theological and practical shift has proven particularly popular among Pentecostal youth and their organisations, like EVASU, the Evangelical Student Union of Ethiopia, causing a generation friction within the Pentecostal movement. One the one side, the oldest generations and the mainline churches remain recalcitrant to get actively involved in politics. Their representatives mostly motivate this stand by recalling the persecutions suffered under the *Derg*. In this respect, the most frightening event was the killing in 1979 of Gudina Tumsa, the secretary general of the Evangelical *Mekane Yesus* Church, who sympathised with the instances of social justice and ethnic emancipation promoted in the first phase of the Ethiopian Revolution (Eide 2000). On the other side stand the young leaders of the churches that within the Ethiopian Pentecostal movement are labelled as "young" or "new", which do not bear such burdensome memory; their enthusiasm is rapidly contaminating the whole Pentecostal movement, as acknowledged by an elder of the *Mulu Wengel* Church:

> My sons are going to Exodus church. They have a holistic vision: they want to get involved in the economy in order to transform the country. Their church is full of young, energetic and skilled people. They want to see the society transformed in all sectors: economy, politics, development. . . . Their programs are much more ambitious than those of the traditional churches and their development wings, like ours. The mainline denominations are a little bit suspicious about the young churches, also because there is a fear from the past experience during the *Derg*

time. But this attitude is spreading from the young churches to influence the whole Pentecostal movement.
(Interview, Addis Ababa, 6 November 2012)[2]

This theological and practical shift promoted by" entails a corrosive critique of the corruption governing politics and the economy. Pastors insist on the need for Pentecostal involvement in these realms in order to fight corruption and to bring righteousness according to Christian values and God's will. The most vocal among those groups also introduced in Ethiopia notions and practices which they described as borrowed from North American or Nigeria Pentecostalism, such us the spiritual warfare and the governmental prayer. By referring to these notions, they challenge the secular distinctions set by the government between spiritual and material transformation, politics and religion, state and church, like it happens in other contexts such as Nigeria (Marshall 2009). As explained by Pastor Abby, founder of the Unic7000 church:

> we pray for our nation, to redress current situations where our nation is affected by evil forces. According to the scripture, we believe that the reality of the present is not just the product of historical conditions, but it has also a deep relationship with the spiritual realm. That is why we engage ourselves in spiritual warfare: we believe that there are spiritual agents of evil and Satan, principles and powers. We engage through governmental prayers those evil forces that influence the institutions, the systems and the leaders of the nation. We have really seen a great change through our prayer efforts. Many things have happened. For instance during the 2005 elections the situation was very volatile. We fasted and prayed through governmental prayers, because the country was divided in half and the intent of the enemy was to steer us toward civil war. People were predicting ethnic tensions and politicians telling that the next Rwanda was going to happen. So we prayed and we saw God changing things. It was a miracle to avoid such chaos.[3]

On the other side the critique of corruption and the call for good governance is balanced by the adoption of a patriotic message, announcing "an era of glory Ethiopia" and echoing EPRDF official discourse on growth and transformation. As explained by Fitsum Negussie, Development Director at SACRED International Ministry,

> Our objective is to offer a positive outlook on the current transformation that the country is experiencing. We encourage in particular the youth to participate in government efforts to transform the country, like those promoted in the Growth and Transformation Plan. We empowered the youth with leadership and excellency, reflecting the image of Christ in their life, in order to offer a positive contribution to their nation.[4]

122  *Emanuele Fantini*

The ambiguity of this call to a new generation of Christian citizens are evident in the plurality of practices and itineraries it legitimised when they have to confront and navigate the tenets of developmental citizenship as it will be explained in the following section.

## Pentecostals and ethnic federalism

While Pentecostalism is usually portrayed as an urban phenomenon, in Ethiopia it remains mostly a rural one: the map in Figure 7.1 shows how the vast majority of Ethiopian registered as Protestants still live in rural areas – in line with the trend of the overall population. They are mainly located in the southwestern regions of the country: Southern Nations, Nationalities and People Regions (SNNPR), Gambella, Benishangul and the western zones of Oromia region. These are the regions of historical missionary presence and where Evangelicals and Pentecostals expanded at the expenses of traditional beliefs (Dewel 2014). The spatial concentration in these regions, featured by a fertility rate above the national average, contributes to explain why Protestants are the fastest growing religious group in the country (Dewel 2014). It is also worth noting that in the regions where Pentecostals are a tiny minority, such as the northern and

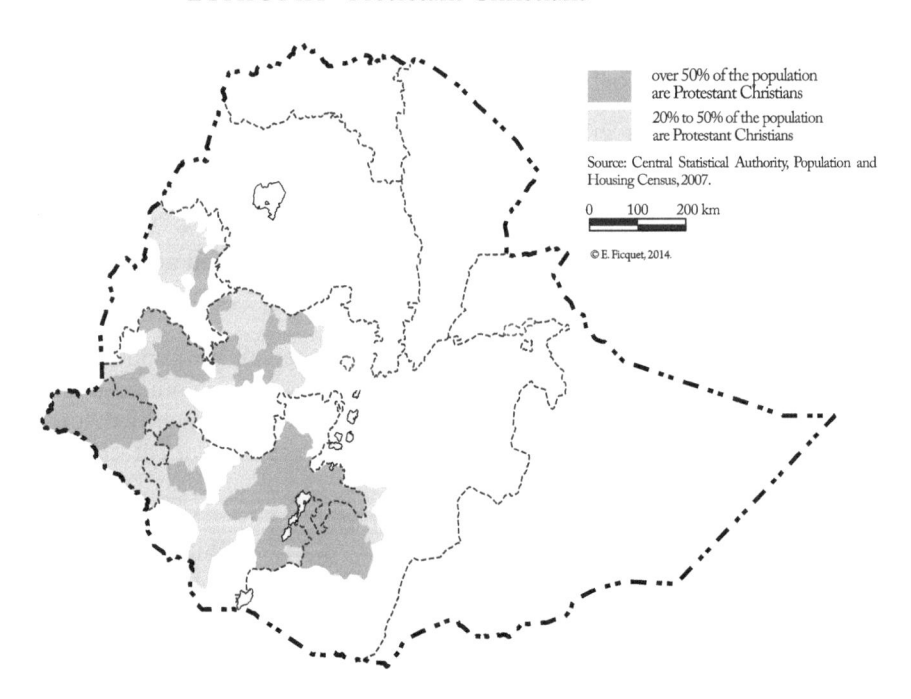

*Figure 7.1* Density of Pentecostal population in different regions (Source Prunier & Ficquet 2015)

traditionally Orthodox Tigray and Amhara, they are mainly located in urban centres, posing significant challenges in terms of coexistence and competition between different religious groups for the occupation of public spaces, including land for religious buildings and airwaves to disseminate religious messages.

In spite of Pentecostals' regional concentration, their ethos of engagement in public affairs is translated into different itineraries, displaying distinct and controversial relationships with the first predicament of developmental citizenship, namely the organisation of political life and institutions along ethnic lines. In some cases, Pentecostalism shares an elective affinity with the ethnic federalism, reinforcing political allegiances and careers within ethnic parties, both in the government and in the opposition. Here Pentecostal faith reinforces local ethnic identities and self-determination claims related to the disputed history of the country, particularly in terms of relationship of domination between different national groups. This is particularly evident for people from the areas characterised by a traditional Protestant missionary presence, such as SNNPR or Western Oromia. In these areas Pentecostalism represents the religion of the majority of the population. Missionary schools were the only opportunity for people belonging to subaltern groups to be educated without being assimilated to the Amhara culture of the ruling elite. The translation of the Bible and worship into local languages by Evangelical and Pentecostal foreign missionaries – soon followed by autochthonous churches – was reinforced and amplified by the emphasis on the right to self-determination and the official recognition of local languages promoted by the 1994 Constitution. Both these factors foster a sentiment of rupture with the historical Amhara dominion during the imperial times ended with the 1974 Revolution, legitimating claims about the rights and the political dignity of the "southern marches" of the former Empire. In those cases, the religious allegiance reinforces the ethnic identity of specific groups, belonging to local and regional elites (Donham 2002; Sato 2002). Occasionally, members of these elites managed to acquire national relevance, as in the case of the public figures that are usually mentioned as examples of "good Christians" involved in politics, the most relevant being the current Prime Minister Hailemariam Desalegn.

By reinforcing its belonging to local elites, Pentecostalism offers the opportunity for a dialectic adhesion to the national establishment, dominated by Amhara and Tigrean ruling classes that are traditionally associated with the EOC. For instance, this is the case of a new generation of dynamic party cadres belonging to the Oromo People's Democratic Organisation (OPDO), the Oromo wing of the EPRDF, and presenting themselves as "pure Christians and pure Oromo".[5] In this case Pentecostal affiliation allows politicians to remain politically loyal to the EPRDF while at the same time distancing themselves from its Tigrean and Amhara establishment, both in religious and ethnic terms. Within the same ethnic group, Pentecostalism might also support political identities entailing a fierce opposition to the government, as in the case of the Oromo Liberation Front (OLF).

The identity of the OLF's main constituencies in Western Oromia has been shaped by the historical presence of Evangelical missionaries and in particular of the Ethiopian Evangelical Church Mekane Yesus (Eide 2000). In this case, the religious factor is controversially interwoven with the OLF's claims for self-determination and its struggle against the EPRDF.

In other contexts, Pentecostalism upholds identities that challenge the institutional ethnic boundaries of the federal state. This applies in particular to urban areas, where ethnic ties are relatively weak, given the historical tradition of inter-ethnic marriages and internal migration. In these cases, Pentecostalism promotes paths of individualisation and a sense of belonging to "a new nation and a new people in Christ" that challenge the foundations and the legitimacy of the ethnic federal architecture. The message sounds particularly appealing to young generations and educated professionals. Usually these people present themselves as willing to contribute to the success of a prosperous Ethiopia, regardless of its internal divisions between nations, nationalities and peoples. This critical stand vis-à-vis ethnic divisions inspired, for instance, a season of political engagement of several supporters with a Pentecostal background within the Coalition for Unity and Democracy (CUD) that during the 2005 electoral campaign questioned the constitutional premises of ethnic federalism and was considered the heir of historical pan Ethiopian political forces.

These examples show the ambiguous relationship between Pentecostalism and ethnic federalism, and the resulting plurality of political itineraries that it contributes to legitimate. The historical legacy of a contested past interwoven with spiritual belief in shaping different political identities. This plurality, matched with the generation frictions described in the previous section, recalls that the Ethiopian Pentecostal movement is not a homogeneous entity and cannot be considered a single political constituency.

Furthermore, both in the cases of negotiated adhesion or of opposition to the current regime, the religious allegiance remains ancillary to the ethnic and party allegiance. In the context of a polarised national political space and a pluralistic society, the adoption of a confessional stand does not appear suitable for any party or coalition aiming at ensuring nationwide support and representativeness. The ethnic marker continues to represent the main frame to mobilise political subjects and to represent their interests, as the 2016 protests in Oromia and Amhara seem to confirm (Lefort 2016). Both within the government and the opposition, political leaders do not publicly flaunt their religious allegiance. Party members are also very cautious in offering a partisan interpretation of their religious affiliation, in order not to compromise their church or create tensions within it. Religious beliefs fail therefore to enter into competition with the secular programme of the EPRDF, whose strong ideology remains almost impermeable to spiritual claims.

The effort of keeping politics and religion separate characterises the approach of traditional mainline churches. Churches like the Mennonite *Meserete Kristos* or the *Mulu Wengel*, for instance, forbid political party members to become church elders or ministers. This position prevails among the generation of believers who bear direct memory of the political persecutions suffered by religious groups under the *Derg* and who fear the possibility of new conflicts as a consequence of a more proactive role of the church in public affairs. This caution nourishes the apolitical register adopted by representatives of mainline churches and of the ECFE., as well as the sense of mistrust towards politics, widely considered among Pentecostals as a dangerous and corrupt game (Haustein 2011). Consequently, the believers who bear a genuine interest and vocation to politics have found themselves caught in a moral conflict when trying to reconcile their political commitment with the official positions of their church and the perception of the majority of their fellow believers.

## Pentecostals and the developmental state

Pentecostals' relations to economic development are as much variegated as the one to ethnic federalism: they legitimise personal aspiration to worldly economic success and they encourage a proactive Christian presence in business by resorting to different theological approaches. A common denominator within the movement seems to be the general rejection of the prosperity gospel, as emerged interviews with pastors and believers of mainline and "new" Pentecostal churches. (Fantini 2016). The miracle-based approach emphasising the power of God in offering wealth and abundance to his people, like the promises of wonders, miracles and easy money performed by foreign pastors visiting the country, are mostly received with suspicion. Pentecostal leaders seem to stick to a "theologically correct" parlance that considers these approaches as a degeneration of Christian doctrine and that labels them as alien to Ethiopian tradition (Fantini 2016 and interviews conducted with pastors between 2010 and 2014). However, inside the Ethiopian Pentecostal movement there seems to be an increasing trend to embody the prosperity gospel spirit in practice, for instance by adopting the language of marketing, and a growing interest in upward mobility. Some of the Pentecostal groups catering to Addis Ababa's middle and upper classes increasingly display economic success as sign of blessing and righteousness of faith and behaviours.

Most of Ethiopian "new" Pentecostal groups adopt an approach linking economic success to spiritual and individual change. Consequently, the call to work for the transformation of the society passes through individual conversion and governing of the self: economic success is conceived as the result of the adherence to rigorous self-discipline and techniques of the body, control of desires, honesty, faith and prayers, but also hard work, technical knowledge and skills. Thus, economic success becomes part of the broader "remaking of the individual" inherent in the Pentecostal conversion (Maxwell 1998:352). Here the emphasis is on a double break with the past. On the one hand, a break with the ascetic ideals of mainline Evangelical churches, and with the suspicion of economic success and the lack of entrepreneurial mentality that permeate the Ethiopian society. On the other hand, a break with personal attitudes and behaviours described in terms of sin and corruption, towards the adoption of an ethic of purity and hard work. In this respect, the Pentecostal message of spiritual and economic empowerment implies the transition from a state of disorder to righteousness.

The promise of economic success combines Pentecostal theology with notions borrowed from the manuals on management, consultancy, self-development and psychology. Consequently, Pentecostal churches and business fellowships offer training opportunities on entrepreneurial and managerial skills for their members. This training addresses both business basics (accountancy, management, marketing, leadership . . .) and moral and spiritual topics (business ethics, social responsibility, Bible study . . .). In addition, the fellowships promote networking among church members, to uphold existing business and inspire the establishment of new ones, such us micro-finance institutions, banks, joint ventures. As explained by Pastor Johannes "Johnny" Girma, leader of the Exodus Apostolic Reformation Church,

> The Church has to teach to work diligently. It has to teach entrepreneurship, in order to provide material means for transformation. God is a provider who cares for you, otherwise poverty affects also your spiritual transformation. Our God is a God of creativity, of development. An entrepreneur. We bring together capitals and vision, and they work together.[6]

By encouraging upward mobility and adopting the register of leadership, excellence and the fight against corruption, Pentecostals endorse the neoliberal narrative, echoing and legitimising the official Government's discourse on the transformation of the country into a mature middle-income market economy. In focusing on individual transformation, Pentecostals do not seem to be condemning structural imbalances within the political or economic systems, neither seeking their structural change.

This preaching legitimises different trajectories and practices in the field of economic development. For instance Dena Freeman emphasises the elective affinity between Pentecostalism and development in rural Ethiopia (Freeman 2012, 2013). She analyses how the Pentecostal "holistic ministry" or "transformational development", understanding economic transformation strictly connected with subjective change, has proved particularly effective in promoting pattern of development and accumulation in rural communities in the Gamo highlands of southwestern Ethiopia. Here, conversion to Pentecostalism facilitated the behavioural changes towards risk assumption and entrepreneurial attitudes, and a break with traditional kinship obligations, advancing individual accumulation by exploiting development opportunities offered by the project of an international NGO promoting cash crop (apple trees) in the area. At the same time, the concept of "holistic ministry" and the practices of "transformation development", with their emphasis on the need to serve the whole person, transcend the official secular approach to development adopted by the Ethiopian government as well as by international NGOs.

Similar patterns of economic success and resource accumulation are present in urban contexts too. Within Addis Ababa business circles there are several entrepreneurs, owning malls, hotels, private schools or companies, whose Pentecostal background is widely known.[7] However most of the time they do not publicly display their faith and their religious networks when dealing with business. Thus, in spite of amplifying vocal discourses on the need to strengthen Christian values in the economy, the development of a flourishing Pentecostal business community at national level has not yet materialised. First of all, these efforts have suffered the effects of the internal fragmentation within the Pentecostal movement, which makes it hard to coordinate the work of churches and para-churches organisations or to establish a unitary businessmen fellowship.

Moreover, these shortcomings are attributed to an attitude of suspicion within the movement towards the involvement in the business sector, or to a lack of appreciation of its importance, as well as to the difficulties of honestly competing in a market where other players – including Christian themselves – recur to fraudulent practices. As acknowledged by Pastor David of the City of Refugee Church,

> Pentecostalism is a relationship with God rather than a religion. Everybody that has a direct relationship with Jesus is a productive person, a good citizen, and a hard worker with a caring attitude towards the family and the nation. God is a God of prosperity who works hard. Therefore also in Ethiopia *Pentes* can help in transforming the country: we need a productive and educated society. But I do not see a contribution by Christians as much as I would like. Why? Some people are not totally committed. As Christian we should have integrity, but because of our culture people do not always respond to their word. There is lack of integrity, due to the prevalence of traditional culture. There is a lack of attitude to renew our mind according to the word of God. Christians are still going for shortcuts in business. Sometimes is very difficult to be honest, when everybody around is corrupted. You need deep spiritual change.[8]

Finally, Pentecostal business endeavours have to deal with the contradictory approach of the EPRDF to both religious and economic liberalisation. On the one hand, the government institutionally authorises spaces for religious and economic freedom. On the other hand, the EPRDF aims at controlling such spaces, perceiving both religious actors and private economic entrepreneurs as potential competitors in terms of popular legitimacy and support. In doing this, the EPRDF does not seem to fully grasp – and consequently does not accommodate – the quest for freedom and autonomy engendered among the population by its own policies of economic and religious liberalisation. Thus, in the name of the secular approach, the developmental citizenship keeps the religious realm separated from the economic and development ones, assigning to the sole government competence on the latter, and thwarting at the same time the space of independent private business. As explained by Mekonnen, chairman of the CCCM Businessmen Fellowship,

> In the Ethiopian context, officially displaying your religious affiliation when doing business might not be a wise economic strategy. Our vision is to play as businessmen and professional an important role in the growth and transformation of the country, as stated in the government plan, the GTP. However, the government does not perceive the private sector as its main development partner and does not encourage it. Therefore it is difficult to measure the practical contribution by Pentecostals to the economy.[9]

Those who are the most vocal and active in affirming themselves as Christian businessmen appears to be also the ones that find themselves in the position of outsiders, both inside the Pentecostal movement and in the broader national political economy. An example of this situation is the Unic 7000 Church in Addis Ababa and its Absolute Value Fellowship. This church stands among the most proactive neo-charismatic and independent groups advocating in advancing Pentecostal public presence through crusades, evangelism conferences or mass-prayers at Addis Ababa national stadium. The church mainly caters to Addis Ababa's upper and middle class; among its members there are lawyers, professionals, businessmen, Ethiopians working in foreign embassies or international NGOs, and a few politicians. These groups are animated by a strong desire of upward mobility and success. They are equipped with the theological notions and practical knowledge to prosper in a neoliberal economy. However, their plans and ambitions to engage in financial and real estate projects have been so far frustrated by their incapacity to access the material opportunities offered by the right political and economic networks fed by developmental patrimonialism (Fantini 2016). This example recalls the plurality of practices in economy and politics legitimised by Pentecostalism. Further case studies are badly needed to better assess and weight these different trajectories and the directions they are taking. This seems a particularly up-to-date agenda at a time when private companies and business logics are increasingly influential in the field of international aid and development cooperation, as for instance preached by the "aid for trade" agenda.

In conclusion, what do Pentecostals' engagement in public affairs tell us about how do people understand and navigate the predicaments of developmental citizenship imposed by the Ethiopian government? Pentecostalism seems to hold a contradictory relation with these predicaments. On the one side, the Pentecostal call for moral regeneration of the country apparently echoes the Ethiopian government's official discourse on good governance, development and economic transformation. This contributes to a widespread – also outside the Pentecostal movement – culture of aspiration to partake the development cake. On the other side the Pentecostal logics challenges the secular division between state and church, religion and politics, spiritual and material transformation, thus undermining the very foundation of the Ethiopian federal state. This contradiction results in a plurality of itineraries, imaginaries and practices, resulting in moral conflicts within and outside the Pentecostal movement, and failing in ensuring a coherent "alternative civic identity". The rigid tenets of developmental citizenship fail to fully accommodate this plurality of logics and aspirations, further delegitimising the state in the eyes of Pentecostals, while reinforcing their faith in God's redeeming role against spiritual crisis and moral corruption.

## Notes

1 On the origin of the term, initially considered socially denigrating, see J. Haustein (2011:229–232) and Donham (1999).
2 The real names of most of the informants have been changed or omitted to protect their privacy.
3 Interview, Addis Ababa, 17 March 2011.
4 Interview, Addis Ababa, 8 November 2012.
5 Interview to OPDO official, Addis Ababa, 23 March 2011.
6 Interview, Addis Ababa, 23 March 2011.
7 Fieldwork observation, Addis Ababa, between 2010 and 2014.
8 Interview, Addis Ababa, 3 May 2012.
9 Interview, Addis Ababa, 27 April 2012.

## References

Abbink, J. 2011. 'Religion in Public Spaces: Emerging Muslim – Christian Polemics in Ethiopi'a'. *African Affairs*, 110(439): 253–274.Bach, J.N. 2015. '"Peurs" et pratiques répressives : mobilisations musulmanes et pouvoir éthiopien (2011-2014)' *EchoGéo* 31. 10 April 2015. URL: http://echogeo.revues.org/14119 DOI : 10.4000/echogeo.14119

Central Statistical Agency. 2012. *Ethiopia Demographic and Health Survey 2011*. Addis Ababa: Central Statistical Agency.

Chang, K. S. 2012. 'Economic Development, Democracy and Citizenship Politics in South Korea: The Predicament of Developmental Citizenship'. *Citizenship Studies*, 16(1): 29–47.

Dewel, S. 2014. *Mouvement Charismatique et Pentecôtisme en Éthiopie: Identité et Religion*. Paris: L'Harmattan.

Donham, D. L. 1999. *Marxist Modern: An Ethnographic History of the Ethiopian Revolution*. Berkeley, Los Angeles: University of California Press.

Donham, D. L. 2002. 'Old Abyssina and the New Ethiopian Empire: Themes in Social History'. In D. L. Donham & W. James (Eds.) *The Southern Marches of Imperial Ethiopia Essays in History & Social Anthropology*. Oxford: James Currey.

Eide, O. M. 2000. *Revolution and Religion in Ethiopia: The Growth and Persecution of the Mekane Yesus Church in Ethiopia 1974–85*. Oxford: James Currey.

Fantini, E. 2013. 'Transgression and Acquiescence: The Moral Conflict of Pentecostals in Their Relationship With the Ethiopian State'. *PentecoStudies*, 12: 198–223.

Fantini, E. 2016. 'Crafting Ethiopia's Glorious Destiny'. *Archives de Sciences Sociales des Religions*, 175: 67–86.

Federal Democratic Republic of Ethiopia. 2010. *Growth and Transformation Plan 2010/11–2014/15*. Addis Abeba: MoFED.

Freeman, D. 2012. 'Development and the Rural Entrepreneur: Pentecostals, NGOs and the Market in the Gamo Highlands, Ethiopia'. In D. Freeman (Ed.) *Pentecostalism and Development: Churches, NGOs and Social Change in Africa*. London: Palgrave-Macmillan: 159–180.

Freeman, D. 2013. 'Pentecostalism in a Rural Context: Dynamics of Religion and Development in Southwest Ethiopia'. *PentecoStudies*, 12(2): 231–249.

Gascon, A. 2008. 'Shining Ethiopia: l'Éthiopie post-communiste du nouveau millénaire'. *Autrepart*, 4: 141–152.

Haustein, J. 2011. *Writing Religious History: The Historiography of Ethiopian Pentecostalism*. Wiesbaden: Harrassowitz.

Lefort, R. 2010. Powers – Mengist – and Peasants in Rural Ethiopia: The Post-2005 Interlude'. *The Journal of Modern African Studies*, 48(3): 435–460.

Lefort, R. 2016. 'Ethiopia's Crisis: Things Fall Apart: Will the Centre Hold?' *OpenDemocracy*. 19 November. Available at: www.opendemocracy.net/ren-lefort/ethiopia-s-crisis (accessed 16 March 2017).

Marshall, R. 2009. *Political Spiritualities: the Pentecostal Revolution in Nigeria*. University of Chicago Press.

Maxwell, D. 1998. 'Delivered From the Spirit of Poverty?' Pentecostalism, Prosperity and Modernity in Zimbabwe'. *Journal of Religion in Africa*, 28(Fasc. 3): 350–373.

Office of the Population and Housing Census Commission. 1991. *The 1984 Population and Housing Census of Ethiopia*. Addis Ababa: Office of the Population and Housing Census Commission.

Office of the Population and Housing Census Commission. 2008. *Summary and Statistical Report of the 2007 Population and Housing Census*. Addis Ababa: Population Census Commission.

Østebø, T. 2008. 'The Question of Becoming: Islamic Reform Movements in Contemporary Ethiopia'. *Journal of Religion in Africa*, 38(4): 416–446.

Pankhurst, A. (Ed.) 2017. *Change and Transformation in Twenty Rural Communities in Ethiopia*. Addis Ababa: EthiopiaWide.

Pew Forum on Religion & Public Life. 2010. *Tolerance and Tension: Islam and Christianity in Sub-Saharan Africa*. Washington, DC: Pew Research Center.

Prunier, G. & Ficquet, É. 2015. *Understanding Contemporary Ethiopia: Monarchy, Revolution and the Legacy of Meles Zenawi*. Oxford: Oxford University Press.

Sato, R. 2002. 'Evangelical Christianity and Ethnic Consciousness in Majangir'. In W. James, D. Donham, E. Kurimoto & A. Triulzi (Eds.) *Remapping Ethiopia: Socialism and After*. Oxford: James Currey.

Skjerdal, T. S. 2011. 'Development Journalism Revived: The Case of Ethiopia'. *Ecquid Novi: African Journalism Studies*, 32(2): 58–74.

Vaughan, S. & Gebremichael, M. 2011. *Rethinking Business and Politics in Ethiopia, Africa Power and Politics Programme Research Reports*. London: Overseas Development Institute.

Villanucci, A. & Fantini, E. 2016. 'Santé publique, Participation communautaire et mobilisation politique en Éthiopie: la Women's Development Army'. *Politique africaine*, 2: 77–99.

Zenawi, M. 2011. 'States and Markets: Neoliberal Limitations and the Case for a Developmental State'. In A. Noman, K. Botchwey, H. Stein & J. E. Stiglitz (Eds.) *Good Growth and Governance in Africa: Rethinking Development Strategies*. Oxford: Oxford University Press.

# Part 3
# Regenerating morality
Values, public beliefs and morality

## 8 Sexual citizenship in postcolonial Zambia

From Zambian humanism to Christian nationalism

*Adriaan van Klinken*

"All citizenship is sexual citizenship". This claim made by David Bell and Jon Binnie (2000:10) foregrounds the sexual nature of citizenship; it expresses, as they put it, that "the foundational tenets of being a citizen are all inflected by sexualities". The relationship between sexuality and citizenship has become subject of historical and social science scholarship especially from the late 1990s, complementing the already existing work on the gendered as well as racialised nature of ideas and discourses around citizenship (Lister 2002; Richardson 2000). However, as Basile Ndjio observes, the mainstream literature on African sexuality pays little attention to nationalism and citizenship, while literature on citizenship in Africa pays little attention to sexuality. This is all the more surprising, he argues, because,

> across the continent, the refoundational aspirations of pan-Africanist thought and Afrocentrist philosophies sustained the nationalist ambition to constitute an exclusive African sexual identity. They also provided an ideological justification for the exclusion by many African postcolonial states of a variety of sexual experiences, expressions, and desires from the realm of respectable citizenship.
>
> (Ndjio 2013:120)

Only recently, links between sexuality, citizenship and ideologies of nationalism have begun to be explored, especially in the emerging body of literature addressing the current politics of homosexuality in Africa (Nyeck & Epprecht 2013; Nyanzi 2011). However, these accounts tend to focus on contemporary contexts and do not provide in-depth insight in the *longue durée* of sexual citizenship in African societies. As Ndjio (2013) demonstrates in his work on Cameroon, contemporary politics of homosexuality, and the promotion of a strictly heterosexual notion of 'African' citizenship, stand in a long tradition of politicising sexuality in postcolonial African states.

This chapter gives an account on the continuity and change of sexual citizenship in postcolonial Zambia, especially in relation to religion. In Zambia, like in other African contexts, religion cannot be separated from politics as both spheres are intricately connected (Ellis & Ter Haar 2007). Among other things, religious ideologies inform and shape the ways in which the nation and its ideal citizens are being imagined, and how gendered and sexual citizenship are being defined and policed. Exploring these dynamics in the context of postcolonial Zambia, this chapter broadly focuses on the discursive politics of Zambian sexual citizenship in two periods: first, the post-independence period dominated by President Kenneth Kaunda and his United National Independence Party (UNIP) in which Zambian Humanism was promoted as the official state philosophy, and second, the period after the 1991 multiparty elections, in which Zambia was officially declared a Christian nation by President Frederick Chiluba and in which Christianity, especially in its Pentecostal form, became a major factor in public and political life.

Humanism and Christian Nationalism represent two narratives of nationhood that have dominated the history of Zambia as a postcolonial state. This chapter introduces, contextualises and examines these narratives, highlighting some crucial differences but also some striking continuities, particularly with regard to the politics of sexual citizenship. Doing so, the chapter hopefully resists and overcomes 'the lure of a simplistic binary' between Kaunda's Humanism and Chiluba's Christianity that occurs in some accounts (Hinfelaar 2011:129).

## UNIP, Kaunda and the philosophy of Zambian Humanism

Zambia's colonial and postcolonial history reveals a continuous contestation over the nature of nationhood. In fact, the country's nationalist movement emerged in 1953 in opposition to the plans for creating a settler-dominated Central African Federation uniting Southern Rhodesia (now Zimbabwe), Nyasaland (Malawi) and Northern Rhodesia (Zambia). This opposition was organised in the African National Congress under the leadership of Harry Nkumbula. One of the younger, emerging voices in the nationalist movement was Kenneth Kaunda, the son of a Protestant missionary and teacher. After his break with Nkumbula over the political future of Northern Rhodesia, Kaunda in January 1960 was elected as president of the newly established United National Independence Party (UNIP). He became prime minister in the government leading Northern Rhodesia into independence, and once that stage had been reached he became the first president of the independent Republic of Zambia in October 1964.

There is an ongoing academic debate about the UNIP and Kaunda-centeredness of Zambian historiography (Gewald, Hinfelaar & Macola 2008; Englund 2013). Yet one cannot deny that the construction of Zambian nationhood, even though contested and challenged from both within and outside, was dominated by UNIP, "which sought to imprint its ideas of what a Zambian nation should be on a diverse territory and its peoples" (Larmer et al. 2014:896). An important means to this was the development of a new philosophy, created by Kaunda and called 'Zambian Humanism', which in 1967 was adopted by UNIP as the official national ideology. Some scholars have been sceptical about the impact that Zambian Humanism has had. According to Vaughan, the structural features which characterised the politics of the Kaunda administration "had nothing to do with 'Humanism' or socialism, except when represented rhetorically by the leadership" (Vaughan 1998:178). Gordon does not deny the strongly rhetorical dimension of Humanism, yet he suggests that the philosophy should be considered "a serious moral and ideological intervention that guided the interactions between individuals and the postcolonial state" (Gordon 2012:160).

Historian David Gordon traces the development of Humanism back to 1964, when Kaunda gave a speech at the annual UNIP conference taking place just a month before independence and shortly after the violent confrontation between UNIP and the Lumpa Church of Alice Lenshina.[1] According to Gordon, the latter conflict strengthened Kaunda in his idea that UNIP "should be a sovereign instrument of morality and guidance for his sometimes confused Zambian flock" (Gordon 2012:161). In his speech Kaunda portrayed Lenshina and her followers as "not only fanatics but lunatics" and as "anti-society" (quoted in Gordon 2012:162) – they represented 'savagery' while what Zambia needed was 'civilisation'. His initial ideas were further developed in subsequent speeches and writings, such as in a series of letters published as *A Humanist in Africa* (1966) and in a pamphlet submitted to the UNIP national conference, entitled *Humanism in Zambia and a Guide to its Implementation* (1967, complemented by Part II in 1974). The philosophy has been described as a mixture of "Fabian socialism, nineteenth-century liberalism, Christian morality and idealisation of the communal values of Zambia's pre-capitalist past" (Vaughan 1998:178).

The introduction of Humanism did spark debate and interest in Zambia. One of the controversies was about the presumed secular and Marxist orientation of the state philosophy and the way it was implemented. Yet as much as Zambian Humanism had secular undertones, it was not anti-religious and in fact was inspired by Christian vocabulary. According to Gordon, it was "a state religion with its own secular invisible world: a modern nation that would resemble heaven" (Gordon 2012:158). Helped by economic growth, the UNIP government initially was well able to meet the expectations of development. Yet with the collapse of the copper price (of which the Zambian economy was, and still is, largely dependent) in the early 1970s, the nationalised economy was deeply ravaged. In response to increased opposition, UNIP in December 1972 introduced a system of 'one-party participatory democracy'. In the subsequent years, the philosophy of Zambian Humanism was applied more and more in the area of morality, individually and publicly, including in relation to issues of sexuality.

## Sexual citizenship under Zambian Humanism

Of particular interest here is a booklet published by UNIP in 1975, entitled *The Zambian Moral Code – A Programmatic Approach*. Addressing the question, 'Why do we need a code?', the introduction refers to Kaunda's publicly expressed concern that he could not watch TV in presence of his children because of the "considerable immorality carried on the Screen of the Television [in] Zambia" (Research Bureau 1975:1). Reference is also made to the party's concern about mini-skirts, tight trousers, jeans, unaccompanied girls in the streets at night and to the 'indiscipline in schools' manifested in the intake of alcohol and drugs. All these expressions of 'indiscipline' and 'immorality', according to the booklet, demonstrate the need for a moral code.

Referring to "all the prophets of God" – and the booklet is religiously inclusive here, as it refers to key figures in a wide range of traditions: Zoroastrianism, Hinduism, Buddhism, Shinto, Judaism, Islam, Baha'i Faith and Christianity – who have "sung hymns against immorality", the *Moral Code* argues that moralising individuals in society cannot be left to religion but is a task of all sectors of society, including the state:

> We have left the Clergy to try to live moral and spiritual lives on our behalf. We only join them for worship on the holy day of the religion concerned. . . . One-day a week morality cannot cleanse the nation. . . [and therefore] every individual and each institution of the state must become part of the struggle. It is in pursuit of this humanist tenet that the party and President Kaunda have enjoined political solution as the guiding star against national pervertion (sic) and immorality.
> (Research Bureau 1975:2)

In the remainder of the booklet, the moral code is introduced and applied to various spheres, such as politics, economics, labour, education, art and entertainment, and it further has sections on 'love and sex', 'marriage', 'cosmetics and dress' and even 'nudes'. Thus, it presents an example of the politics of sexual citizenship under Zambian Humanism. Yet what are these politics?

The gendered nature of sexual citizenship becomes immediately clear in the section on love and sex. The section first addresses the topic of 'the position of women', recognising the rights of women and stating that "one of the tasks of the moral revolution [is] to eliminate cruelty to women" (Research Bureau 1975:14–15). The suggestion here is that women are full citizens. The apparent concern about gender inequality is, however, directly undermined in the next paragraph. Here it is argued that when it comes to "soliciting for love", a woman "shall at all times wait until she is loved or approached by a man to engage her in a decent love affair" (Research Bureau 1975:15). This argument is made with reference to "the Zambian traditional customs and indeed the African customs in general" (ibid.) which would not allow women taking initiative in love-making. The patriarchal view of love-making that is reflected here and supported with a reference to so-called Zambian and African traditions fits in one of the strategies distinguished by Ndjio – of the essentialisation and racialisation of Africans' sexuality – through which sexuality in postcolonial African contexts has been made a site "where the myth about African cultural unity is enacted" (Ndjio 2013:126).

Interestingly, in the same section the booklet has a rather peculiar statement saying: "It is beseeming for a humanist whether male or female to engage in a decent free love affair in accordance with Zambian Customary law or according to new style law" (Research Bureau 1975:15). It is not explained what is meant by such a 'decent free love affair', but the next section on marriage might throw light on this. It discusses the practice of the 'exchange of wives', which refers to a situation where a married woman by arrangement of her husband is involved in sexual relations with another man. This is presented as a morally acceptable arrangement, with the implicit underlying notion that a woman's body and sexuality belong to her husband and that he can decide, for various reasons, to share her.[2]

Another concern in the moral code is with cosmetics and dress. Any form of 'defacing' – the painting of finger and toe nails, lips, eye-lids, etcetera – as well as the use of cosmetics that bleach the skin are labelled as immoral here, because they are "copied from foreign standards" (Research Bureau 1975:17). Also very precise prescriptions are given regarding appearance and dress: afro-wigs, bell-bottom jeans, tight trousers and mini-skirts are all considered as immoral. Even though some of the prescriptions are directed to men, most of them concern women's dress and appearance, making the female body in particular the site of morality. Similar concerns had been expressed earlier by Vice-President Simon Kapwepwe who in 1969 had called for a 'Cultural Revolution' – "in a bid to rid the nation of alien cultures" (Mwangilwa 1986:111) –, as part of which he particularly denounced the use of lipstick, stretching of hair and wearing of mini-skirts, among other things.

Last but not least, the moral code addresses the issue of 'nude and love exposures in public'. It refers to the publication of nude pictures and the showing of 'indecent love affairs' on television or in cinemas as "uncalled for and immoral" (Research Bureau 1975:18). Kaunda himself, in his 'Watershed speech', which he delivered at a UNIP national council meeting in 1975, had also argued that the moral standards in Zambian society are a matter of concern for the party, and had particularly raised the issue of nude pictures. Referring to a Zambian newspaper that had recently published such a picture, Kaunda stated:

> Now when you publicise such things, you are appealing to the instinct of men. You are sabotaging their morality – that is what you do in a permissive society. . . . You are promoting prostitution in the nation. You are appealing to the most base instincts in man, destroying him morally. . . . The capitalist society is permissive. Whatever money can be raised will be raised, even if it means destroying man morally, spiritually, materially and physically.
>
> (Kaunda 1975:31)

In the speech Kaunda announced a concrete measure to prevent things like this happening again: the newspaper concerned will be taken over by, and brought under control of UNIP.

Of particular interest here is how his argument against nude pictures led Kaunda into an argument against capitalism. The same move is made in the moral code, which states: "In Capitalist Countries, all morals are orientated to Capitalist system, outlook and the whole army of morals are designed to protect capitalism" (Research Bureau 1975:3). Humanism is presented as an ideology that, different from capitalism, is able to protect the moral foundations of the nation. Related to this anti-capitalist argument is a strong anti-Western stance. According to Kaunda, the moral purity of Zambia is under threat because,

> There has been a successful invasion of our cultural values by those of the west. Any erosion, countrymen, of our cultural values is a threat to Zambian personality. While we are free to borrow positive aspects of foreign culture to enrich our own, we must defend ourselves against undermining our nationhood through cultural conquest. The whole issue, therefore, becomes one of . . . rejection and indeed fighting those cultural activities from other lands which may destroy our cultural values, thereby not only dehumanising us, but also making us faint carbon copies of themselves.
>
> (Kaunda 1975:28)

There is clearly an echo here of the 'Cultural Revolution' that had been initiated by Vice-President Kapwepwe a few years earlier. The explicitly anti-Western rhetoric evoked by Kaunda in his quest to defend the moral purity of the Zambian nation is even more explicitly reflected when he states: "This is Zambia with its own way of life and not Europe. This is Zambia and not the United States of America. We take our cultural values very seriously" (Kaunda 1975:31).

The rather extensive discourse of Zambian Humanism covers many different social, political and public issues, and sexuality is certainly not the most prominent theme. However, it does receive substantial attention, especially in speeches and publications in the mid-1970s. No systematic concept of sexual citizenship is being developed, but it is clear that citizenship under Zambian Humanism certainly is sexualised – the state inflicts upon its citizens certain notions of what it considers as moral and appropriate in the areas of both public and private sexuality. These notions are presented as being inspired by and derived from 'Zambian culture' and as opposed to the foreign influences from Western capitalist cultures. Yet Gordon's (2012:160) comment on Zambian Humanism in general certainly does apply to the humanist discourse on sexuality in particular: that it is a consolidation of "the moral reformism of the missionary civilizing mission in which the Kaunda family had been so involved".

# From Kaunda's Humanism to Chiluba's Christian nationalism

In the 1980s – a period of deepening economic problems and misuse of political power –, Kaunda and his UNIP government became increasingly subject of criticism, among others of the churches and the trade unions. In 1990, Kaunda gave in to the pressure for democratisation and he signed a new constitution putting an end to the system of one-party democracy. In the 1991 elections, UNIP was defeated by the Movement for Multiparty Democracy (MMD) under the leadership of Frederick J. T. Chiluba, a former trade union leader who succeeded Kaunda and became Zambia's second president.

The Christian churches, united in the Zambia Episcopal Conference (ZEC, Catholic Church), the Christian Council of Zambia (CCZ, mainline Protestant churches) and the Evangelical Fellowship of Zambia (EFZ, evangelical and Pentecostal churches), had played an important role, both in bringing about the democratic change that made the elections possible and in promoting Chiluba as the preferred candidate (Gifford 1998:190–197). Chiluba himself was a member of the United Church of Zambia (UCZ)[3] who had undergone a 'born-again' experience in 1981while being imprisoned by Kaunda for his trade union activities, and who had received the gift of speaking in tongues at a crusade with German evangelist Reinhard Bonnke. Thus, in the words of Gifford, "as Kaunda came to be increasingly regarded as a renegade Christian, presiding over a corrupt and oppressive government, Chiluba stressed (and his supporters stressed even more) his impeccable credentials as a true spirit-filled believer" (Gifford 1998:193). As a born-again Christian with strong Pentecostal-charismatic sympathies, Chiluba was particularly close to leaders of the Pentecostal forms of Christianity that had grown rapidly in Zambia since the 1970s (Cheyeka 2008). Prominent Pentecostal leaders supported him publicly in his campaign and continued to have a strong influence on him once elected.

Only two months after being voted into office (a period in which State House had been ceremonially cleansed by charismatic pastors from 'evil spirits', and in which an 'anointing ceremony' had been held in the Anglican cathedral in Lusaka), on 29 December 1991 President Chiluba declared Zambia to be a Christian nation. He did so in a ceremony broadcasted on national television, surrounded by several Pentecostal leaders. His own government ministers had not been invited because Chiluba did not consider it a 'political' function. Chiluba's speech at this occasion, however, demonstrates the fluid boundaries between 'religion' and 'politics' and can be read as an example of Pentecostal political theology:

> On behalf of the people of Zambia, I repent of our wicked ways of idolatry, witchcraft, immorality, injustice and corruption. I pray for the healing, restoration, revival, blessing and prosperity of Zambia. On

behalf of the nation, I have now entered a covenant with the living God. . . . I submit the Government and the entire nation of Zambia to the Lordship of Jesus Christ. I further declare that Zambia is a Christian nation that will seek to be governed by the righteous principles of the Word of God. Righteousness and justice must prevail in all levels of authority, and then we shall see the righteousness of God exalting Zambia.

(Quoted in Koschorke, Ludwig & Delgado 2007:273)

According to Amos Yong (2010:9), the declaration reveals a sense of 'Pentecostal nationalism', with born-again ideology being applied not just to individuals but to the nation as a whole. In other words, the declaration made Zambia into 'a nation reborn' (Gordon 2012:178), although this does not mean that Zambian Christianity as a whole has been Pentecostalised as other denominations remain strong (Cheyeka, Hinfelaar & Udelhoven 2014).

Welcomed enthusiastically by many born-again Christians as well as Pentecostal leaders and EFZ officials, the reactions of the two other main Christian bodies, ZEC and CCZ, to the declaration were more reserved (see Gifford 1998:198–199; Hinfelaar 2011; Phiri 2008). A couple of years later, in 1995, when Chiluba proposed to include the declaration of Zambia as a Christian nation in the preamble of the country's new Constitution, CCZ and ZEC publicly opposed this, expressing their belief in a plural society. This opposition appeared to be futile, and since 1996 the Zambian Constitution opens with the statement that "We, the people of Zambia . . . declare the Republic a Christian nation". The debate about the declaration re-emerged in 2003, with the installation of a constitutional review commission (Hinfelaar 2011:60) and has continued to date. As recent as April 2013, the delegates at the national constitution making convention, where a new draft constitution was discussed, voted in favour of upholding the declaration as part of the preamble. This indicates that the idea of Zambia as a Christian nation has become rather popular and has remained so many years after Chiluba – who had lost popularity because of corruption and political machinations – left office.

Isabel Phiri (2008:105) points at several tangible consequences of the Christian nation declaration. Under Chiluba's government, diplomatic links with Israel were being re-established, while the ties with Iran and Iraq were cut; several pastors were appointed as members of the cabinet, and a Department of Christian Affairs was opened in the President's office; the relations between Christians and Muslims soured, with the small Muslim minority in Zambia feeling increasingly marginalised; there was an influx of Christian missionaries (mainly from the US) in Zambia and many new churches were established with 'discretionary support' from the president. Regardless of these policies and results, Chiluba himself has hardly articulated the meaning of the Christian nation declaration in official documents and speeches. Subsequent political leaders have either supported the declaration (especially those with Pentecostal sympathies) or have paid lip service to it, probably realising that there is little electoral gain in opposing it. Prominent Pentecostal figures, as well as the influential Evangelical Fellowship,[4] have continued to express and mobilise support for the declaration until to date, and successfully so. But different from Zambian Humanism, Zambian Christian nationalism has never been systematically developed into a political ideology. However, as shown in the next section, it has shaped public and political debates especially in the area of sexuality (cf. van Klinken 2014).

## Sexual citizenship in a 'Christian nation'

The notion of Zambia as a Christian nation has become central in public and political discourse. It shapes debates on matters of public morality and is also used to legitimise certain actions policing public morality, in particular relating to sexuality.

One example is the issue of pornography, which was strictly controlled under Kaunda. Surprisingly, in 1993 the Chiluba government announced that it was lifting the ban on the sale and possession of pornographic material. This was much to the dismay of Christian leaders such as EFZ General Secretary Joseph Imakando who stated that "we do not believe that democracy means that you should have loose morals" (quoted in Third Way 1993). Thus after a massive outcry Chiluba re-imposed the ban, and it has been in tact till to date. In 2014 there was a prominent case when a popular Zambian musician and his girlfriend were fined for producing an 'obscene video'. In its commentary, government-owned newspaper *Times of Zambia* expressed its concern that "such videos are now becoming a norm", and it stated:

> This not only shows the moral degradation levels in our society but brings shame not only to the affected persons and their families but the nation at large. Zambia is a Christian Nation and filming and circulating of such materials is against the Christian values. Such conduct should therefore be curbed at all costs and culprits punished to preserve our good Christian values.
>
> (Kabaila 2014)

A similar use of the Christian nation argument can be found in debates on prostitution – another practice that was prohibited under Kaunda and has remained so to date. Under the current laws, sex workers are frequently arrested by the police and are at risk of harassment and abuse, illustrating their status as secondary citizens. In recent years, sex workers have become more self-organised and are campaigning for decriminalisation. Yet in the media this generally receives a negative response, and again references to the Christian character of the country prevail. The formulation of the question with which a Zambian radio station opened a discussion on the topic is typical and telling: "Commercial sex workers want prostitution to be legalized.

What's your say on this topic bearing in mind that Zambia is a Christian nation?" (Flavafm 2012).

Another moral issue of public concern under Zambian Humanism, as mentioned above, was mini-skirts. This concern has also continued to exist and frequently emerges in public debates. For example, after Uganda in 2014 had passed a law prohibiting mini-skirts (the Anti-Pornography Act), the popular Zambian radio station Radio Phoenix asked on its Facebook page whether Zambia should follow that example. Several respondents referred to the status of Zambia as a Christian nation to argue that indeed, the Ugandan example should be followed (Radio Phoenix 2014). There have even been cases where people took matters in their own hand and publicly undressed and shamed girls whom they considered to be dressed in 'indecent' ways, while appealing to the need of "preserving Christian and cultural values" (Kudakwashe 2012). Both in the case of sex work and mini-skirts, the moral concern appears to be primarily with women, demonstrating that female bodies, in particular, are being policed by the state as well as by the general public.

All these are examples of policing sexual citizenship, and disciplining Zambians as sexual citizens, in the self-declared Christian nation. They illustrate the continuity between the discourses of Zambian Humanism and Christian nationalism in the area of public morality. The most prominent issue emerging in public debates about morality and sexuality in recent years, however, is homosexuality – an issue that was not explicitly discussed in the time under Kaunda. Homosexuality became subject of heated public debate for the first time in Zambia in 1998, after independent newspaper *The Post* on 14 July published an interview with the first Zambian to publicly identify himself as gay, Francis Chisambisha. Then 25 years old, Chisambisha also announced that he planned to launch an association. His public coming out sparked 'a mammoth scandal', and when a couple of weeks later the Lesbian, Gays, Bisexual and Transgender Persons Association (LEGATRA) was presented this caused even more public outrage (Long, Brown & Cooper 2003:34–46). Both political and church leaders expressed their disgust of Chisambisha's actions, and doing so they also denied the place of same-sex sexuality in Zambian history, culture and society. In their response they would typically refer to the Christian character of the country which was under threat by 'foreign influences' – an idea that was only reinforced by the fact that several Western NGOs and governments expressed their support of Chisambisha and LEGATRA. Analysing this dynamic, Charlotte Cross (2007:9–10) argues:

> Although much of the nationalist rhetoric defined itself only by virtue of what was not Zambian or African, the claims of a minority for recognition forced the majority to consider its own self-identity. The strongest alternative to Western decadence, which resonated with the 'moral' aspects of the crisis, was the 'Christian nation' of Zambia, whereby God could act as benefactor and guide, replacing secular and corrupted donors.

Then President Chiluba contributed to the debates in a speech, symbolically delivered on the thirty-fourth anniversary of Zambia's independence, where he stated: "Homosexuality is the deepest level of depravity. It is unbiblical and abnormal" (quoted in Long, Brown & Cooper 2003:40). The opposition was so strong that LEGATRA was never able to register as an NGO and ceased to exist within a few months after its launch, with Chisambisha having left the country to apply for asylum in South Africa.

The pattern emerging from this controversy – of the constitutional Christian status of Zambia being used as a key argument against any public expression of homosexuality and public advocacy for lesbian and gay (or LGBT) human rights – has repeated itself several times since then. Thus, when in February 2012 United Nations Secretary General Ban Ki-moon in an address to the Zambian parliament called upon the country to recognise and protect the rights of all citizens "regardless of . . . sexual orientation", political and religious leaders rejected his call. For diplomatic reasons the government did not respond directly, but Member of Parliament and President of the opposition party MMD, Felix Mutati, pre-emptively ruled out his support for any possible legislation decriminalising homosexuality, arguing that "Zambia is a Christian nation and Christianity is against homosexuality" (Mwaanga 2012:1). In the public debate following Ban's visit, his call was even linked to the Devil who would have set his mind on Zambia because of it being a Christian nation, and participants on online Zambian discussion forums called upon their fellow Zambians "to be strong, to resist the international pressure to recognise gay rights, to protect Zambia's status as a Christian nation and to oppose this demonic attack" (Van Klinken 2013:529). A year later, when another controversy about homosexuality emerged following a European Union advert in a Zambian newspaper announcing a call for funding scheme, ministers of the Patriotic Front (PF) government fuelled public debate with strong statements. Then Minister of Home Affairs (and current Zambian President), Edgar Lungu, undiplomatically stated that the EU should "take the fight for gay rights to Europe" because homosexuality "is not part of our culture" (Zambian Watchdog 2013) – a statement that reads like an echo of Kaunda's anti-Western rhetoric quoted above: "This is Zambia with its own way of life and not Europe. . . . We take our cultural values very seriously" (Kaunda 1975:31). In addition to Lungu, then Minister of Justice, Wynter Kabimba, argued that there is "No room for gays in Zambia". Explaining this, he said: "As Zambians, we declared that we are a Christian nation and there is no way we can allow this un-Zambian culture" (Namaiko 2013). In other words, he literally denied gay Zambians their legitimate status as citizens and defined Zambian citizenship as exclusively and normatively heterosexual. Shortly after these statements were made, indeed a gay rights activist and some alleged gay coupled were arrested by the police and prosecuted, leading Amnesty International (2014) to express its deep concern about the "systematic persecution" of individuals based on their perceived sexual orientation in Zambia (for a more detailed account see Van Klinken 2017).

In these public debates on homosexuality a similar concern about foreign 'immoral' influences, and a defence of 'Zambian culture', can be observed as in the discourse of Zambian Humanism, however with two notable differences. First, in the recent debates on homosexuality there is a much more direct and explicit appeal to Christianity, with 'Christian values' being presented as more or less coinciding with 'Zambian values', which illustrates the impact of the Christian nation declaration in shaping the perception of national identity. For many people – both religious and political leaders and ordinary Zambians – homosexuality appears to be the litmus paper for the Christian character of the country as well as for its independence and sovereignty. Second, where the Zambian humanist discourse rejected Western cultural influences because of their capitalist nature, in the post-Kaunda era Zambia has more or less adopted neoliberal capitalist principles; Western influences are now (very selectively) being rejected, not because of the capitalist but the secular nature of Western societies. As I have argued elsewhere, the framing of homosexuality – and of gay rights and human rights in general – as a 'secular thing' in popular Zambian discourses is informed by a dualist worldview in which Zambia has the divine mission to defend truly Christian values and principles in a world that is believed to have become "secular, immoral and humanistic; a world of shifting norms" (Van Klinken 2014:267–268).

## Conclusion

Accounts of Zambia's political and nationalist history sometimes present a somewhat simplistic binary between Kaunda's Humanism and Chiluba's Christian nationalism as two different, if not opposite, narratives underlying the project of nation building in postcolonial Zambia. This chapter does not deny that there are significant differences in the content and tone of both nationalist narratives. Yet it has highlighted the striking continuities, especially in the area of public and private morality such as relating to matters of sexuality. Both the humanist and the Christian narratives of nation building demonstrate an explicit concern with respectable citizenship and inflict upon Zambians more or less similar notions of what is considered morally appropriate in the area of sexuality. This is not surprising given the fact that Zambian Humanism, especially its moral reformist agenda, was a continuation of the civilising mission of missionary Christianity – a mission that in recent decades has been taken up with new energies by Pentecostal churches, concerned as they are not only with religious revival but also with a particular Christian vision of nation building and political renewal. In Zambia, Pentecostal churches have come to realise that declaring the nation to be Christian is not the end but the beginning of a project of national redemption which requires ongoing investment. To this aim, they actively make use of the media, engage in public debate, work with political bodies and civil society organisations, but the key strategy is possibly what Ruth Marshall (2009) has called the born-again programme of conversion through which Pentecostalism seeks to produce the ideal Christian citizen who is the cornerstone for the building a Christian nation (Van Klinken 2016). In this chapter I have not so much discussed the role of Pentecostal churches as such, but the influence of Pentecostal Christian ideology on Zambian politics and notions of citizenship, especially in relation to sexuality. As much as Pentecostalism presents a new religious narrative discourse for public and political debate on issues of sexuality and citizenship, I also have observed striking continuities with the earlier political narrative of Zambian Humanism.

Throughout the 50 years of independence, Victorian notions of decency and morality have shaped the discursive politics of sexual citizenship in Zambia and have defined the boundaries of legitimate sexual expressions and practices. These boundaries, as has become clear above, are implicitly or explicitly heteronormative and patriarchal – with female bodies, in particular, being scrutinised, and non-heterosexual sexualities being marginalised and excluded from the realm of citizenship. What is particularly striking is how sexuality, in both narratives of nationhood, has been used as a key site to define Zambia's identity status as an independent nation vis-à-vis the West. In a further analysis such moral identity politics of 'Zambian-ness' need to be interpreted through a wider political economy analysis of Zambia's position in the global neoliberal political and economic order. As James Ferguson (2006:144) suggests, the moral concern with sexuality in Zambia might have to be understood from a context "where what is endangered is less biological reproduction than [reproduction of] the cultural and social sort".

## Acknowledgement

I am grateful to David Gordon for providing me with e-copies of relevant pages of *The Zambian Moral Code*.

## Notes

1 Alice Mulenga (1920–1978) in 1953 had a radical conversion experience, and subsequently started the revivalist Lumpa Church movement. The church's rejection of earthly authority resulted in a violent conflict between church followers, members of the United National Independence Party (UNIP), and state security forces in 1964, after which the church was banned.
2 The booklet suggests that in case a couple's marriage is childless, a husband might arrange for his wife to sleep with another man; also, a husband can share his with a friend as a "gesture of friendliness".
3 According to Phiri (2008:101), he was involved in charismatic fellowships within the UCZ and was also attached to Northmead Assembly of God, which is a prominent Pentecostal church in Lusaka.
4 The Evangelical Fellowship of Zambia (established in 1964) is an umbrella body for over 200 evangelical and Pentecostal churches and organisations. Together with the Zambian Episcopal Conference (Catholic Church) and the Council of Churches in Zambia (mainline Protestant churches), EFZ is one of the three so-called Christian 'mother bodies' that are official consultation partners of the Zambian government and that actively contribute to public debates on social and political issues in the country.

# References

Amnesty International. 2014. 'Zambia: End State-Sponsored Persecution as Same-Sex Trial Reaches Verdict'. Available at: www.amnesty.org/en/news/zambia-end-state-sponsored-persecution-same-sex-trial-reaches-verdict-2014-02-21 (accessed 30 October 2015).

Bell, D. & Binnie, J. 2000. *The Sexual Citizen: Queer Politics and Beyond*. Cambridge: Polity Press.

Cheyeka, A. 2008. 'Towards a History of the Charismatic Churches in Post-Colonial Zambia'. In J. B. Gewald, M. Hinfelaar & G. Macola (Eds.) *One Zambia, Many Histories: Towards a History of Post-Colonial Zambia*. Leiden: Brill: 144–163.

Cheyeka, A., Hinfelaar, M. & Udelhoven, B. 2014. 'The Changing Face of Zambia's Christianity and Its Implications for the Public Sphere: A Case Study of Bauleni Township, Lusaka'. *Journal of Southern African Studies*, 40(5): 1031–1045.

Cross, C. 2007. 'A Human Wrong: Denial of a Right to Be Homosexual in Zambia'. M.Sc Dissertation, University of Oxford.

Ellis, S. & Ter Haar, G. 2007. 'Religion and Politics: Taking African Epistemologies Seriously'. *Journal of Modern African Studies*, 45(3): 385–401.

Englund, H. 2013. 'Zambia at 50: The Rediscovery of Liberalism'. *Africa*, 83(4): 670–689.

Ferguson, J. 2006. *Global Shadows: Africa in the Neoliberal World Order*. Durham: Duke University Press.

Flavafm. 2012. 'Commercial Sex Workers Want Prostitution to Be Legalized'. Facebook Post. 29 April. Available at: www.facebook.com/flavafm/posts/10150712104438715 (accessed 30 October 2015).

Gewald, J. B., Hinfelaar, M. & Macola, G. 2008. 'Introduction'. In J. B. Gewald, M. Hinfelaar & G. Macola (Eds.) *One Zambia, Many Histories: Towards a History of Post-Colonial Zambia*. Leiden: Brill: 1–13.

Gifford, P. 1998. *African Christianity: Its Public Role*. London: Hurst & Co.

Gordon, D. M. 2012. *Invisible Agents: Spirits in a Central African History*. Athens, OH: Ohio University Press.

Hinfelaar, M. 2011. 'Debating the Secular in Zambia: The Response of the Catholic Church to Scientific Socialism and Christian Nation, 1976–2006'. In H. Englund (Ed.) *Christianity and Public Culture in Africa*. Athens: Ohio University Press: 50–66.

Kabaila, M. 2014. 'Crack Down on Web Pornography'. *Times of Zambia*. 9 July. Available at: www.times.co.zm/?p=26544 (accessed 30 October 2015).

Kaunda, K. D. 1966. A Humanist in Africa. London: Longman Greens.

Kaunda, K. D. 1967. *Humanism in Zambia and a Guide to Its Implementation. Part I*. Lusaka: Zambia Information Services.

Kaunda, K. D. 1974. *Humanism in Zambia and a Guide to Its Implementation. Part II*. Lusaka: Division of National Guidance.

Kaunda, K. D. 1975. *The Watershed Speech*. Lusaka: Zambia Information Services.

Koschorke, K., Ludwig, F. & Delgado, M. (Eds.) 2007. *A History of Christianity in Asia, Africa, and Latin America, 1450–1990: A Documentary Sourcebook*. Grand Rapids, MI: Eerdmans.

Kudakwashe, P. 2012. 'Maureen Mwanawasa Speaks on Mini Skirts'. *Lusaka Times*. 9 July. Available at: www.lusakatimes.com/2012/07/09/maureen-mwanawasa-speaks-mini-skirts/ (accessed 30 October 2015).

Larmer, M., Hinfelaar, M., Phiri, B. J., Schumaker, L. & Szeftel, M. 2014. 'Introduction: Narratives of Nationhood'. *Journal of Southern African Studies*, 40(5): 895–905.

Lister, R. 2002. 'Sexual Citizenship'. In F. Enging, B. Isin & B. S. Turner (Eds.) *Handbook of Citizenship Studies*. London: Sage Publications: 191–207.
Long, S., Brown, W. & Cooper, G. 2003. *More Than a Name: The Spread of Homophobic Rhetoric in Southern Africa*. New York: Human Right Watch. Available at: www.hrw.org/sites/default/files/reports/safriglhrc0303.pdf
Marshall, R. 2009. *Political Spiritualities: The Pentecostal Revolution in Nigeria*. Chicago, London: University of Chicago Press.
Mwaanga, D. 2012. 'Gay What? It's Criminal in Zambia – Shamenda'. *Zambia Daily Mail*, 2 March.
Mwangilwa, G. 1986. *The Kapwepwe Diaries*. Lusaka: Multimedia Publications.
Namaiko, C. 2013. 'No Room for Gays in Zambia – Kabimba'. *Times of Zambia*, 22 April. Available at: www.times.co.zm/?p=6574 (accessed 6 December 2013).
Ndjio, B. 2013. 'Sexuality and Nationalist Ideologies in Post-Colonial Cameroon'. In S. Wieringa & H. Sivori (Eds.) *The Sexual History of the Global South: Sexual Politics in Africa, Asia, and Latin America*. London: Zed Books: 120–143.
Nyanzi, S. 2011. 'Unpacking the [Govern]mentality of African Sexualities'. In S. Tamale (Ed.) *African Sexualities: A Reader*. Nairobi: Pambazuka Press: 477–501.
Nyeck, S. N. & Epprecht, M. (Eds.) 2013. *Sexual Diversity in Africa: Politics, Theory, Citizenship*. Montreal: McGill-Queen's University Press.
Phiri, I. A. 2008. 'President Frederick Chiluba and Zambia: Evangelicals and Democracy in a "Christian Nation"'. In T. O. Ranger (Ed.) *Evangelical Christianity and Democracy in Africa*. Oxford, New York: Oxford University Press: 95–130.
Radio Phoenix. 2014. 'Uganda Has Passed a Law Which Prohibits Mini Skirts'. Facebook Post. 25 February. Available at: www.facebook.com/RadioPhoenixZambia/posts/10152248642678748 (accessed 30 October).
Research Bureau. 1975. *The Zambian Moral Code – A Programmatic Approach*. Lusaka: Freedom House.
Richardson, D. 2000. 'Constructing Sexual Citizenship: Theorizing Sexual Rights'. *Critical Social Policy*, 20(1): 105–135.
Third Way. 1993. 'Porn Legal in Zambia'. *Third Way: Christian Perspectives on Today's World*, 16(1): 10.
Van Klinken, A. 2013. 'Gay Rights, the Devil and the End Times: Public Religion and the Enchantment of the Homosexuality Debate in Zambia'. *Religion*, 43(4): 519–540.
Van Klinken, A. 2014. 'Homosexuality, Politics and Pentecostal Nationalism in Zambia'. *Studies in World Christianity*, 20(3): 259–281.
Van Klinken, A. 2016. 'Pentecostalism, Political Masculinity and Citizenship: The Born-Again Male Subject as Key to Zambia's National Redemption'. *Journal of Religion in Africa*, 46(2–3): 129–157.
Van Klinken, A. 2017. 'Sexual Orientation, (Anti-)Discrimination and Human Rights in a "Christian Nation": The Politicization of Homosexuality in Zambia'. *Critical African Studies*, 9(1): 9–31.
Vaughan, M. 1998. 'Exploitation and Neglect: Rural Producers and the State in Malawi and Zambia'. In D. Birmingham & P. M. Martin (Eds.) *History of Central Africa: The Contemporary Years Since 1960*. London: Longman: 167–202.
Yong, A. 2010. *In the Days of Caesar: Pentecostalism and Political Theology*. Grand Rapids, MI: Eerdmans.
Zambian Watchdog. 2013. 'Edgar Lungu Tells off EU Over Gay Rights Advert in Zambia'. 25 March. Available at: www.zambianwatchdog.com/edgar-lungu-tells-off-eu-over-gay-rights/ (accessed 30 October 2015).

# 9 'I will make you into a Great Nation, and I will Bless you'[1]

## Citizens, traitors and Christianity in Kenya

*Gregory Deacon*

Since the very founding of the country, and establishment of the state, Christianity has played an integral role in shaping ideas of citizenship and exclusion in Kenya and it has remained intertwined with its development as a nation. Indeed, there are well-established descriptions of Kenya as a Christian nation and consideration of concomitant defining of citizenship by closing that group in this manner and portrayal of others such as Muslims as 'strangers,' in Georg Simmel's classic description (1971143–148). In this chapter I explore the idea of *Kenyan Christianity*. The suggestion is not that Christianity in Kenya should be seen as monolithic; rather, as with Weber's *Protestant Ethic*, the attempt is to elaborate "an historical concept" (2006:13) – or rather a current concept that cannot be understood without awareness of its historical development and antecedents. The aim is to unpick varied threads of historical reality, and undertake the complex task of looking at how this concept is formed by, as it concurrently influences and constructs, society, economics and politics – moving far beyond theological, liturgical and denominational understanding (c.f. Deacon 2015a). This is a challenging task, further complicated by the fluidity of such a concept in time and space.

There is broad acceptance that, in Kenya, Pentecostalism is a "prominent feature of the country's religious and political landscape and now commands a massive following" (Parsitau & Mwaura 2010:96). However, beyond even descriptions of prominence, Christianity in Kenya in general may currently even be described as Pentecostalised (Deacon 2012; Deacon & Lynch 2013; Deacon 2015a; Deacon 2015b; Deacon et al. 2017). There are many exceptions to this assertion – such as the young, Catholic, political operative who told me "I don't want Jesus to be my friend" (personal communication 2014). Nevertheless, the analytical approach undertaken here is that of a Weberian ideal type (Deacon 2015a), or "abstracting the outstanding features from some (more or less clearly demarcated) historical complex, and by organising these into a coherent word-picture" (Watkins 1952:23). The chapter therefore aims to construct a coherent description of the ideological components that can be seen running through contemporary Christianity in Kenya and that are manifest in public discourse. In particular, the chapter seeks to highlight the powerful presence of Evangelical Protestantism, and theological ideas and themes that are often called Pentecostal, or neo-Pentecostal. The chapter aims to move well beyond reference to, for example, "the experiential presence of the Holy Spirit as part of normal Christian life and worship" (Asamoah-Gyadu 2005:97). Instead, the intention is to consider how this locally constructed and conceptualised Christianity has evolved historically and its contemporary implications for citizens and how citizenship is conceptualised, expressed and defined in Kenya.

This theoretical consideration uses secularisation theories to unpick a range of approaches grounded in Western Enlightenment thought. As the chapter will demonstrate, these secular approaches are unable to account for the current nature of Christianity in Kenya, although inverting discursive models proves valuable in describing the nature of Kenyan, neo-Pentecostal Christianity and its role in citizenship. The chapter then examines the case study of a prayer rally held in April 2016 to celebrate the vacation of charges against Kenya's president and deputy president of crimes against humanity. This was an occasion when the dominant, homogenising narrative of Kenya's current rulers and their supporters was on clear display. This represents the crux of the matter because, as I have already alluded to, it is not my contention that a monolithic Kenyan Christianity exists and is held by all Kenyans; rather, a dominant discourse has evolved in Kenya that is Christian, Pentecostalised and extremely popular but contains particular ideological and political elements that exclude many Kenyan citizens through portrayal of them as non-citizens, because they do not hold to implicitly prescribed standards of Christianity, which is bound up with national identity.

## "Kenya Is a Christian Country"[2]

One of the most telling examples concerning the integral, intimate, inescapable place of Christianity in Kenyan identity and citizenship can be seen in the title of a 2013 news piece from the Kenya Television Network (KTN). Still available online the video, which reports on responses to former US President Barrack Obama's comments on gay rights whilst he was visiting Senegal, features Uhuru Kenyatta and William Ruto (both in church) describing Kenya as a "God fearing nation".[3] However, what is most significant is that the headline, at the time I watched the report in Kenya and retained in the online video, is in fact "Barack Obama endorses gayism as Uhuru and Ruto claim Kenya is a *Christian* country" (my emphasis). More than "dog-whistle politics", the assumption that reference to God would necessarily mean the Christian God reflects deeply entrenched views in Kenya and understandings of the country, its foundations and its current construction. On 15 April 2016, for example, a number of church leaders (contesting the official registration of an Atheist Society of Kenya) stated that: "According to our Constitution, this nation acknowledges the Almighty God and the same is enshrined in our National Anthem (Oh [sic] God of all creation)" (*Daily Nation*, April 15 2016). Even more explicitly though, on 27 November 2016, whilst "At Kaaga Methodist Church, North Imenti Constituency, Meru County" William Ruto Tweeted that "We are a prayerful and God fearing nation".[4]

This situation is, according to many commentators, actually very longstanding: Alamin Mazrui argues that the Kenyan state, as well as Tanzania and Uganda, are "secular only in the sense that their constitutions do not specifically state that they are based on Christian Laws" (Mazrui 1993:199). The foremost historian of Kenya's Christian construction, John Lonsdale, describes the processes by which its "highland hinterland became the region's vanguard of cultural, political, and economic change. Biblical literacy, state institutions and export agriculture all clustered inland. A Christian colony gave birth to a largely Christian post-colonial state" (Lonsdale 2008:311). This historical and institutional legacy is very much felt today, although a great deal of change and evolution has taken place with regards to what Christianity is in Kenya and what it does.

As throughout sub-Saharan Africa, it has been argued that in Kenya there was "an intimate, inevitable connection between missions and 'cultural imperialism'" (Porter 2004:367). Postcolonial critiques of missionaries are persuasive in the Kenyan context – with strong arguments for the case that they operated as "ideological shock troops" (Silverman 2005:144) and that "social welfare projects and infrastructure were provided by missions (often funded by subscription and collections in Europe) and this supported [the colonial state] that would have been unable to fund such activities otherwise" (Deacon & Tomalin 2015:71; c.f. Manji & O'Coill 2002:569). Education and homiletic practice can also be seen as more intangibly involved in the "incorporation of human subjects into 'natural,' taken-for-granted forms of economy and society" or "the internalization of a set of values, an ineffable manner of [colonial] seeing and being" (Comaroff & Comaroff 1986:2). By contrast, African Independent Churches (AICs) may be seen as contesting colonial, mission Christianity (Deacon & Lynch 2013; Deacon 2015b) or even constituting "a stage in the evolution of anti-colonial protest, lying between early armed resistance and the rise of modern mass nationalist parties" (Ranger 1986:2). Similarly, mission educated subjects came to interrogate biblical texts and express "open resistance to the colonial order by pointing to its inconsistency with biblical injunction, and by freeing from the holy text itself a charter for liberation: the message of the chosen suffering in exile, whose historical destiny was to regain their promised land" (Comaroff & Comaroff 1986:2).

Whilst the mainline missions were important in the building of colonial Kenya, whatever their role or otherwise in colonising the minds of the Crown's new subjects, Evangelicalism was also extremely significant – even with a purported focus on "personal salvation" rather than "social involvement" (Gifford 2009:33) In fact, groups such as the Baptists and Methodists were at the very heart of, in particular, producing an administrative and executive elite that would go on to run the nation at independence. Evangelical missions in Kenya were involved from the get-go in more than simple evangelisation – they were an essential part in the founding of the Alliance High School, for example, one of the country's foremost educational institutions that that has produced so very many of Kenya's leaders. Evangelical Christian adherence was also essential for becoming, and involved in class-distinction amongst, the Kenyan, colonial state's first bureaucratic chiefs (Anderson 2005:11–12). In sum, Evangelicalism in varied forms has been of huge import in Kenya since the foundation of the country – indeed, Paul Gifford argues furthermore that even mainline missions, especially "Anglican and Presbyterian missions (respectively the Church Missionary Society, CMS, and the Church of Scotland Mission, CSM)[5] . . . were conservative evangelical" (2009:33).

Post-independence, new forms of "urban, revivalist Protestantism" (Deacon 2015a: 228) grew, particularly on university campuses, as well as representing responses to the "temptations of urban life in new bureaucratic lives" (ibid.). The mainline churches were more consumed with development activities – infrastructure and education – as they sought to maintain a role in the new nation, and to justify their place in a state whose colonial abuses they at best might have contested more strongly, and at worst condoned, excused or explained away (Anderson 2005). Where the Anglicans in particular adopted a new silence over arguments that Christianity represented a necessary belief system to move into modernity (c.f. Branch 2009:7) and reject backward African beliefs, as well as the "disease" of the Mau Mau insurgency (ibid.), Evangelical churches, particularly the Baptists, forged ahead as an intimate part of Kenya's actual modernity. Such churches catered to urban, wealthy Kenyans of mixed races – and then Africanised.

The place of Christianity in Kenya's *status quo*, and role in elite hegemony was contested in the late 1980s and 1990s when some churches were involved in campaigning for a return to multiparty politics (Gifford 1994:528). The churches in question, or really a limited number of individuals with international linkages within those organisations, were almost exclusively contemporary forms of the mainline churches (Sabar-Friedman 1997). Many Kenyans still ostensibly belong to those churches, and they continue to play an important role in the provision of social services – particularly health and education (Gifford 2009). Since the country's puported return to national, electoral, multiparty democracy in the mid-1990s though, and in tandem with the neoliberal turn – producing greater movement of capital, goods and people as well as burgeoning inequality – the number and variety of churches in Kenya has exploded, as has the number of adherents (Deacon & Lynch 2013). These are churches that may be seen as blurring distinctions between Pentecostal and Evangelical (Gifford 1994:524–525), and might be called neo-Pentecostal – as per extensive debates over contemporary Pentecostalism, its relation to classical Pentecostalism (for example Anderson 2001; Martin 2002), its place in modernity (for example Englund & Leach 2000) and its developmental role (for example Freeman 2013, 2015). However, they require consideration in their particular continental, regional, national and historical context (Deacon 2015a).

Such churches display vigorous forms of worship, and a particular blend of the prosperity Gospel; this is pertinent to local conditions in its discussion of wealth and inequality, and their causes, meaning that it is well understood by Kenyan Christians of most nominal denominational affiliations (Deacon & Lynch 2013; Deacon 2015a; Deacon 2015b). Such churches also blur categories of adherence – many, perhaps the majority of Kenyan Christians, interact with a variety of churches, attending (for example) a traditional family institution on Sunday morning and engaging in a newer form of worship, expression and action at other times (Deacon 2015b:205). This is extremely widespread (though almost impossible to quantify) particularly since the decade, following the eventual peaceful transfer of power from Kenya's long-time dictator Daniel arap Moi to Mwai Kibaki in 2002, which concomitantly and relatedly saw "denominational differences reduced dramatically" (Deacon 2015a:228). At that point, the public and political role of neo-Pentecostalism really took off, or at least achieved a new level of visibility – with the need for involvement in competition for resources (Deacon 2015a:229) and the basic success of new forms of belief, worship and adherence (Deacon et al. 2017). In essence, Kenya does not have an official or state religion, nor is it a theocracy. Nevertheless, devotional practices, attitudes and understandings have very much converged amongst Kenyan Christians, who represent the majority of Kenyans[6] (Deacon 2015b:204).

## Discursive Christianity

On 13 May 2015, on the popular American topical comedy programme *The Daily Show*, public intellectual Reza Aslan discussed religious adherence in the United States and referred to statistics that "seven out of 10 Americans are Christian", in order to rhetorically question *"what does that mean?"*.[7] Similarly, extremely high levels of Christian adherence are hard to deny in Kenya; what is important to discern is the nature of adherence – what does it mean that the vast majority of Kenyans are Christian, and does it matter? On one level, our interest is that "many Kenyans voluntarily associate themselves with religious networks, which they use for a variety of purposes – social, economic and even political – that go beyond the strictly religious aspect" (Theuri 2013:57). However, to conceptualise Kenyan Christianity in this sense is, as Callum Brown argues of analytical misjudgments regarding the UK and secularisation, to consider religion only "by measure of members or worshippers" and this is problematic as by "doing so social science dichotomises people: into churchgoers and non-churchgoers, into believers and unbelievers" (Brown 1994). Such counting or institutional observation cannot cope, for example, with the seemingly simple challenge of multiple church membership, or visitation. This is particularly important for Kenyan Christians who, as mentioned above, may attend the mainline (mission or historical) church that has been the family's congregation for generations but deem such a church to be insufficient if they wish to worship in an exuberant, Evangelical, neo-Pentecostal manner or for those who need healing, especially in cases of witchcraft and other demonic attacks that mainline churches do not account for and generally deny the existence thereof (Deacon 2015b:205).

As the foundation of our current analysis, it is well worth quoting Brown in depth:

> Broadly speaking, virtually all historical and sociological studies of religion and society have envisaged the "role" of religion in four "forms": *institutional Christianity* (the people's adherence to churches and practise of worship and religious rites), *intellectual Christianity* (the influence of religious ideas in society at large and of religious belief in individuals), *functional Christianity* (the role of religion in civil society, especially local government, education and welfare, and *diffusive Christianity* (the role of outreach religion amongst the people.
> (Brown 1994:11)

Each of these elements, Brown states, depend upon the higher form of *discursive Christianity* – or:

> the people's subscription to protocols of personal identity which they derive from Christian expectations, or discourses, evident in their own time and place. Protocols are rituals or customs of behaviour, economic activity, dress, speech and so on which are collectively promulgated as necessary for Christian identity. The protocols are prescribed or implied in discourses on Christian behaviour. The discourses may be official ones from churches or clergy, public ones from the media, "community" ones from within an ethnic group, a street or a family, or private ones developed by men and women themselves.
> (Brown 1994:12)

Essentially, the contention is this: Christianity is institutional, intellectual, functional and diffusive in Kenya – it is in these ways that Kenya can be considered a Christian nation. Furthermore, discursive Christianity is highly Pentecostalised in Kenya. Official discourse by churches or clergy is of course found in Pentecostal churches themselves, but pastors appear regularly in the media, for example – shifting such discourse into the wider public. Pentecostal, Evangelical media is widely consumed and enjoyed by many Kenyans (Deacon 2015b:204). Most important, however, is the constant discussion of events and expression of experience through Christian, neo-Pentecostal idioms and theological concepts such as health, wealth, healing, success and spiritual warfare (Deacon 2012; Deacon & Lynch 2013; Deacon 2015a, b; Deacon et al. 2017). Thus, even though Uhuru Kenyatta is a Catholic for example and frequently attends Mass, his political Jubilee alliance used such ideas, images and themes during Kenya's general election in 2013 and they were "comprehensible and attractive to the majority of Kenyans" (Deacon 2015b:215). Furthermore, a narrative of national healing and progress has increasingly become dominated by the result of the election that heralded this process and the Jubilee alliance (now party: JAP) sets out with greater and greater rigidity an authoritarian depiction of its leadership as chosen by God, and thereby infallible and unquestionable, and those who seek to criticise them as not only disruptive but as terrorists and traitors. Indeed, as Christian ideas, they are inherently exclusionary to those who are not Christian.

To some extent Islam happens to be the religion and corresponds to the identity of many of those who are marginalised in Kenya: as Otenyo argues, "In comparative terms, Muslims regions [sic] were perceived as most underdeveloped. Curiously, at the lower primary and secondary levels, schools associated with Christian churches always performed better than most" (Otenyo 2004: 79). However, exclusion is connected to religion in and of itself because citizenship is so bound up with Christianity – leaving those who are not Christian in an almost inescapable situation of being "other," or "strangers". Alamin Mazrui argues that

> while Kenya is constitutionally a secular state which upholds the principles of non-discrimination on ground [sic] of religion, non-Christian citizens have nonetheless been known to suffer gross inequalities in their post-colonial experience. The ascendancy of Christianity to a position of dominance in Kenya's body politic has partly resulted in a systematic imbalance that has allowed the management of national and public affairs to assume a peculiarly Christian bias.
>
> (1993:199)

Inequality in Kenya is immense and poverty widespread, whatever the faith of those who do not have access to money, property and power (Deacon & Lynch 2013; Deacon 2015a, b). Nevertheless, the religious construction of citizenship in Kenya means that "Muslims have felt still more permanently, deeply, and unjustly marginalised than Kalenjin or Luo" (Lonsdale 2008:311). However, as I will argue in the next section using the case study of the prayer rally of April 2016, contemporary events and the evolution of Christian understandings are increasing exclusion and extending portrayal of terrorists and traitors not only to those of other faiths, but to those who question a particular narrative of God's place in the nation and God's purported choice of leadership.

## Jubilee Christianity triumphant

Kenya's neo-Pentecostal churches as institutions are rarely, if ever, involved in challenging Kenya's government and the *status quo*. However, homiletic and theological disengagement from temporal issues (Ngunyi 1995:126–129) does not necessarily lead to apolitical outcomes. On the one hand, some may explicitly support the ruling regime, as was particularly the case under former president Daniel arap Moi (Deacon & Lynch 2013:110).

Furthermore, churches and senior figures were drawn into the botched election and subsequent violence of 2007–2008 (Gifford 2009:43–45; 221–223) and many were also involved in opposition to constitutional reform, defeated in a 2005 referendum but passed in 2010.[8] In the main, however, this approach has been and continues to be inclined to conservatism in political terms. This overt depoliticisation can distract from, but does not preclude, the extent to which Evangelical or Pentecostalised Christianity constitutes a dominant discourse that is closely involved processes of homogeneity and in producing and reproducing the current political and social order in Kenya (Deacon & Lynch 2013, 112; Deacon 2015a, b). Indeed, such themes, especially those of wealth, success and receipt of blessings as reward for abstract repentance and forgiveness were extremely important and popular during Kenya's general election in 2013 in the context of preceding disputed vote counts and violent protests in 2007 (Deacon 2015a, b).

The events of 2007 and 2008 led to ultimately failed prosecutions on charges of crimes against humanity against now President Uhuru Kenyatta and his deputy William Ruto at the International Criminal Court (ICC). On 5 April 2016 the charges against William Ruto, and radio journalist Joshua arap Sang, were vacated. The decision from the ICC noted that "The Chamber declined to acquit the accused due to the special circumstances of this case. In so doing, the Chamber endorsed the Prosecution's position that this case has been severely undermined by witness interference and politicisation of the judicial process" (ICC 5 April 2016). These 'special circumstances' were essentially ignored in the triumphant celebration seen in Kenya of the end of the judicial processes in the Netherlands. Uhuru Kenyatta's case had been terminated a year earlier, and he had stated at the time that he "could not celebrate until all the cases had been terminated" (Government of Kenya 2016). This outcome now having been realised, he immediately called "upon all Kenyans of goodwill to join us at the Afraha Stadium, Nakuru, on Saturday 16th April 2016, for a thanksgiving service" (ibid.).

In 2013 Deputy President William Ruto declared "Where we came from it's taken God to get us here and we trust in God for the future" (Deacon 2015a:234). On 16 April 2016, at Afraha Stadium in Nakuru, following arrival in the back of a pickup truck as part of an enormous motorcade, he once again stated his amazement that God had so clearly selected him and his president to lead Kenya in a new era of peace and prosperity.[9] Imams were present during the proceedings but, in religious terms, Christian discourse was far more dominant. Speaker after speaker, for example, knew that the crowd would participate in the call and response that opens the majority of sermons, testimonies and prayers in Kenya: "God is good/all the time and all the time/God is good" (ibid.). Furthermore, the Nakuru prayers continued and further entrenched a narrative of repentance and forgiveness bringing about national rebirth and prosperity through divine blessing.

Kenya's general election in 2013 was overwhelmingly understood as an opportunity to save Kenya from its past sins and the horrors of the violence Kenyatta and Ruto were accused of orchestrating in 2007–2008 (Deacon

2015b). The April 2016 rally was a triumphal restatement of the belief held by JAP and their supporters – who are a numerical electoral majority – that God chose Kenya to be reborn in 2013 through its election and the coming together of the anointed leaders of two warring (but both victimised, in this understanding) communities. Satan was said to have entered the nation in 2007 and collective effort was imperative to drive him out again. Jubilee campaigned using a narrative according to which, through their détente and individual repentance and forgiveness, the nation was being washed clean of past sins, redeemed and born again (ibid.).

Jubilee's 2013 election narrative was explicitly maintained on 16 April 2016, as Kenyatta stated that the rally would be "an opportunity for prayers for healing, reconciliation and unity of Kenya as we push on the path of inclusive *prosperity for all*" (*The Standard*, 5 April 2016). Duly, at Afraha, Henry Kosgey – a former politician who had also been indicted by the ICC – began his speech saying that God is good, and the crowd responded ecstatically that this is so "all the time", and when Kosgey posited "all the time" the crowd roared that "God is good".[10] Kosgey then juxtaposed Christian Kenya against atheist Europe, as he thanked God for freedom from the bondage of neo-colonialism; he quoted Psalm 91 verse 11 that God will send his guardian angel to guard you and in the fullness of time he will keep his promise – saying that the fullness of time came and God freed the accused "Ocampo six" as they are known (named for the original ICC prosecutor) (ibid.). Kosgey went on, quoting Romans 8:31 and asking "if God is for us who can be against us?" Answering his own rhetoric, Kosgey stated that "God is with Kenya" and incorporated this into the Jubilee narrative that the nation was born again, it was "time to start afresh", this process would continue in the 2017 general election, and that "Kenyans are a forgiving people and they have forgiven the past. It is time to forgive and move into the future" (ibid.).

In his comments, William Ruto acknowledged his legal team but was unequivocal in arguing that "God was the true victor, without Him we would not have won" (ibid.). Ruto also opened his speech with the ubiquitous call and response that "God is good, all the time, all the time God is good" before referring to 2 Chronicles 7:14: "If my people who are called by my name will humble themselves and call to me, I will heal their land" (ibid.). Ruto introduced Kenyatta and both led the crowd in The Lord's Prayer in Swahili (ibid.). Those who were prosecuted by the ICC, Kenyatta continued, were "falsely labelled as aggressors" but God had "proven them innocent" (ibid.). It was, he said, "time to rededicate ourselves to reconciliation" and that it was "not a time for bitterness but for reconciliation that heals the wounds of the nation" (ibid.). Kenyatta tied the, by now, well-established theological threads together, declaring that God gave them "the victory in elections even when people didn't believe they could do it and He has continued to prove victorious now with the case collapse" (ibid.).

The Afraha prayers thus maintained the narrative of reconciliation pleasing God and leading Him to bless Kenya that it might prosper. This is an explicitly neo-Pentecostal narrative and despite the presence of a few imams at the event, and an Islamic blessing recited by Kenyatta's lead lawyer, when Kenyatta said that all should "believe in what God says in Genesis 12:2" (ibid.) he was using what is in this context an exclusionary passage of scripture. Genesis 12:2 says that "I will make you into a great nation and I will bless you" – but the Kenyan nation, that Kenyatta asked to continue to be blessed, has been defined as Christian, and those who are not Christian will therefore not be blessed. Beyond restriction of blessings to those who are Christian, however, the nature of reconciliation and forgiveness was also reaffirmed as requiring obedience and the absence of criticism – these being divisive, and therefore preventing peace, blessing and prosperity, as well as necessarily being made against leaders who (no matter the process) had been chosen by God; God is for the Kenyan nation, to oppose His leaders would be to go against His will, this is therefore to go against Kenya and thereby, *ipso facto* a critic is a traitor.

The Jubilee narrative includes the violence of 2007–2008, but rather than a phenomenon of human conception, organisation and execution, the events are portrayed as "a painful journey" in which the nation was beset by demons, invaded by Satan and Kenyans fighting "in the name of politics" conceptualised in broader terms of spiritual warfare (ibid.). Through the coming together of Kenyatta and Ruto, the two men argue, there is no longer "any enmity between the Kikuyu and Kalenjin", (ibid.) moves which acted as prayer, as well as being accompanied by prayer, heard by God who "healed us and helped us build a government that is able to lead Kenyans to a better future" (ibid.). This was, Kenyatta and Ruto contend, the covenant they as Jubilee "made to the people when they were elected" (ibid.) and with God – and to question their actions is to move to break that covenant. To do so is to use "divisive language" (ibid.) – in Kenya's recent and longer history it is simple to equate division with "tribal strategies", (ibid.) and to refer to such strategies is to allude to the creation of violence such as occurred in 2008.

Consideration is required of the ramifications of these approaches and a plea that Christianity's immense importance in Kenyan citizenship be taken seriously (c.f. Ellis & ter Haar 2007) by social scientists working on Kenya, who can be inclined to dismiss what they perceive as a matter for the private sphere or, at most, political manipulation. The narrative that is set out with increasing confidence and authoritarian determination by Kenya's current rulers continues to squeeze the nation's already limited democratic space. The contention is that in circumstances where to be Kenyan, or "Kenyan-ness" is so bound up with one religion, those who adhere to another – Muslims in particular – face evolving forms of exclusion, discrimination and marginalisation in ways that are pressing for development, security and national cohesion, by contrast with the dominant Jubilee narrative of social harmony. Division is equated with 'tribal strategies' which are equated with 'hate speech' – this having been subject to enormous discourse as well as arrests and prosecutions in 2013 (Deacon 2015a; Deacon 2015b); thus when Kenyatta says he "will not allow hate speech" because it would "pit Kenyans against each other" and those who engage in it will "face the full force of the law" it is a definitive statement that to criticise is equivalent to treason; it is to speak against the country, which is formed of and blessed by the Christian God.

## Conclusion

Formally and constitutionally Kenya is a secular state. However, it is dominated by a Christian elite, reflecting its colonial foundations – though the nature of Christianity and its societal role has evolved in form and content since independence. *Kenyan Christianity* has been co-opted by the nation's rulers who increasingly bolster their power by making "strangers" of those who do not conform to a growing authoritarian construction, whether they be non-Christians (i.e. Muslims) or even Christians of differing political (and thereby ethnic) persuasions. If we understand Jubilee as a Christian alliance, who see themselves as charged with a Holy mission, we gain some insight into the struggles of Kenya's opposition to present a significant challenge to them in the 2013 general election; attempts by the Coalition for Reform and Democracy (CORD) to call for redistribution of wealth appeared weak, obstructive and lacked the immediacy of Jubilee's portrayal of the country being swiftly blessed with success (Deacon 2015b). However, since the election, this narrative has become much more than an electoral strategy, and ingrained in current conceptions of Kenya, the direction of the nation and what it is to be Kenyan and who is not Kenyan. Uhuru Kenyatta has, since the election and at the Nakuru prayer rally on 16 April 2016, been able to warn of dire consequences for those who stand in any way against God's chosen rulers or who might make criticisms that must necessarily be divisive if they differ from the singular, divine path to glory that Jubilee describe and believe they must lead. Afraha was much more than a party – it was a ringing statement of a concord between Jubilee and God, and woe betide those who attempt to stand in the way of divine prophecy or the power of the Lord.

Since the Afraha prayers Jubilee has conducted considerable outreach to Muslims – declaring Idd-ul-Adha a public holiday for example. This would appear to constitute moves in the search for votes and an attempt to crushingly dominate the upcoming 2017 general election. Nevertheless, on 6 November 2016 for example "at PCEA Zimmerman Parish, Roysambu Constituency, Nairobi County" William Ruto Tweeted that "We owe each other the debt of friendship, brotherhood & unity. A fulfillment [sic] of this debt will result in a harmonious and prosperous nation".[11] This is very much a return to the neo-Pentecostal narrative of unity and peace, which require the absence of criticism, and outspoken faith of a particular form – incorporating the Faith Gospel – leading to prosperity.

The role of Christianity is immense in current state building projects and religious conflict in Kenya and Africa. Christianity and the Kenyan state are inextricably linked, and have evolved together into, as well as reflecting and reproducing, the unique forms that we see today. Therefore, conceptualising and theorising the nature of Kenyan, African Christianity, which is highly Evangelical and 'Pentecostalised', is impossible without a deep understanding of Kenya and 'Kenya-ness'. Furthermore, grasping contemporary socio-economic and political issues in Kenya requires extensive reference to Kenyan Christianity. There is also a need for exploration of Kenyan Christianity's relationship to and interaction with other faiths and this is of great importance in conceptualisation and generation of policy with regard to the nature of apparently religious conflict. Currently, political events in Kenya reflect and reproduce a dominant narrative of Kenyan, Christian citizenship that excludes other, already marginalised faiths – especially Islam – as well as increasingly setting out an authoritarian depiction of the country's leaders as chosen by God and inescapably entwined with national wellbeing, meaning that those who might question and oppose them being against God and nation, and thus traitors, unworthy of citizenship; this exclusion further solidifies the narrative of a particular Christian citizenship in a nation whose boundaries are determined by socio-theological understandings.

## Notes

1. Genesis 12:2 – scripture quoted by President Uhuru Kenyatta on 16 April 2016: field notes.
2. From a Kenya Television Network (KTN) News headline, 30 June 2014.
3. www.youtube.com/watch?v=HI7zGUfb2LM
4. https://twitter.com/WilliamsRuto/status/802844662235021313
5. It was the CSM that notably provided Kenya's first president, Jomo Kenyatta, with his school education.
6. The Pew Forum reported Kenya's Christian population as being some 88.5% with 56% of those specifically considering themselves to be "renewalist" (Pew Forum. 2006. *Spirit and Power: a 10-Country Survey of Pentecostals*. Washington D.C: Pew Forum).
7. www.cc.com/shows/the-daily-show-with-jon-stewart/interviews/8dwtnx/exclusive-reza-aslan-extended-interview
8. It was opposed as not containing sufficient measures against abortion, gay marriage and Muslim 'Kadhi courts' (Gifford 2009:41).
9. Field notes 16 April 2016.
10. *Ibid*.
11. https://twitter.com/WilliamsRuto/status/795207028679602176

## References

Anderson, A. 2001. 'Pentecostals in Africa: The Shape of Future Christianity?' In M. Viggo (Ed.) *The Charismatic Movement and the Churches*. Copenhagen: University of Aarhus.

Anderson, D. 2005. *Histories of the Hanged: The Dirty War in Kenya and the End of Empire*. New York: W. W Norton.

Asamoah-Gyadu, K. 2005. 'Christ Is the Answer: What is the Question? A Ghana Airways Prayer Vigil and Its Implications for Religion, Evil and Public Space'. *Journal of Religion in Africa*, 35(1): 93–117.

Brown, C. 1994. *The Death of Christian Britain: Understanding Secularisation, 1800–2000*. London: Routledge.
Comaroff, J. & Comaroff, J. 1986. 'Christianity and Colonialism in South Africa'. *American Ethnologist*, 13(1): 1–22.
Daily Nation. 15 April 2016. 'Religious Leaders Want Atheist Group Deregistered'. Nairobi.
Deacon, G. 2012. 'Pentecostalism and Development in Kibera Informal Settlement, Nairobi'. *Development in Practice*, 22(5–6): 663–674.
Deacon, G. 2013. 'Satan's Snake and Political Violence in Kenya'. In H. Moksnes & M. Melin (Eds.) *Faith in Civil Society: Religious Actors as Drivers of Change*. Uppsala: Uppsala University: 158–163.
Deacon, G. 2015a. 'Kenya: A Nation Born Again'. *PentecoStudies*, 14(2): 219–240.
Deacon, G. 2015b. 'Driving the Devil Out: Kenya's Born Again Election'. *Journal of Religion in Africa*, 45(2): 200–220.
Deacon, G., Gona, G., Mwakimako, H. & Willis, J. 2017. 'Preaching Politics: Christianity and Islam on Kenya's Coast'. *Journal of Contemporary African Studies*: 35(2): 148–167.
Deacon, G. & Lynch, G. 2013. 'Allowing Satan in? Toward a Political Economy of Pentecostalism in Kenya'. *Journal of Religion in Africa*, 43(2): 108–130.
Deacon, G. & Tomalin, E. 2015. 'A History of Faith-Based Aid and Development'. In E. Tomalin (Ed.) *The Routledge Handbook of Religions and Global Development*. Oxford: Routledge: 68–79.
Ellis, S. & Ter Haar, G. 2007. 'Religion and Politics: Taking African Epistemologies Seriously'. *The Journal of Modern African Studies*, 45(3): 385–401.
Englund, H. & Leach, J. 2000. Ethnography and the Meta-Narratives of Modernity'. *Current Anthropology*, 41(2): 225–248.
Freeman, D. (Ed.) 2013. *Pentecostalism and Development: Churches, NGOs and Social Change in Africa*. Basingstoke: Palgrave Macmillan.
Freeman, D. 2015. 'Pentecostalism and Economic Development in Sub-Saharan Africa'. In E. Tomalin (Eds.) *Routledge Handbook of Religion and Global Development*. Abingdon: Routledge: 114–126.
Gifford, P. 1994. 'Some Recent Developments in African Christianity'. *African Affairs*, 93(373): 513–534.
Gifford, P. 2009. *Christianity, Politics and Public Life in Kenya*. London: Hurst & Co.
Lonsdale, J. 2008. 'Soil, Work, Civilisation, and Citizenship in Kenya'. *Journal of Eastern African Studies*, 2(2): 305–314.
Manji, F. and O'Coill, C., 2002. 'The missionary position: NGOs and development in Africa'. International Affairs, 78(3): 567–584.
Martin, D. 2002. *Pentecostalism: The World Their Parish*. Oxford: Wiley-Blackwell.
Mazrui, A. 1993. 'Ethnicity and Pluralism: The Politicization of Religion in Kenya'. *Journal of the Institute of Muslim Minority Affairs*, 14(1–2): 191–201.
Ngunyi, M. 1995. 'Religious institutions and political liberalization in Kenya'. In Gibbon, P. (ed) Markets, civil society and democracy in Kenya. Uppsala: Nordiska Afrikainstitutet : 121–178.
Otenyo, E. 2004. 'New Terrorism'. *African Security Review*, 13(3): 75–84.
Parsitau, D. & Mwaura, P. 2010. 'God in the City: Pentecostalism as an Urban Phenomenon in Kenya'. *Studia Historiae Ecclesiasticae*, 36(2): 95–112.
Porter, A. 2004. *Religion Versus Empire? British Protestant Missionaries and Overseas Expansion 1700–1914*. Manchester: Manchester University Press.

Ranger, T. 1986. 'Religious Movements and Politics in Sub-Saharan Africa'. *African Studies Review*, 29(2): 1–69.

Sabar-Friedman, G. 1997. 'Church and State in Kenya, 1986–1992: The Churches' Involvement in the "Game of Change"'. *African Affairs*, 96(382): 25–52.

Silverman, D. 2005. 'Indians, Missionaries, and Religious Translation: Creating Wampanoag Christianity in Seventeenth-Century Martha's Vineyard'. *The William and Mary Quarterly*. 62(2): 141–174.

Simmel, G. 1971. *On Individuality and Social Forms*. Chicago: University of Chicago Press.

*The Standard*. 5 April 2016. 'President Uhuru Kenyatta, Raila Odinga Applaud "No Case to Answer". Verdict Against DP William Ruto and Joshua Arap Sang'. Nairobi.

Theuri, M. 2013. 'The Relationship Between Christianity, Education, Culture and Religion in Kenya Since Political Independence in 1963'. *Research on Humanities and Social Sciences*, 3(16): 52–61.

Throup, D. 1995. 'Render Unto Caesar the Things That Are Caesar's: The Politics of Church-State Conflict in Kenya 1978–1990'. In H. Hansen & M. Twaddle (Eds.) *Religion and Politics in East Africa*. London: James Currey: 143–176.

Watkins, J. 1952. 'Ideal Types and Historical Explanation'. *The British Journal for the Philosophy of Science*, 3(9): 22–43.

Weber, M. 1930/2006. *The Protestant Ethic and the Spirit of Capitalism*. London: Routledge.

# 10 Citizenship beyond the State

Pentecostal ethics and political subjectivity in South African modernity

*Marian Burchardt*

If by citizenship we mean the bundle of claims to participation people make in a given polity as well as their capacities to enforce such claims,[1] then Pentecostal Christianity has indeed become central to citizenship in post-apartheid South Africa. Therefore, in this chapter I explore Pentecostal conceptions of political subjectivity and situate them within the analysis of post-apartheid modernity.[2] By modernity I mean the assemblage of cultural ideas and political projects geared towards collective emancipation, equal citizenship and personal freedom as well as the power relations and disciplinary effects that paradoxically arise through their enactment (Bauman 2013; Wagner 2002; Eisenstadt 2000).

Among the religious changes that occurred after the end of the apartheid system of racist oppression, the rise of Pentecostal Christianity is arguably the most important one. While Pentecostalism was present in South Africa early on following the Asuza Street revival in Los Angeles in 1906, it did not spread as dramatically as in other African countries until the early 1990s. As other religious communities, Pentecostal groups were divided through apartheid's official racial categories. Politically, they occupied an uneasy position between Anglophone mainline Christians' this-worldly, socialist oriented attitudes and politicisation on the one hand, and African Initiated Churches other-worldly politics on the other (Comaroff 1986; Balcomb 2004; Bompani 2006).

Pentecostalism's phenomenal rise over the last 20 years can, to a great extent, be explained by people's twin aspiration to become modern citizens and to be protected against misfortune (Burchardt 2017). Pentecostals promised to do both. Pentecostals thus became the fiercest competitors of traditional healers in an already crowded field of spiritual actors who lay claims on protection against "spiritual insecurity" (Ashforth 2005) and witchcraft as their chief domain. But they also came to confront social movements and non-governmental organisations with whom they vie over hegemony with regard to defining rights (Burchardt 2013 and 2016a). Both fields – spiritual protection and citizenship rights – are mediated by particular understandings of political subjectivity.

In the few anthropological studies on South African Pentecostalism (Helgesson 2006; Frahm-Arp 2010; Van Wyk 2014), neither modernity nor citizenship play a central role. Contrary to that, I suggest that both concepts are central for understanding contemporary Pentecostalism. Therefore, I begin by describing the links between Christian citizenship and perceptions of modernity where I also compare Pentecostal to African Traditional Religion's and mainline Christian concepts of citizenship. This section draws up contrasts between Pentecostalism and other sacred traditions such as human rights-oriented activism, especially around issues of sexuality, gender and healing. By emphasising Pentecostalism's political conservatism, however, such contrasts sometimes conceal alternative political possibilities South African Pentecostals create for themselves. In order to elucidate these alternative possibilities, I recount the story of an engaged pastor from Cape Town's township of Khayelitsha whom I will call Pumzile, and explore the grounds that allowed him to thwart established pathways. This ethnographic case leads me to conclude that while Pentecostal professions of faith and human rights-oriented social movements pursue contradictory goals, they sometimes converge around the cultural form of personhood they articulate: radically autonomous in its value commitment, and dramatically subjective in aesthetic expression (Burchardt 2016b). On the one hand, Pentecostalism contests many of the claims to cultural emancipation and liberal politics of post-apartheid modernity, especially those around gender equality and sexual freedom. Pentecostal leaders loudly rejected same-sex marriage, the liberalisation of abortion laws and sexual education oriented towards HIV prevention (Burchardt 2013). However, it simultaneously and unwittingly endorses and promotes important elements of a specific notion of personhood. Thus, at the interface of Christianity and social movements we see the emergence of new repertoires around the aesthetics and enactments of personhood that are shaping the cultural contours of South African modernity.

Methodologically, the chapter draws on data gathered through field research in Cape Town and Johannesburg between 2010 and 2015. These data include ethnographic observations in the township of Khayelitsha and interviews with leaders from Pentecostal, mainline Christian and African Traditionalist communities as well as interviews with members of religious lobby organisations (such as the Family Policy Institute or the South African Council of Churches [SACC]) that represent religious groups vis-à-vis the state.

## Understanding post-apartheid modernity

Pentecostal notions of citizenship and the way they take shape through contestations over competing claims to citizenship are best appreciated when placed within the broader context of South African post-apartheid modernity. Inspired by Ann Swidler's work (2010), I suggest that South African modernity should be seen as constituted by three distinct sacred traditions that are expressed in different institutional spheres: i) the modern democratic state with non-governmental organisations and progressive social movements; ii) world religions; and iii) the institutions of African traditionalism. Each of these traditions embodies specific visions of community, authority and personhood.

The modern state and NGOs envision authority as democratic, community as civic, and sacred personhood as rooted in individual autonomy, anchored in legally enforceable human rights, and backed by global discourses about democracy, education and empowerment. World, or "axial", religions imagine the religious community as voluntarily chosen and horizontal,

> with the sacred located in transcendent symbols that bind a community of equals together (even though such communities may be quite hierarchical, with pastors or sheiks exercising local authority and claiming special access to the sacred [Englund 2003], and with prestige flowing to elders and other influential members of the community).
> (Swidler 2013:681)

Institutions of African traditionalism comprise customary law, traditional healing, traditional authority, African traditional religion and kinship. In contrast to world religions, they construe community as compulsory and hierarchical, authority as hereditary and personhood as enshrined in kinship obligations.

Yet importantly, in South Africa the institutional expressions of traditionalism (customary judiciaries; the Congress of Traditional Leaders [Contralesa]; the Traditional Healers Organization [THO]) are seen by many as modern not only because they are bound by the rules of constitutional democracy but also because their influence expresses modern values of cultural autonomy and self-determination (Oomen 2005). These three sacred traditions provide the central symbolic resources South Africans draw on when making claims to citizenship. Situating themselves within these sacred traditions allows people to mobilise particular hermeneutics of the political and the legitimacy they afford their claims. Forms of political subjectivity flow from these particular concepts of authority, community and personhood and then come to underpin citizenship practices.

Many scholars have pointed to the foundational tensions between citizenship as a project of universal inclusion, the nation as the collective of rights-bearing individuals and nationalism as a political and cultural force of exclusion (see for example Anderson 1983). Each of the above-mentioned sacred traditions is articulated to current expressions South African nationalism. Similar to other African countries, South African Pentecostals as well as representatives of African traditionalism frequently engage in discourses in which legitimate membership in the national community is rendered dependent upon the commitment to heteronormativity (Burchardt 2013). Their citizenship project is thus tied to a deeply sexualised nationalism and carved out through the dramatisation of sexual difference. Less clear are the ways in which these sacred traditions are linked to the violent manifestations of nativist nationalism and xenophobia (Hayem 2013) that repeatedly erupt since 2008.

The analytical triangle described above is first and foremost a heuristic tool inspired by Weber's concept of the ideal type (Weber 1985). In other words, the sacred traditions I address are analytical abstractions that do not exist as neatly separated entities in social reality but in fact have fuzzy boundaries and overlap. African Traditional Religion (ATR), for instance, is peculiarly placed between axial religions and African traditionalism and indeed makes claims on both sacred traditions. Its most energetic proponents, Nokuzola Mndende and the Icamagu Heritage Institute, mobilise with the aim of reformulating parts of African tradition such as ancestor worship and ritual *as a religion*, claim public and governmental recognition of it in these terms but also modernise it by crafting new forms of training, education and ordinance. Mndende also bitterly protested against the exclusion of ATR representatives from interfaith forums such as the National Religious Leaders Forums (NRLF), created in 1997 by Nelson Mandela, and the presumed oblivion with which the African National Congress (ANC) treated African Traditional Religion. More than ten years later, things had changed only slightly. One of the priests Mndende had ordained told me in a conversation in 2010:

> Recently the premier of the Eastern Cape, Noxolo Kiviet, organized an inter-congregational prayer after a road accident in which seven people had died. But it was not interfaith because we were never invited. Only Christians were invited to go and pray for these accidents that often happen in the Eastern Cape. But I also said I was happy that we were not invited there because we do not pray the same way. We pray to the same God but not the same way. Now we will not know whether it is because of our prayers or their prayers that made it happen [. . .] Even in the interfaith forum here in Cape Town, when Father John [spokesperson of the Western Cape Interfaith Council], is there and the Jewish and Islam guys, the archbishop will say "Can you give us a prayer" but he refers to the so-called world religions. Maybe he is talking to a Hindu or a Jewish guy. Several times I was there, he never said to me "Can you give us a prayer" because he sees me like a traditional healer.

While claiming both inclusion and the right to religious difference, he felt that the grounds on which they made their claims were misrecognised – being seen as a healer instead of a priest, which is what ATR leaders really are in their own view. For them, being viewed as healers means being denied the status of priests. If adherents of ATR are thus sometimes viewed by others as occupying unclear positions this is also true for "mainline" Christians such as Anglican, Quakers or Methodists and the SACC as their umbrella body. These churches' notions of citizenship are peculiarly placed between world religions on the one hand, and NGOs and social movements on the other. In 2010, I visited mainline organisations such as the SACC headquarters in Johannesburg and their parliamentary liaison office in Cape Town. They were actively mobilising around domestic violence, renewable energy for the poor, sustainable water use and religious freedom and were central actors in the campaigns on the Basic Income Grant (Ferguson 2015) and People's Budget Campaign. In keeping with their ideology of social justice, they lobbied government on an impressive array of issues and spearheaded almost all religious movements toward the "moral regeneration"[3] of the state that this volume addresses.

However, from participant observations it emerged that there was a widespread perception that mainline Christians had become too similar to social movements. Simultaneously, Anglican, Methodist and Catholic activists were often frustrated about the ways in which Pentecostals easily move into the spotlight of media attention with their moralising discourses about sexuality. They staked their claims to citizenship on notions of human rights, democracy and justice that also constituted the "sacred tradition" of social movements and NGOs. While perfectly illustrating the kind of modern "public religion" Casanova (1994) described mainline Christians increasingly struggled to unite people around their projects. But how can we explain Pentecostalism's success in this regard?

## Pentecostal citizenship: ethics

Pentecostal Christians' engagements with politics are characterised by two competing tendencies: political skepticism on the one hand, and activism and demands to be heard on the other. I describe both of these tendencies in the following.

As elsewhere in the world, many South African Pentecostals tend to view the world as a battleground between the forces of good and evil, between Jesus and Satan, and as a place that oscillates between light and darkness. In this battle, people are called to take sides by converting and accepting Jesus as their personal saviour. Anthropologists such as van Dijk (2001) and Meyer (1998) have highlighted how this Manichean dualism structured Pentecostal worldviews, beliefs and ritual. How does this dualism play out with regard to notions of citizenship?

For many Pentecostals the domain of politics, parties and electoral competition is a part of the fallen world, which they view as essentially corrupt. In the post-apartheid period, people have of course witnessed the continuous proliferation of stories about corruption. At the top is the case of the US-$ 23 million of public money that, according to a public anti-corruption body, had been improperly spent on current president Jacob Zuma's rural home in KwaZulu Natal. In addition, in April 2016 the Constitutional Court found that Zuma's failure to repay parts of the money as the anti-corruption agency had been demanded, violated the constitution.[3] This story is followed by numerous others involving government institutions such as the South African Police Forces and the public tender system. Between 2001 and 2013 South Africa dropped in the global Corruption Perception Index 34 places while the percentage of people who think fighting corruption should be a government priority rose from 14 to 26%.[4] Corruption is perceived to be very real and is taken as a proof that evil is all around. Pentecostal discourse offers theological interpretations of corruption stories and suggests particular ways to make sense of politics.

Still more than corruption, for Pentecostals discourses about gender rights, sexual rights and homosexuality have become proof of the fact that politics belong to the sphere of evil. One central implication is that born-again people who have "crossed to the realm of light and salvation" cannot interfere with the "fallen world" without running the risk of being drawn into its evil course. When I asked Pentecostals whether they should engage in politics they often answered: "We as a church must stand aside". One pastor gave me an elaborate the explanation for his reluctance to engage:

> No, Christians shouldn't be in politics. You know Mandela? Mandela said one day, politics is a dirty game. So you can't get involved in a dirty game if you are a Christian, you can't do that as a Christian. If I am a member of a political party, and the members of that political party decide to kill someone, I must support those members but I think it is evil. So I can't do that. So there are many things that are not good in politics. If you are in a member in politics, you must be a liar. In our religion, you can't be a liar. You must lie there in order to make things right. You must not tell the truth, you must lie. So in our religion you mustn't be a liar, and so I can't get involved in politics.

The passage illustrates the reproduction of theological dualisms and divisions and the dramatic effects this has for notions of citizenship. There is a tendency to withdraw from politics, voting and other kinds of participation, for instance, in civil society organisations or voluntary community organisations. While there are Pentecostal pastors and groups active in civil society, such as Cape Town's "Great Commission" for instance, they do not represent the mainstream of independent Pentecostalism. Such pastors are either exceptional Pentecostal activists or actors modelling their politics on those of US-American evangelicals. In general, according to my own observations independent Pentecostals are less active in organised politics and civil society than mainline Christians. This tendency is paralleled by discourses that fashion Pentecostals as the nation, the Bible as its constitution and the church as its government (Comaroff & Comaroff 2003). One pastor expressly proclaimed: "I am like a government". Through these comparisons Pentecostals contrast the mundane spheres of politics and law with a religious domain *in the same terms*, rendering it as one of quasi-judicial legislation. Importantly, this religious domain does therefore not have a lesser, but a peculiarly enhanced ontological status.

Contrary to these attitudes of political skepticism, there are other Pentecostal groups who fashion political involvement both through extra-parliamentary pressure group politics and party politics (especially the African Christian Democratic Party) as their Christian duty. Again, these Pentecostal groups' discourse chiefly revolves around issues of sexual morality and "traditional" family values. These Pentecostals see South African Christianity as increasingly under siege through the onslaughts of secular liberalism, for which, in their view, the legalisation of same-sex marriage is the clearest proof. In an interview, the president of the "Family Policy Institute" – one of the most vocal Evangelical leaders[5] in Cape Town and central figure in the so-called "Marriage Alliance" – in fact assimilated the position of Christians in post-apartheid South Africa to that of oppressed racial groups under the apartheid regime. In order to clarify this point, Evangelicals often had recourse to statistics, specifying how many South Africans were Christians or adherents of other religious traditions that shared their moral concerns, opposed same-sex marriage, and felt abhorred by ANC sexual politics and secular liberalism.

These two orientations – political skepticism and activism focused on issues around biblically based sexual morality – are arguably the hegemonic discourses connecting and severing Pentecostals from contestations around citizenship. However, there is a third type of Pentecostal political subjectivity that I illustrate through the story of a pastor from the city of Cape Town. The story shows up the limitations of hegemonic discourses and therefore also opens new avenues for thinking about Pentecostal politics.

## Political pathways and possibilities: the morality of activism

When I got to know Pumzile[6] in 2010, the house in which he lived with his wife and two children was one of the biggest in the neighbourhood called "Town Two" located in the township of Khayelitsha. Pumzila was born in 1970 in the small Eastern Cape town of Stutterheim where he grew up with his grandparents. His parents were unmarried and he felt "anger and hatred, and unforgiveness coming up in me about that kind of life, coming from a poor family such as mine", as he told me.[7] Already as a child, he started to pray for other people, felt the gift to do so and told his family that he wanted to become a pastor. However, South Africa's historical circumstances – the massive deprivations and racist oppression non-whites suffered during the apartheid period, the lack of opportunities in education and professional careers – initially moved his life into a different direction. Early on, he began seeing himself as a politicised person. As so many others during that period he dropped out of school because of his involvement in political campaigns and underground activities.

At the same time, he had to navigate the complicated moral terrain of township life characterised as it was during the 1980s by rising levels of violence, increasing political chaos engineered by apartheid security forces and massive poverty. He did so by foregrounding two orientations: politics and ethics.

> As a black person you were involved in politics, whether you were a leader of a certain way of fighting the system, or you were just involved by supporting the leaders against the suppression . . . I was just a

comrade, not a leader in a so-called leadership structure, I was just a comrade who was influential amongst other comrades.

Many times he had to escape during nocturnal police raids as they hid other comrades in his grandmother's house. Several times he was also beaten up by the police during protest marches in his hometown. Simultaneously, he realised the disorderliness in life that necessarily came with participation in underground activities and emphasised the importance of having been brought up as a Christian in his Anglican home. "As an Anglican child I knew my morals, I knew how to treat the elderly and because my grandparents told me I knew how to behave when I am alone", he explained.

By the late 1980s, he started to become actively involved several religious groups and became a leader an Anglican youth movement and an Evangelical movement called the "conquerors". One of their main activities was to visit schools and other places where young people would meet to address people through public speeches in which they would testify and talk about their experiences with Jesus Christ. These "testimonies" were often made up people stories about their past lives and how they encountered Jesus and the power of the Holy Spirit against the odds of life in these difficult times they often experienced as a trial. Importantly, Pumzile described his activities of giving political speeches and his testimonies as a Christian in homologous terms: both involve biographical accounts as people suffering because they belong to oppressed social categories with a specific dramatic structure. Both are public performances of citizenship, despite the fact that they draw on divergent sacred traditions (Burchardt 2016a).

Several times, these practices of speaking out publicly at Christian gatherings animated people to encourage him to become a pastor. He experienced these encouragements as prophesies that called for a more radical change than he had hitherto envisioned. The notion of becoming "born-again" and "saved" encapsulated this idea of radical change and slowly he became acquainted with the world of Pentecostals, chiefly, as it were, through meeting Christians from different denomination over time, not through a dramatic sudden experience of conversion. He recognised that for many years he remained a "backslider".

And yet the need to be protected by the Holy Spirit became dramatically clear already in 1991 when in the context of a fight his uncle stabbed him with a scissor. "It still makes me cry", he told me, "because this is when I saw Jesus. It was like how can I be able to trust him?" Pentecostals often construe such experiences as ordeals that eventually shape the world as a place between good and evil, and survival as the work of Jesus.[8] He recalled how he felt the blood in his abdomen. For a month he stayed in the hospital and was in coma.

However, there were more serious trials to come in the future: as so many others who did not complete schooling as a result of their political involvement during the 1980s he lacked the credentials to get a job in South Africa's depressed post-apartheid labour market; he moved from city to city, living with different relatives, in search of a job and often ended up drinking, having girlfriends and also fathered a child out of wedlock. He got by with poorly paid jobs as a security guard, quit his job several times just in order to take it up and only slowly got on his feet again.

In 2000 he moved to Cape Town, feeling he heard a voice that called him. "Cape Town was corrupt, it was a city of gangsters and there was no moral fiber in Cape Town and no respect", he observed. While again taking up jobs as a security guard he also became victim of a car accident, broke his legs and jaws and again had to stay in hospital for a month. Finally he responded to the "voice" that asked him to preach. He became a member of the Apostolic Faith Mission, married the mother of his child, and after years of Bible study, ordinance and slowly being promoted within the hierarchies of the church he was allowed to plant his own church in Khayelitsha. However, he did not receive financial contributions from the mother church and, as in the numerous independent Pentecostal churches that dot Cape Town's urban landscape, had to become self-reliant: "When you are called you have to look for people to support you financially, for the building of the church, for your family, money to eat and buy clothes" (see also Englund 2003).

Pumzile was a definitely a gifted speaker and it seemed that this was one of the main reason of his success as a pastor. His Sunday services gathered around a hundred followers turning his congregations into one of the largest in the area. He became engaged in Pentecostal counselling as a way of teaching people Christian conduct, that is, a particular way of refashioning the self "in terms of a 'born-again' conversion to the faith, moral imperatives for people's intimate lives and strictures vis-à-vis social behavior" (van Dijk 2013:510; Burchardt 2009). Pumzile shared in this idea: "People still practice adultery and sexual immorality, they know that they are not supposed to have girlfriends, smoke, drink and use drugs. They know it that but they find it difficult to practice, so you have to teach and counsel them". However, he also realised that what attracted people most immediately is deliverance and doing miracles as they read this as a sign that "this church is blessed by the spirit of the Lord".

In many ways, Pumzile shared the view that sexual morality is central to moral personhood and citizenship that dominates Pentecostal political agendas across many African countries. Thus, when asked about his views on same-sex marriage, he argued:

> When you create such laws or rights, such an understanding of human rights, and if you support such human rights for such kind of people [gays and lesbians] who are doing this, you are against God, that is what the bible says, and I am following the bible. And the constitution may say that, but what about the bible? But the bible is *our constitution*, as Christians!

However, much more important is the fact this was not his *only* politics and that his notion of citizenship went beyond the established discourses on sexuality in several ways. First, he tied his idea about reforming people's lives to the idea of reforming the "whole community" and on many occasions talked about social development. He described his idea of the church as follows:

> This church does not belong to the congregation only. Christ has done and fed people, and the church today has to feed people. Not in terms of the soup kitchen. To feed the church is go to the houses if there is a need, because there are elderly people and children that are left in many houses, women that are abused and so on. Gender equality, the church needs gender equality because there mustn't be anyone who suppresses anyone else. Women can be leaders, in the church, in the NGOs, in the country.

Second, he did not only address issues of social justice on occasions of all kinds but also had a clear idea of the social position that he needed to fashion for himself in order to so. For him, being a pastor was about "being vocal on issues, being heard" while simultaneously keeping distance to the field of party politics. He felt that party politics was inevitably based on divisions that ran counter to the unity in the church. "I serve the purpose of Christ in government by talking to government, not being part of it".

Finally, anchoring his political subjectivity in the Bible he remained faithful to Pentecostal tenets but also transcended them by claiming that "praying alone is not enough" neither to be saved nor to improve people's lives. This view contrasts with 'world-rejecting' versions of Pentecostalism that view 'modern', state-led efforts to improve people's lives such as biomedicine (as in HIV/AIDS responses) with suspicion. Generally, Pumzile drew on individualist rather than socialist vocabularies when describing his ideas about citizenship. But he also emphasised the fact the church was an essential part of the community of citizens rather than standing apart. I suggest that this kind of Pentecostal political subjectivity is intimately tied to Pumzile's biographical experiences of politicisation under apartheid. These experiences certainly reflect the particularities of South African history but it is not impossible that similar subjectivities also emerge under different conditions of political oppression.

## Conclusion

As participants in social movements and NGO-driven civil society, Christian communities promote modern human rights and activist visions of democracy and personhood. Contrary to other African societies where the organisational forms imposed by the state and NGOs "have induced a proliferation of ornately ritualized practices that symbolically enact rational modernity" (Swidler 2013:682) with no significant rationalising consequences, in South Africa Christianity social movements do engage in overlapping discourses centred on emancipation, autonomy and democratic control. Within these discourses, activists and participants envision themselves as autonomous individuals with legitimate claims on the social order construed as progressively of their own making. While the claims of mainline Christianity are more overtly political and collectivist, those promoted by Pentecostal Christianity are more individualistic.

Beyond the specific content of claims to citizenship, one powerful impact of Pentecostalism on post-apartheid modernity lies in the ways in which personhood is culturally imagined and expressed. Post-apartheid history came along with the creation of numerous arenas in which people would offer narrative accounts of themselves in front of others: they would talk about their lives as victims of racism, as HIV-positive people, as women and members of oppressed or empowered sexual minorities. They would enact their personhood by speaking as victims of state-led eviction campaigns or as urban marginals who are excluded from the basic forms of "infrastructural citizenship" (Burchardt & Höhne 2016), i.e. access to urban services that is actually one of the most contested terrains of citizenships struggles in South Africa (see also Schnitzler 2008). Invariably, these accounts would take the shape of what Foucault termed "confessional technologies". These acts of telling the truth about oneself, replete with instances of leaving behind or moving out of states of ignorance or blindness and seeing the light of truth and wisdom, unfolded as staged and highly dramatic performances of authenticity in which powerful claims to subjectivity and personhood were made. In other words, citizenship is "speaking the self". As I showed, these very same practices of dramatic storytelling were cultivated within the spheres of Pentecostal and Charismatic Christianity, but also in the world of movement activism and everyday life in NGOs. In other words, the most powerful articulation between Pentecostalism and other axis of post-apartheid modernity lies in the narrative and performative practice of claiming, expressing and enacting political subjectivity. Pentecostals believe in the value of enthusiastic professions of faith. Invariably, the most dramatic instances of such professions are those related to conversion. The reason is that religious conversion is construed as structurally homologous to political forms of the speaking and fashioning the self in that both temporal ruptures (between past passivity and present agency) and social distance (between the faithful and others, see also Meyer 1998 and van Dijk 2001). But also after conversion, the importance of professions of faith as rituals of subjectivity for their religious lives continues. Believers continually narrate their everyday experiences during Sunday services and other occasions as they search for the presence of Jesus Christ in their lives and for some kind of meaning that offers coherence.

While the Pentecostal professions of faith and the rituals of testimony in the world of social movements and NGOs may seem unrelated or even contradictory, I suggest that they converge around the cultural form of personhood they articulate: radically autonomous in its value commitment and dramatically subjective in aesthetic expression. While Pentecostalism certainly contests many of the claims to cultural emancipation and liberal politics of post-apartheid modernity, especially those around gender equality and sexual freedom, it simultaneously and unwittingly endorses and promotes important elements of its notion of personhood. Thus at the interface of Christianity and social movements we see the emergence of new repertoires around the aesthetics and enactments of personhood that significantly shape the cultural contours of South African modernity.

There is thus a Pentecostal type of modernity that rests on the insistence of radical change, implacably and incessantly demanded by Pentecostal pastors and believers on all sorts of public gatherings across Africa today. The notion of radical change is fundamental to Pentecostals' religious life. dramatised in rituals of conversion and linked to the promise to "become saved", Pentecostals' discourse on change, to be brought about by personal effort and Godly support, creates expectations that one's life can indeed be transformed. During many Sunday services and countless other occasions, I observed how Pentecostals told stories about the presence and work of Jesus Christ in their everyday lives confirming to themselves in front of others that change for the better is possible and actually happening. Such occasions therefore function as ceremonies in which claims to modernity in terms of rupture and radical change are collectively validated.

Testimonies are extremely important instruments in which accusations against injustices and the experiences of those suffering from them are packaged. They transform individuals into citizens called forth as specific categories of people with fundamental rights that have been violated. Testimonies invoke discrete categories of right-bearing subjects that would remain abstract and 'bloodless' without the affective force of the testimony.

The important point here is that the structure of these narrative practices as well as their import on conceptions of personhood is similar to Pentecostal practices of testimony that serve to validate *Christian* vision of radical change. My argument is that both coalesce to shape notions and technologies of the self that have ideas of people as agentive, autonomous and modern at their centre; people whose life has a purpose that they actively chose and that becomes a project through the practices of working towards that purpose. What emerges is a cult of subjectivity that willy-nilly binds Pentecostal Christianity and progressive social movements within a shared project of modernity.

## Notes

1 This conceptualization of the term citizenship broadly corresponds to the way it is used in recent anthropological scholarship (e.g. Holston 2008, Ong 2006).
2 In this chapter, I use the term Pentecostal as a shorthand for independent Pentecostal-charismatic communities.
3 www.bbc.com/news/world-africa-35943941
4 Newham, G. 'Why is Corruption Getting Worse in South Africa?' www.corruptionwatch.org.za/why-is-corruption-getting-worse-in-south-africa/
5 Most scholars subscribe to the notion of fundamentalism and Pentecostalism forming the two major expressions, or sub-currents, of the broader notion of

Evangelicalism. In this context, actors such as the Family Policy Institute as well as the Church His People to which it is tied, bear relatively strong resemblance to American-style fundamentalism while locally in South Africa there are also viewed as Pentecostals. Significantly, with their positive attitude towards political involvement they differ from what I call independent Pentecostals, i.e. the small township-based community organised along the one-pastor/one-church model.
6 This name is a pseudonym used to protect the informant's anonymity.
7 The following quotes are all taken from personal interviews carried out during fieldwork in 2010, 2014 and 2015. I transcribed these interviews and interpreted them with an interest in the specific biographical experiences that shaped Pumzile's political subjectivity.
8 Other informants told me to have been poisoned by relatives or by healers and similarly experienced their survival as the work of Jesus.

# References

Anderson, B. 1983. *Imagined Communities: Reflections on the Origin and Spread of Nationalism*. London: Verso Books.
Ashforth, A. 1998. 'Reflections on Spiritual Insecurity in a Modern African City (Soweto)'. *African Studies Review*, 41(3): 39–67.
Ashforth, A. 2005. *Witchcraft, Violence, and Democracy in South Africa*. Chicago: University of Chicago Press.
Balcomb, A. 2004. 'From Apartheid to the New Dispensation: Evangelicals and the Democratization of South Africa1'. *Journal of Religion in Africa*, 34(1): 5–38.
Bauman, Z. 2013. *Modernity and Ambivalence*. New York: John Wiley & Sons.
Bompani, B. 2006. 'Mandela Mania: Mainline Christianity in Post-Apartheid South Africa'. *Third World Quarterly*, 27(6): 1137–1149.
Burchardt, M. 2009. 'Subjects of Counselling: Religion, HIV/AIDS and the Management of Everyday Life in South Africa'. In P. W. Geissler & F. Becker (Eds.) *AIDS and Religious Practice in Africa*. Leiden, Boston, MA: Brill: 333–358.
Burchardt, M. 2013. 'Equals Before the Law? Public Religion and Queer Activism in the Age of Judicial Politics in South Africa'. *Journal of Religion in Africa*, 43(3): 237–260.
Burchardt, M. 2016a. 'State Regulation or "Public Religion"? Religious Diversity in Post-apartheid South Africa'. In A. Dawson (Ed.) *The Politics and Practice of Religious Diversity: National Contexts, Global Issues*. New York: Routledge: 187–204.
Burchardt, M. 2016b. 'The Self as Capital in the Narrative Economy: How Biographical Testimonies Move Activism in the Global South'. *Sociology of Health & Illness*, 38(4): 592–609.
Burchardt, M. 2017. 'Pentecostal Productions of Locality: Urban Risk and Spiritual Protection in Cape Town'. In A. Strhn & D. Garbin (Eds.) *Religion and the Global City*. London: Bloomsbury: 78–94.
Burchardt, M. & Höhne, S. 2016. 'The Infrastructures of Diversity: Cultural and Materiality in Urban Space – An Introduction'. *New Diversities*, 17(2): 1–13.
Casanova, J. 1994. *Public religions in the modern world*. Chicago: University of Chicago Press.
Comaroff, J. 1986. *Body of Power, Spirit of Resistance: The Culture and History of a South African People*. Chicago: University of Chicago Press.
Comaroff, J. & Comaroff, J. 2003. 'Reflections on Liberalism, Policulturalism, and ID-Ology: Citizenship and Difference in South Africa'. *Social Identities*, 9(4): 445–473.

Eisenstadt, S. N. 2000. 'Multiple Modernities'. *Daedalus*, 129(1): 1–29.
Englund, H. 2003. 'Christian Dependency and Global Membership: Pentecostal Extraversions in Malawi'. *Journal of Religion in Africa*, 33(1): 83–111.
Ferguson, J. 2013. 'Declarations of Dependence: Labour, Personhood, and Welfare in Southern Africa'. *Journal of the Royal Anthropological Institute*, 19(2): 223–242.
Ferguson, J. 2015. *Give a man a fish: Reflections on the new politics of distribution*. Durham: Duke University Press.
Frahm-Arp, M. 2010. *Professional Women in South African Pentecostal Charismatic Churches*. Boston, MA, Leiden: Brill.
Hayem, J. 2013. 'From May 2008 to 2011: Xenophobic Violence and National Subjectivity in South Africa'. *Journal of Southern African Studies*, 39(1): 77–97.
Helgesson, K. 2006. *"Walking in the Spirit": The Complexity of Belonging in Two Pentecostal Churches in Durban, South Africa*. Uppsala: DICA.
Holston, J. 2008. *Insurgent Citizenship: Disjunctions of Democracy and Modernity in Brazil*. Princeton, NJ: Princeton University Press.
Meyer, B. 1998. ' "Make a Complete Break With the Past": Memory and Postcolonial Modernity in Ghanian Pentecostal Discourse'. In R. Werbner (Ed.) *Memory and the Postcolony: African Anthropology and the Critique of Power*. London: Zed Books.
Ong, A. 2006. 'Mutations in Citizenship'. *Theory, Culture & Society*, 23(2–3): 499–505.
Oomen, B. M. 2005. *Chiefs in South Africa: Law, Power and Culture in the Post-Apartheid era*. London: James Currey.
Schnitzler, A. V. 2008. 'Citizenship Prepaid: Water, Calculability, and Techno-Politics in South Africa'. *Journal of Southern African Studies*, 34(4): 899–917.
Swidler, A. 2010. 'The Return of the Sacred: What African Chiefs Teach Us About Secularization'. *Sociology of Religion*, 71(2): 157–171.
Swidler, A. 2013. 'African Affirmations: The Religion of Modernity and the Modernity of Religion'. *International Sociology*, 28(6): 680–696.
Van Dijk, R. 2001. 'Time and Transcultural Practices of the Self in the Ghanian Pentecostal Diaspora'. In A. Corten & R. Marshall-Fratini (Eds.) *Between Babel and Pentecost: Transnational Pentecostalism in Africa and Latin America*. Bloomington, Indianapolis: Indiana University Press.
Van Dijk, R. 2013. 'Counselling and Pentecostal Modalities of Social Engineering of Relationships in Botswana'. *Culture, Health & Sexuality*, 15(supp 4): S509–S522.
Van Wyk, I. 2014. *The Universal Church of the Kingdom of God in South Africa: A Church of Strangers*. Cambridge: Cambridge University Press.
Wagner, P. 2002. *A Sociology of Modernity: Liberty and Discipline*. New York, London: Routledge.
Weber, M. 1985. 'Die "Objektivität" sozialwissenschaftlicher und sozialpolitischer Erkenntnis'. In J. Winckelmann (Ed) *Gesammelte Aufsätze zur Wissenschaftslehre*. Tübingen: J.C.B. Mohr: 146–214.

# 11 Moral models, self-control and the production of the moral citizen in the Ugandan Pentecostal movement

*Alessandro Gusman*

In the last 15 years, Pentecostal-charismatic churches have gained a significant role within the Ugandan public and political spheres, becoming one of the most significant religious voices in the country. One of the reasons for its success has been the movement's ability to propose alternative models of behaviour to traditional mechanisms of social control, that were based on a gerontocratic system in which sexuality and other spheres of young people's life were under the control of the elders. The models proposed by Pentecostals, based on the idea of self-control as a way of creating an ethical subject, have proved to be especially effective to young people in the urban context. In the face of an experience of "radical uncertainty" (Marshall 2009), Pentecostalism produces new social and political topographies, in which the "Christian citizen" is socialised to individual responsibility in order to counter the moral and social crisis in the country. Individual conversion and salvation has thus to be seen in the broader context of a political project to save and redeem the whole nation.

This implies a new form of citizenship, that Ruth Marshall (2009) defined "redemptive citizenship", in which the religious and the political are not mutually exclusive, but on the contrary are inextricably linked. In this view, the Pentecostal movement is a highly public religion in the African continent, and its call for social redemption and moralisation is a political programme: that of a collective political redemption that has to be realised through the formation of responsible individuals, honest leaders in their families, local communities and in the nation. With this rhetoric and the models it proposes, Pentecostalism operates as a prescriptive regime that produces new forms of subjectivities, also on gendered basis (Van Klinken 2016). In this way, Pentecostalism has been able to put itself forward as an agent of transformation and moralisation for the country, self-representing itself as able to strengthen the presence of Christianity and to put an end to the corruption, both physical and spiritual, of the social body.

Throughout this period of time, a significant number of young Ugandans have entered Pentecostal congregations attracted by discourses on how to change their lives, find success in relationships, work and studies, and become true "Christian citizens" by following the normative models proposed by Pentecostalism. This first implies the acceptance of strict regulations concerning sexual life, ways of behaving in public and of doing business; as a consequence, those who do not conform to Pentecostal models of living are considered "unsaved", and thus potentially immoral, corrupt or even a danger for the integrity of society, as in the case of the anti-homosexuality campaign (Boyd 2013; Cheney 2012; Nyanzi 2013; Sadgrove et al. 2012).

Based on long-term research on Pentecostalism in Kampala beginning in 2005, this chapter aims to show how these moral models have become central in defining the identities of the young born-agains in Uganda and directing the movement's political agenda.[1] To do this, I will focus especially on abstract ideals, rather than on real practices, recognising that individuals often have to find a compromise in their everyday lives between these asserted ideals and actual situations (Daswani 2013).

After introducing the link between the feeling of insecurity and the creation of 'folk devils' who are blamed for social decay, in the second section I will analyse in more detail how three consecutive waves of 'moral panic' around sexuality have worked to reinforce mechanisms of social control in Uganda and increased the political influence of the Pentecostal movement. I will then discuss the importance of the models proposed by Pentecostal churches that shape young people's worldviews and ways of behaving.

## From the feeling of insecurity to the idea of social contamination

In recent decades, 'insecurity' has become a widely used category to explain the existential conditions of people in Africa (as elsewhere); in the face of the powerful socio-economic transformations driven by globalisation processes and the neoliberal economy, individuals and groups – youth, especially – have come to be seen as "dealing with uncertainties" (Haram & Yamba 2009) and "navigating" (Christiansen, Utas & Vigh 2006) to find a way to reduce vulnerability and access adulthood.

Insecurity is a polyvocal concept that indicates a plurality of different kinds of situations: physical and spiritual conditions, as well as social and economic situations. Insecurity undermines the regularity – real or perceived – of human existence: the more rapid the social transformation, the less predictability is likely to be found in individual life. Yet, human beings privilege regularity, acts of classification and finding the cause of individual and social problems. This is of course not restricted to African contexts, but in sub-Saharan Africa conflicts, epidemics, famines, forced displacement and other such phenomena make insecurity an existential condition for a large part of the population.

As I will show in this chapter, Pentecostalism provides young Ugandans with social networks and prescriptive models that help reduce the feeling of insecurity and provide reference points, especially in town, where according to Pentecostals systems of social control are considered to be loose and where the danger of losing direction and living 'immorally' are always present.[2] Thus, moral models proposed to and from young born-again in Kampala are focused on the construction of an ethical, responsible and accountable subject, especially through the reference to the ability of 'self-control'. I will return to this in more detail in the next sections.

In addition to the above characteristics, it is important to note that insecurity is a rather impalpable phenomenon for social actors, linked as it is to wide social transformations that largely exceed the local and even the national level; this makes insecurity something difficult to perceive in everyday life and to express verbally. It is thus possible to consider the frequent emergence of discourses concerning the 'risk' or the 'danger' represented by certain social phenomena or groups not so much as a mirror of a feeling of widespread insecurity within a society, but rather as the source of the words and categories used to express a feeling of anxiety and loss of control in one's own life. This loss of existential security and of cognitive certainty is translated into the idea of 'safety at risk' in the public discourse. Pentecostal groups are skillful in presenting themselves as closed, safe and saved communities, able to contrast this insecurity and to protect believers against external dangers. The Pentecostal topic of 'spiritual warfare' against evil forces thus also assumes a political meaning: contrasting dangerous individuals and groups does not only mean praying for protection against the spiritual forces that they embody, but proposing and supporting laws against the social danger they represent.

In this way, discourses about insecurity and social contamination become a frame through which people read social life; individuals and groups labelled as 'dangerous' for the integrity of the social fabric are turned into "folk devils"[3]: real, physical enemies against whom society must defend itself (Cohen 1972). The struggle against these personified threats is much more effective in the creation of a feeling of shared identity and social cohesion than less palpable entities such as epidemics, economic global forces or natural disasters; and they are more likely to become targets for acts of hostility. In the Ugandan case, the anti-homosexuality surge, sustained by the local media and pushed by political and religious groups who sustained the so-called "Anti-Gay Bill",[4] led during the discussion of the law to a sort of witch-hunt that culminated in October 2010 with the publication of a list – with photos – of 100 alleged homosexuals on the first page of the newspaper "Rolling Stone", with the writing "Hang them!".[5] The public and media debate on homosexuality was accompanied by a growth of homophobia in the country and by acts of hostility and violence towards sexual minorities; the murder of an activist for sexual minorities rights – David Kato – in 2011 has been interpreted by some as a consequence of the stigmatisation and social tension created by media attention as well as political and religious campaigns during the discussion of the draft law (Ward 2013).

## Ugandan Pentecostals and the moral imagination: creating 'folk devils' to build shared identities

Let me now turn to the question of how a social reality, such as a sexual behaviour, can become a 'social problem' in a specific period. Here, I will not discuss the political motivations behind the decision to sustain the anti-homosexuality campaign; other works (Demange 2012; Sadgrove et al. 2012; Boyd 2013; Bompani & Valois 2017) have already stressed this aspect of the Ugandan case. Rather, my contribution to this debate focuses on the sociocultural mechanisms underlying the construction of such 'folk devils', with specific attention for the moral component involved in this process.

To start this discussion, I briefly analyse the concept of 'frame' as it was introduced by Erving Goffman (1974) and further elaborated by David Snow (Snow et al. 1986). According to these scholars, a frame is an interpretative structure that allows people to make sense of their everyday experience, for instance by locating an event within a setting that classifies it as a specific 'social problem', necessitating a political solution.

In the case under analysis, sexuality has been represented in Uganda as a moral as well as a social problem, one that needs to be confronted with a public campaign and political action. Here, Pentecostal theology, with its frequent reference to the presence of evil spirits acting in the physical world, facilitates the creation of a specific religious moral frame in which social problems are seen as the result of the satanic presence in the world; this frame pushes believers, especially in some more socially active congregations, to call for social and political mobilisation to contrast the danger and change the situation (Smilde 1998; Gusman 2013). In the widespread moral worldview among Ugandan Pentecostals, sexual 'immorality', identified especially in premarital sex and concurrent relationships (and thus with the spread of the AIDS epidemic), pornography and homosexuality, has to be seen as a field of political, as well as of spiritual, struggle.

From this perspective, the anti-homosexuality campaign takes on a different meaning; far from being an isolated action, it can be better analysed as part of a broader programme for the control of sexuality and the moralisation of social and public discourse in Uganda; a process that started with the abstinence campaign and continued with the anti-pornography and anti-homosexuality campaigns.[6] There is a continuity among these three cases, mainly found in the role Pentecostals played both in spreading these topics in the public sphere and in inscribing them in the Ugandan political agenda (Demange 2012).

On this basis, it seems possible to assert that during the last 15 years the Ugandan public sphere has been swamped by subsequent waves of 'moral panic' around sexuality and the perceived dangers connected to sexual immorality. In this period, some religious groups (mainly Pentecostal congregations) put sexuality at the centre of their ideology and action, and sustained programmes promoting the 'natural family' (heterosexual and monogamous) and the so-called 'AB' model (Abstain, Be faithful) for sexual relationships and AIDS prevention. These programmes have been instrumental in imposing control on people's behaviours, starting from the intimate sphere of sexual intercourse and expanding to other sectors of everyday private and public life.

In this process of the creation of 'folk devils' the role of institutions is double: on the one side, they are challenged by waves of moral panic and pushed to react to them; on the other side, they are "primary definers" (Hall et al. 1978) as institutional decisions and actions come to define the debate around supposed social enemies. It is interesting to note some of the characteristics that theorists of 'moral panics' assumed as common for this social phenomenon and that can be useful in analysing the Ugandan case. First of all, to make social mobilisation more sustainable, it is necessary to renew the panic, focusing it on different supposed emergencies. In Uganda, while maintaining a common frame based on the link morality-sexuality-salvation, we can observe at least three consecutive waves of moral panic around sexuality, focused respectively on premarital sex, the spread of pornography and homosexuality. Moreover, it has been observed that the longer the period of moral panic, the more social and political reactions are likely to include mechanisms of control and disciplining. Finally, these panics stimulate a cultural anger that can be used to invoke moral regulation, so that at the end moral panics "provoke new techniques for governing others or for governing the self in the effort to strengthen well-being and social rights" (Herdt 2009:2).

The Ugandan case fits well within the theoretical framework of moral panic: individuals and groups around whom panics are created are in fact seen as signs of a moral decay that needs to be stopped. Society itself is considered at risk of survival, due to this decay: significantly, homosexuality has been represented as a potential cause of social death, because it implies the impossibility of reproduction. More generally, those who do not conform to models of sexuality proposed by Pentecostals become targets for moral blame and are considered the mirror of a morally collapsed society, unable to reproduce itself.

To better understand how folk devils and moral panics are produced, we can start with a simple observation from my own fieldwork in Kampala: when I first arrived in Uganda, in 2005, the streets of the capital city were literally filled with three types of fliers. The first group showed images of famous Ugandan musicians, able to attract crowds of young people. The second group advertised Pentecostal 'crusades' held in stadiums or other public spaces. However, what attracted my attention the most was the third group: hundreds of fliers promoting sexual abstinence for unmarried people, mainly youth.

This marked the height of "Abstinence campaign",[7] promoted by the Office of the First Lady and current minister for Education and Sport, Janet Museveni. The campaign involved a number of Pentecostal congregations who actively promoted abstinence among young people, organised parades in town, travelled to schools to encourage students to sign 'abstinence cards', and other initiatives. These techniques mobilised young believers and created a feeling of shared identity around the "moral mission" of the Pentecostal movement in Kampala and in Uganda (Gusman 2013).

Billboards promoting abstinence gradually replaced those illustrating the use of condoms to avoid AIDS infection (Epstein 2007). The "ABC strategy" (Abstain, Be faithful, use Condoms) almost became 'AB' only, with a strong emphasis on abstinence and focus on youth. In the same period, several Pentecostal churches in town were developing a discourse in which the need to "save a generation" to use as a guide for the country became a central subject (Gusman 2009). The discourse particularly stressed the need for a morally righteous generation, one that could turn Uganda into a 'real Christian country' by avoiding 'dangerous' behaviour and respecting a strict moral code, including abstinence, prohibiting alcohol, smoking and wearing mini-skirts and other 'immoral' clothes. It is clear that the effort to control and discipline young people's bodies began before the proposal of laws against homosexuality and pornography. In 2004 sexuality – with a clear focus on youth sexuality – had begun to be described as a 'social problem'; according to some Pentecostal pastors, the country was in a very risky situation and, without a radical change in sexual behaviours, it could self-destruct. The sentiment is made clear from an excerpt from a Sunday service in a Pentecostal church: "We lost a generation; our fathers were killed by their immoral habits; do you want to be the next? Or you want to be remembered as the generation that brought a moral revolution in Uganda?".[8]

In this rhetoric the righteous Christian citizen is someone who is able to self-control, to act according to Pentecostal moral norms and to present himself as an accountable subject. The creation of physical enemies is an important step to make these ideas more effective and to push young believers to change their behaviours and accept severe moral norms. Gilbert Herdt (2009) underlines how very often moral panic crises are structured around individuals and groups represented as agents of moral decay, and as a sign that society is on a 'slippery slope' that can eventually result in its own destruction. In such situations, "moral imagination" is at work or the aptitude to evaluate one's actions by projecting them on future scenarios and considering their potential effects (Coeckelbergh 2007). Pentecostal community building, with its focus on the need to combat 'moral chaos' and prevent the moral destruction of the community can be read through this concept, based on the need to lift Uganda from a situation of moral decay (represented by the AIDS epidemic and the supposed spread of pornography and homosexuality) to build a 'saved' country.

In this context the Pentecostal focus on discontinuity, often expressed through the idea of the "break with the past" (Meyer 1998) acquires an interesting nuance: that of the urgency, for young believers, to act to build a new saved generation, safe from AIDS, with a strong moral fibre and therefore able to lead the country. This ideology of rupture has a strong attraction to young people, who see in it an opportunity to free themselves from a gerontocratic society and to reshape intergenerational models (Gusman 2012).

## The Ugandan Pentecostal movement 183

In search of new expressive modalities to represent social realities and try to transform them, young people in the African continent often turn to religion, and mainly to Pentecostalism and indigenous Islamic movements. Both groups put the idea of 'rebirth' at the centre of their discourses to emphasise the discontinuity with the past; and are composed of a large majority of young believers. Mamadou Diouf observed that these religious movements are able to attract masses in contemporary Africa "not only because they offer modes of being and belonging, but also because they construct new imaginations of the community and the individual" (Diouf 2003:7). This means that they are particularly effective in reconfiguring the idea itself of 'youth' – no more seen as a "lost generation" (Cruise O'Brien 1996) – but as a project in becoming. The temporal dimension of crisis, that of the day-to-day, is thus replaced by a projection of future changes in which young people will be directly involved. This project of 'becoming someone', both in generational and in individual terms, is expressed through ideologies and models that are pivotal in building a shared identity in a group that is charged with the task of transforming society. In this process, religion makes an important contribution in defining youth identity and at the same time faith itself acquires a youthful appearance (van Dijk et al. 2011).

Conversion to Pentecostalism requires young people embrace (at least nominally) a rigidly normative lifestyle with a severe morality whose precepts are constantly reaffirmed during church meetings and other weekly occasions. The 'rebirth' of becoming born-again is strongly associated to the capacity of the individual to adhere to moral models that have to permeate the everyday life of the believers, if they want to stay away from the spiritual and physical dangers and thus be saved and safe. Conversion and the baptism of the Holy Spirit are necessary to receive divine protection, but they need to be continuously reasserted through the believer's acts. In this discourse 'self-control' is a central concept as it indicates the need for the individual to engage directly with an act of personal will, to reinforce salvation received after conversion to Pentecostalism.

Going a step further we need to consider the interaction between this personal will to adhere to a moral model, and the control exercised by a community of peers, that can be very strict, especially in small and medium sized congregations (Sadgrove 2007). Members of the same 'cell group'[9] are often in charge of controlling each other to prevent potentially dangerous behaviour and ensure everyone follows the moral code of the congregation. During the weekly meetings of cell groups, members are often requested to express their difficulties in keeping promises of purity, abstinence and so on. Confession is a central part of faith for Pentecostals: the group of peers encourages those who admit their weaknesses, condemns faults and prays together with the 'sinner' to make him/her stronger.

The control of sexuality is at the core of this vision: though there is obviously a discrepancy between self-representation and actual practices of young Pentecostals, that can emerge if analysed outside the church context

(Burchardt 2011), the ideology of moral renewal insists on sexual purity and the need to follow the 'abstinence and fidelity' model. For this reason, the control of sexuality is taken away from adults, who have traditionally been in charge of it. For example, in Buganda paternal aunts, called *ssenga*, were charged with monitoring young girls' virginity and teaching them how to be good wives (Parikh 2005).

The ideological dimension of the rhetoric to change pre-existing arrangements and give the control of young people's sexuality to religious groups (for example with the "Abstinence Campaign") becomes clearer when considering it arose around 2003, when the incidence of the AIDS epidemic was at its lowest level in Uganda, having decreased from the peak of 18% at the beginning of the Nineties to around 6% (UNAIDS 2010). Blaming the adult generation for the 'moral decay' of the country and for the resulting spread of AIDS, and preaching the existence of a 'sexual emergency' was thus greatly the result of a representation given by religious and political groups that found an opportunity to gain public visibility.

The starting point for the creation of moral panic around sexuality and the danger of social collapse due to sexual behaviours, can thus be considered as an instrument used to justify a restrictive political and religious response, one that had the idea of 'self-control' at its heart. In the next section, the chapter will show that in the Pentecostal movement in Kampala the topic of self-control was not limited to the sexual sphere, but extended to other domains of the private and public life.

## Models of behaviour 'for' and 'of' young Pentecostals

As I have already mentioned, embracing the Pentecostal faith for many young people in Kampala means adopting models of extremely rigid and regulated behaviour: this implies limiting relationships with those who are not saved and avoiding places and ways of behaving that are considered immoral.

Some of the well-known bars and clubs in town are cited in pastors' sermons and church meetings as places of moral dissolution, and associated to 'devilish' behaviours such as alcohol and drug consumption, as well as promiscuity. The reference to the Devil is not a metaphorical one. In the Pentecostal worldview, only a powerful and evil being as Satan can create these dangerous places and the strong attraction they create on young people. While on one hand Pentecostals harshly condemn these places and those who frequent them, they simultaneously acknowledge their seductive force and the continuous struggle involved in resisting temptation. To resist seduction implies two requisites that are central to the definition of a 'true Christian' for Pentecostals: the ability of self-control and the construction of thick relationships with other born-again believers in order to support each other in the struggle against satanic forces. These social networks, usually established within the congregation, work both to support and to control the believer in his everyday life. The idea of developing self-control is central in building a 'Pentecostal identity' in Kampala. To be born-again means being able to resist temptation by following rigid moral models defined by the group in order to avoid places and behaviours considered dangerous for the spiritual and physical salvation of the believer.

To this aim, Pentecostal churches in Kampala often organise meetings for their members to pray, study, discuss or just socialise. These occasions reinforce sociality and solidarity among young believers. As a counterpart, this implies a moral and physical fracture among 'saved ones' and those who are not. Yet, this does not mean that Pentecostals consider the 'world' a place to avoid. Except in a few cases, Pentecostal churches do not preach isolation from the world, but rather direct action to shape it. For Robbins (2004) this is the Pentecostal two-sided "world-breaking" and "world-making". In this construction of moral imaginaries, models of consumption and concerning the body play an important role, too; distinguish themselves from the 'world' is in fact not a matter of abstract moral rules, but needs to be showed in how one behaves, wears and spends his money.

Before analysing such models, it is interesting to observe that these ideologies 'for' youth are often also ideologies 'of' youth (Van Dijk et al. 2011). On the one hand, young people are the targets and end-users of ideologies, they are shaped and limited by them in their ways of behaving. On the other hand, they are not passive subjects in these processes, but actors who have acquired ideological force and learned how to use it to achieve their goals. Through the rhetoric of the break with a sinful past, of the moral fracture with the world, and of the socio-moral renewal of Uganda, the Pentecostal movement defines models that are not only thought 'for' young people, but also 'through' them. They present themselves as the generation in charge of building a new society. In this self-definition of a 'new generation' to be central is not the age *per se*, but rather the vision of a different future (Stroeken 2008). Instead of considering themselves an 'engendered generation' or passive voice in a gerontocratic society, young Pentecostals in Kampala try to become a 'generating generation', one that is not only subjected to models, but also creates them.

## Body, consumption and self-control

The individual body is central to defining a model of the 'true Christian' with purity and integrity as the two main elements of the young Pentecostal's body. Personal and social bodies are conceived as arenas for the struggle between good and evil. Satanic forces try to possess the believers' body, to submit it. On the other side, according to Pentecostals the baptism of the Holy Spirit – the sign of conversion – washes away sins and corruption and protects the individual against evil attacks. Within this view, only by trusting in Jesus Christ as a personal saviour can the believer be reborn to a new life and transcend an imperfect human nature (Englund 2007). It is thus faith and divine help that make the Christian able to self-control and resist temptations.

Yet, the presence of the Holy Spirit does not guarantee salvation. Faith has to be continuously renewed, and without this effort the believer is at risk to lose Christ's protection. Being born-again is a necessary condition for salvation, but it is not sufficient. Following the ideology of the rational and accountable subject, Pentecostals underline the fact that self-control also requires an individual act of will. The final responsibility for one's own behaviour is thus on the individual himself. According to young Pentecostals in Kampala the 'true Christian' is someone who is able to exercise self-control in all the important aspects of life. In Pentecostal discourse the creation of a 'new generation', that will transform Uganda from an 'immoral' to a Christian country, needs both the protection of Jesus Christ against evil forces and the direct involvement and action of believers, who voluntary choose to adhere to religious models.

Thus, Pentecostal churches present themselves as the true successors of traditional mechanisms of social control, taking on the role that was in the past attributed to village elders. Significantly, many Pentecostal congregations in Kampala have a weekly meeting for 'gender education' with separate classes for males and females. At the core of these teachings are – once again – models of behaviour concerning sexuality, the body and consumption. In the urban context, where mass consumption is quickly growing churches propose models of consumption for young people. Here self-control is also central, as the ability not to be seduced by 'immoral goods' (cigarettes, alcohol, ostentatious clothes, etc.) or spend money on unnecessary goods instead of saving it for the family and church.

The general attitude towards wealth, money and goods is ambiguous. At the same time goods are desired and feared as instruments Satan uses to corrupt people (van Dijk 1999). For this reason, Pentecostal churches in Kampala often try to propose good models of consumption for believers. A young man or woman needs to learn how to dress, adorn the body, what to buy and how much to spend on these goods.

The model of consumption churches propose in most cases is modest. In male classes I often heard discussion about how to be elegant but avoid luxury, while in female classes girls are taught to be "attractive but not obscene". This was stressed during one of the meetings of the *Deborah group* I attended at *Makerere Community Church* (now called *One Love Church*). While there is recognition that one's appearance has a role in different aspects of social life (finding a partner, obtaining a job, etc.) the search for elegance and a smart look should not deviate from the moral models of 'decency' proposed by Pentecostals.

Another common topic during these meetings was that money is a necessary aspect of projects for the future and not just living day by day. For example, during a cell meeting at *Makerere Full Gospel Church* a young pastor better illustrates this point:

> All the members of this group need to have a bank account. If you still don't have one, then open it as soon as possible. You should not use

money as your fathers did. They spent everything, to the last shilling, in bars; they went out to drink every night, and then sometimes came back home drunk and beat you. Or they used it for their lovers, to buy them gifts. And what did they save for you? Nothing, not even the money for their funerals. This was the "traditional" way of living: I want you to leave all these African ideas that stop you from having success, that make us see things in a wrong way, a non Christian way.[10]

Although the most frequent blame goes to the previous generation's inability to develop Uganda and make it a saved Christian country, it is not infrequent to also hear jokes and critics of other social groups, especially non-saved young people, who do not follow Pentecostal models.

Similar arguments are used to propose models for businesses, to assert they can only develop and prosper if run in a Christian way. *Mutundwe Christian Fellowship* is a well-known centre of deliverance in Kampala. Each day hundreds of people from various parts of town and the country reach this small and dusty suburb of the capital city to pray at pastor Tom Mugerwa's church to solve their daily problems concerning love affairs, business, studies, health, and so on. Delivering from the 'spirit of poverty' and from the 'spirit of failure' is one of the centre's specialisations and daily teachings focus on economy and theft. The basic principle behind this teaching, as pastor Roland Kabuye described during a prayer session, is that "if you have a business, and you rob people, then it is not going to prosper. Many people come here arguing because their business is not succeeding; this is because anything that it is not done in God's way, it will be destroyed".

The lesson continued with several examples and testimonies: a butcher who was cheating the weight of meat; an employee who was stealing pens and other objects from office to sell them; a salesperson who was selling clothes at a higher price. Concluding with

> sometimes you get employed but you are not transparent in your job; you'll end up being chased away. Many people here in Kampala, and even in this church, want to have electricity in their homes, but they don't want to pay for it, and they steal it. But when you act in this way, God is not going to listen to your prayers, and your home will not be blessed.[11]

## Conclusion

In this chapter, I have shown that the models of behaviour proposed by Pentecostalism have a strong attractive especially for Ugandan youth who are in search of fixed landmarks amidst the condition of social and ontological insecurity that is common in much of the African continent. In the face of this situation, Pentecostalism has been able to produce a discourse in which spiritual and physical dangers and the need of redemption to save both the individuals and the nation are central. Through this rhetoric, the public space becomes an arena of struggle against forces of corruption, and specific groups and/or ways of behaving are constructed as 'folk devils', dangerous for the integrity of the social body. The anti-homosexual campaign is a clear example of how these systems of social control work. Against the irruption and the potential disruptive action of these supposed chaotic forces, the Pentecostal movement in Uganda has been at the forefront in proposing prescriptive moral regimes, with strict behavioural codes that all born-agains are supposed to follow; these regimes are aimed at producing a form of redemptive citizenship, based on the idea of the moral subject and responsible individual.

Through the refusal of aesthetic, consumption and business models of their fathers' generation and of non-converted youth, Pentecostals present themselves as 'ethical subjects', able to withstand physical and material affliction. Pentecostalism can thus be seen as a "prescriptive regime" (Marshall 2009) that works to shape individual subjectivity, and born-again politics as one that focuses mainly on the moral fashioning of the individual (Boyd 2015). It is thus possible to conclude that in this vision, the failure of a business, not too differently from the fact of being HIV positive or other situations, are mainly explained as the 'moral failures' of an individual who has been unable to follow God's way and Pentecostal models. While structural conditions and global dynamics are not completely out of the picture and are sometimes cited as direct causes, are considered secondary when compared to the centrality of conversion (that is, God's protection) and individual will.

## Notes

1 Within the Pentecostal movement in Kampala the terms 'born-again', 'Pentecostal', 'savedee' and '*mulokole*' (which means "the saved one" in *luganda*, with reference to the East African Revival) are used indifferently as synonyms; for this reason in this chapter I use with no distinction both Pentecostal and born-again.
2 Yvan Droz (2015) has shown that, in the problematic phase of the "coming-to-age", Pentecostalism proposes to young Africans an ethos that at the same time preserves some traditional elements and offers alternative representations of masculinity and femininity and of what a 'real man' and a 'real woman' should be.
3 It is important to stress the role of media in the construction of this securitarian discourse, of which the creation of folk devils is only an aspect. See Bompani and Brown (2015).
4 Proposed by the born-again parliamentarian David Bahati already in 2009, the "Uganda Anti-Homosexuality Act" (also known as "Anth-Gay Bill") was passed by the Ugandan Parliament after long national and international debates and oppositions in December 2013, and signed into law by the President Yoweri Museveni in February 2014. On 1 August 2014 the Constitutional Court of Uganda declared the Act invalid because of procedural failures.
5 Following this episode, the High Court stated the suspension of the publication of the "Rolling Stone".
6 The "abstinence campaign" was one of the main focuses for Pentecostal churches between 2004 and 2010 and one of the main factors of visibility for the movement. It was based on the opposition to condoms as a prevention method for

HIV/AIDS and on the promotion of 'moral values' (abstinence and the exclusive monogamous heterosexual marriage) in the fight against the epidemic. The campaign was supported directly by the Office of the First Lady, Janet Museveni, a declared born-again Christian, and had among its main promoters evangelical organisations such as "True Love Waits", "Family Life Network" and the "Campus Alliance to Wipe Out AIDS". For a detailed analysis of this campaign and its consequences, see Boyd (2015).

Similarly, these and other Pentecostal groups have been vocal in condemning the diffusion of 'pornography' in Uganda as a sign of the moral dissolution in the country. The Anti-Pornography Act, signed in February 2014, is officially aimed at reducing sexual violence; yet, it explicitly contains references to forms of control to individual freedom, especially in the field of clothing, as it condemns mini-skirts and other clothes defined as 'obscene'. For this reason the Act was popularised as the "mini-skirt law".

7 For a detailed analysis of this campaign and its consequences, see Boyd (2015).
8 Ps. Martin Ssempa, Makerere Community Church, Kampala, 20 August 2006.
9 'Cells' are small groups of 10 to 15 members of the same congregation who have a weekly meeting – usually at one of the members' place – to pray together, discuss individual problems, sustain each other and sometimes share a meal.
10 Ps. Sam Muyinda, *Makerere Full Gospel Church*, Kampala, 10 January 2008.
11 Ps. Roland Kabuye, *Mutundwe Christian Fellowship*, Kampala, 11 October 2013.

## References

Bompani, B. & S. T. Brown 2015. 'A "Religious Revolution?" Print Media, Sexuality, and Religious Discourse in Uganda'. *Journal of Eastern African Studies*, 9(1): 110–126.

Bompani, B. & Valois, C. 2017. 'Sexualizing Politics: The Anti-Homosexuality Bill, Party-Politics and the New Political Dispensation in Uganda'. *Critical African Studies*, 9(1): 52–70.

Boyd, L. 2013. 'The Problem With Freedom: Homosexuality and Human Rights in Uganda'. *Anthropological Quarterly*, 86(3): 697–724.

Boyd, L. 2015. *Preaching Prevention: Born-Again Christianity and the Moral Politics of AIDS in Uganda*. Ohio: Ohio University Press.

Burchardt, M. 2011. 'Challenging Pentecostal Moralism: Erotic Geographies, Religion and Sexual Practices Among Township Youth in Cape Town'. *Culture, Health & Sexuality*, 13(6): 669–683.

Cheney, K. 2012. 'Locating Neocolonialism, "Tradition", and Human Rights in Uganda's "Gay Death Penalty"'. *Africa Studies Review*, 55(2): 77–95.

Christiansen, C., Utas, M. & Vigh, H. 2006. *Navigating Youth, Generating Adulthood*. Uppsala: Nordiska Afrikainstitutet.

Coeckelbergh, M. 2007. *Imagination and Principles: An Essay on the Role of Imagination in Moral Reasoning*. Basingstoke: Palgrave Macmillan.

Cohen, S. 1972. *Folk Devils and Moral Panics*. London, New York: Routledge.

Cruise O'Brien, D. B. 1996. 'A Lost Generation? Youth Identity and State Decay in West Africa'. In R. Werbner & T. Ranger (Eds.) *Postcolonial Identities*. London: Zed Books: 55–74.

Daswani, G. 2013. 'On Christianity and Ethics: Rupture as Ethical Practice in Ghanaian Pentecostalism'. *American Ethnologist*, 40(3): 467–479.

Demange, É. 2012. 'De l'abstinence à l'homophobie : la " moralisation " de la société ougandaise, une ressource politique entre Ouganda et États-Unis'. *Politique Africaine*, 126: 25–47.

Diouf, M. 2003. 'Engaging Postcolonial Cultures: African Youth and Public Space'. *African Studies Review*, 46(2): 1–12.
Droz, Y. 2015. 'Jeunesse et âge adulte en pays Kikuyu: Des éthos précoloniaux aux nouveaux mouvements politico-religieux'. *Cahiers d'études Africaines*, 218: 213–230.
Englund, H. 2007. 'Pentecostalism Beyond Belief: Trust and Democracy in a Malawian Township'. *Africa*, 77(4): 477–499.
Epstein, H. 2007. *The Invisible Cure: Africa, the West and the Fight Against AIDS*. New York: Farrar, Straus and Giroux.
Goffman, E. 1974. *Frame Analysis*. Cambridge, MA: Harvard University Press.
Gusman, A. 2009. 'HIV/AIDS, Pentecostal Churches, and the "Joseph Generation" in Uganda'. *Africa Today*, 56(1): 66–86.
Gusman, A. 2012. 'Pentecôtisme ougandais entre individualisme et la formation de la 'new generation'. In M. N. Leblanc & M. Gomez-Perez (Eds.) *L'Afrique des générations : Entre tensions et négociations*. Paris: Karthala: 469–493.
Gusman, A. 2013. 'The Abstinence Campaign and the Construction of the Balokole Identity in the Ugandan Pentecostal Movement'. *Canadian Journal of African Studies*, 47(2): 273–292.
Hall, S., Critcher, C., Jefferson, T., Clarke, J., and Roberts, B. 1978. *Policing the Crisis: Mugging, the State, and Law and Order*. London: Macmillan.
Haram, L. & Yamba, C. 2009. *Dealing With Uncertainty in Contemporary African Lives*. Uppsala: Nordiska Afrikainstitutet.
Herdt, G. 2009. *Moral Panics, Sex Panics: Fear and the Fight Over Sexual Rights*. New York, London: New York University Press.
Marshall, R. 2009. *Political Spiritualities: The Pentecostal Revolution in Nigeria*. Chicago: University of Chicago Press.
Meyer, B. 1998. '"Make a Complete Break With the Past": Memory and Post-Colonial Modernity in Ghanaian Pentecostalist Discourse'. *Journal of Religion in Africa*, 28(3): 316–349.
Nyanzi, S. 2013. 'Dismantling Reified African Culture Through Localised Homosexualities in Uganda'. *Culture, Health & Sexuality*, 15(8): 952–967.
Parikh, S. 2005. 'From Auntie to Disco: The Bifurcation of Risk and Pleasure in Sex Education in Uganda'. In V. Adams & S. L. Pigg (Eds.) *Sex in Development: Science, Sex and Morality in Global Perspective*. London: Duke University Press: 125–158.
Robbins, J. 2004. 'The Globalization of Pentecostal and Charismatic Christianity'. *Annual Review of Anthropology*, 33: 117–143.
Sadgrove, J. 2007. '"Keeping Up Appearances": Sex and Religion Amongst University Students in Uganda'. *Journal of Religion in Africa*, 37(1): 116–144.
Sadgrove, J., Vanderbeck, R., Andersson, J., Valentine, G. & Ward, K. 2012. 'Morality Plays and Money Matters: Towards a Situated Understanding of the Politics of Homosexuality in Uganda'. *The Journal of Modern African Studies*, 50(1): 103–129.
Smilde, D. 1998. '"Letting God Govern": Supernatural Agency in the Venezuelan Pentecostal Approach to Social Change'. *Sociology of Religion*, 59(3): 287–303.
Snow, D., Rochford, E., Worden, S. & Benford, R. 1986. 'Frame Alignment Processes, Micromobilization, and Movement Participation'. *American Sociological Review*, 51(4): 464–481.
Stroeken, K. 2008. 'Tanzania's "New Generation": The Power and Tragedy of a Concept'. In S. R. Whyte, E. Alber & S. van der Geest (Eds.) *Generations in Africa: Connections and Conflicts*. Lit Verlag: Berlin: 289–309.

UNAIDS. 2010. 'Report on the Global AIDS Epidemic'. Available at: www.unaids.org/globalreport/documents/20101123_GlobalReport_full_en.pdf
Van Dijk, R. 1999. The Pentecostal gift. Ghanaian carismatic churches and the moral innocence of the global economy. In Fardon, R., Van Binsbergen, WM., and R. van Dijk (Eds). *Modernity on a shoestring: dimensions of globalization, consumption and development in Africa and beyond.* Leiden: Eidos: 71–89.
Van Dijk, R., de Brujin, M., Cardoso, C. & Butter, I. 2011. 'Introduction: Ideologies of Youth'. *Africa Development*, 36(3/4): 1–17.
Van Klinken, A. 2016. 'Pentecostalism, Political Masculinity and Citizenship: The Born-Again Male Subject as Key to Zambia's National Redemption'. *Journal of Religion in Africa*, 46(2–3): 129–157.
Ward, K. 2013. 'Religious Institutions and Actors and Religious Attitudes to Homosexual Rights: South Africa and Uganda'. In C. Lennox & M. Waites (Eds.) *Human Rights, Sexual Orientations and Gender Identity in the Commonwealth: Struggles for Decriminalisation and Change.* Human Rights Consortium, Institute of Commonwealth Studies, University of London: 409–428.

# Index

Page numbers in *italic* indicate a figure.

Abacha, Sani (death) 38
absolute sovereignty, quest 110
Absolute Value Fellowship 128
Abstain, Be faithful (AB) model 180–182
Abstain, Be faithful, use Condoms (ABC) strategy 182
abstinence 180–184, 188
Acamai Global Workplace Fellowship and Destiny Consult 29
*Accra Charter of Religious Freedom and Citizenship* 90, 91
accumulation 37, 99–101, 109, 126–127
Acheampong Supreme Military Council, replacement 50–51
action, importance 8
activism, morality (South Africa) 169–172
actors, emergence 22
Addo, Nana Akuffo 55, 57
Adeboye, Enoch 38, 42, 87
Adekunle, Julius 39
Afraha prayers, narratives 157–158
Africa: change, vector 35–36; Pentecostal resurgence 46; public life, corruption 95–96; societies, sexual citizenship (longue durée) 133
African Christian Democratic Party 168–169
African Independent Churches (AICs) 4, 35–36, 151; role 50
African National Congress (ANC) 134; ATR treatment 166
African Pentecostal-charismatic discourses 83
*African Postcolonial Modernity* (Osha) 22
'African Rising' narrative, focus 35
African State, moral regeneration 1

African Traditional Religion (ATR) representatives, exclusion 166
Aggrey, Gilbert Abeiku 58, 59
"aid for trade" agenda 128
AIDS: epidemic, incidence/level 184; infection (avoidance), condoms (usage) 182; safety 182
Akuffo, Nana 60
*Aladura* churches 38
All Progressives Congress (APC) 43
Amin, Idi 25
Amoako, Salifu 52, 54
ancestor worship/ritual 166
Anderson, Allan 6
Anglican missions 152
"Anti-Gay Bill" 179, 188
Anti-Homosexuality Bill: formulation 2; introduction 23
anti-homosexuality campaign 180
Anti-Pornography Act 189
apartheid 169
Apostleship 52
Aprako, Emmanuel Kwaku 51, 57
arap Moi, Daniel 153, 155
arap Sang, Joshua 156
Armed Forces Revolutionary Council (AFRC) 58–59
Asamoah-Gyadu, J. Kwabena 7, 13–14, 83
Asante, Emmanuel 53
Ashimolowo, Matthew 87
Aslan, Reza 153
Assemblies of God, Pentecostal church representation 83–84
Asuza Street revival (1906) 163
Atheist Society of Kenya, registration 150
axial religion, community perspective 165

## Index

Babangida, Ibrahim 37
Babirye, Judith 103
backslider, recognition 170
Bahati, David 188
Bakare, Tunde 39–41, 46
Bamugemereire, George 29
Baptist 115
Basic Income Grant 167
Bell, David 133
Bempah, Isaac Owusu 52, 54–55, 59, 60; Ghana Police Service interrogation 55
Benishangual region 122
*Beyond the Rivers of Ethiopia* (Otabil) 87
"biblical perspectives" 88
Binnie, Jon 133
Bompani, Barbara 1, 2, 12
Bonnke, Reinhard 139
born again 6
born-again conversion 171
"born-again experience" 91
"born-again" governance roadmap 41–42
born-agains, impact 28
Brouwer, Steve 94
Buhari, Muhammadu 41, 43
Burchardt, Marian 15, 163
Buturo, James Nsaba 31

Cape Town: corruption 171; "Great Commission" 168
Caritas Zambia 72–73
Carter, Jimmy 38
Catholic Bishops Conference 50, 58
Catholic Church, activism 73
Catholic Justice and Peace Commission (CJPC) 67
CCCM Businessmen Fellowship 128
charismatic, label (refusal) 5
Charismatic Christian Church (Accra) 51
charismatic Christianity (Ghana) 50–51
Charismatic Prophets, self-perception 53
charismatic styled prayer crusades 54
Chiluba, Frederick J.T. 70; Christianity 134; Christian nationalism 139–141
China, collaboration 72
Chisambisha, Francis 142–143
Christian Association of Nigeria (CAN) 38, 45
Christian Churches Monitoring Group (CCMG), formation 73
Christian citizens: becoming 26–30, 177–178; citizenship, conception 7–11; examination 1; formation, Catholic approaches (Zambia) 71–73
Christian citizenship: alternative forms, promotion 69–70; concept 8–9; conceptualisation 63; designation 67; making (Zambia) 70–71; performative dimension 8; visions, divergence 13
Christian Council of Ghana 50, 58
Christian Council of Zambia (CCZ) 139–140
Christian faith, ancestors 92
Christian fundamentalism 94–95
Christian goal 74
Christianity: citizenship, relationship 8; discursive Christianity 153–155; Kenya 149; Pentecostalised discourse, evolution 14; politics, relationship (Zambia) 70–71; types 154; Uganda 22–25
Christian laws, basis 151
Christian morality 135
Christian nation, sexual citizenship 141–144
Christian nationalism 133, 134, 139–144
Christian Orthodox Church, devotion 117
Christian public activism 22
churches: idea, description 172; sermons, teaching opportunities 100; structure/organisation (Uganda) 104–105; work, coordination 127
Church His People 175
Church Missionary Society (CMS) 152
Church of Scotland Mission (CSM) 152
citizens, offensiveness 26
citizenship: bifurcated system, colonial legacy (impact) 10–11; Christianity, relationship 8; constitution 63; construction 65–70; convergence 8–9; dual citizenship 11; features 10; kingdom/responsibility, relationship 90–93; moral 44–45; notions 84; PCC role 99–100; Pentecostal-charismatic narratives (Uganda) 21; Pentecostal-charismatic property discourses, relationship 94–96; Pentecostalism, relationship 84–85; redemptive citizenship 177; responsible citizenship, African Pentecostal-charismatic discourses 83; rights-based notion 10–11; types, arrangements 102; vision 44; *see also* developmental citizenship; sexual citizenship

Citizenship Development Research Center (C-DRC) 63
City of Refugee Church 127
civic identity, alternative 115–116
civil conflict 69
Coalition for Unity and Democracy (CUD) 124
Cold War, cessation 65
Colijn, Brenda 93
collective action, strategy 28
collective bodies, impact 66
collective religious institutions, role 67–68
colonial legacy, impact 10–11
Comaroff, Jean and John 29, 64, 76
community cooperation, norms 66
"Comprehensive Sexual Education Curriculum," change 23–24
Congress of Progressive Change 40
Congress of Traditional Leaders (Contralesa) 165
"conquerors" 170
Convention People Party (CPP) 50
conversion 188; born-again conversion 171; born-again programme 144–145; competition 36–37; concern 46; experience (Mulenga) 145; individual conversion 125–126, 177; Pentecostal conversion 36, 125–126; personal conversion 44; political approach (Nigeria) 9; process, usage 6, 8, 22; rebirth, usage 7; religious conversion 173; religious conversion, sources 35–36; rituals 174; sudden experience 170
Corinthians, book 52
Corruption Perception Index 167–168
Council of Churches in Zambia (CCZ) 73–74
Covenant Nation Church (CNC) 24, 26
'Cultural Revolution' (call) 137–138
cultural values, invasion (Zambia) 138

Deacon, Gregory 14, 32, 149
*Deborah group* meetings 186
democratic backsliding 70–71
democratisation (sub-Saharan Africa) 50–51, 65–70, 76–77
*Derg* military regime 119
*Derg* persecutions 125
*Derg* time 120–121
Destiny Consult, impact 29–30
developmental citizenship (Ethiopia) 115
developmental journalism 116
developmental patrimonialism, impact 128

developmental state, Pentecostals (relationship) 125–129
Development Associates 29
devil, impact 27
dialectics 6
diffusive Christianity 154
discretionary support 140–141
discursive Christianity 153–155; analysis 154; form, heightening 154
divine mandate 53
Divine will, manifestations 6
dog-whistle politics 150
dominion, Pentecostalism worldview 86–90
*Dominion Mandate, The* (Otabil) 87
dual citizenship, defining 11

earthly good 83
earthly use, heavenly citizenship (translation) 93–94
East Asia, developmental success 116
economic citizenship 101–103; forging 99; importance 13–14; Watoto transformative model 102–103
economic success, promise 126
economies 13–14
elections 12–13; prophecies, upsurge (Ghana) 53–56; prophecies (Ghana) 49
Enim, Emmanuel Kofi 57
entrepreneurial spirit 99
'Episcopal Conferences' 66
epistle of John 85
ethics, Pentecostal citizenship (South Africa) 167–169
Ethiopia: developmental citizenship 115–119; Pentecostal population, density 122; Pentecostals 115; religion 116–119; renewed Pentecostal citizens, call 119–122; shining Ethiopia, image 115
Ethiopian Christian Graduates Fellowship 120
Ethiopian Evangelical Church Mekane Yesus 124
Ethiopian Federal Constitution, ethnicity institutionalisation 117
Ethiopian Islamic Affairs Supreme Council 118
Ethiopian Orthodox Church (EOC) 115, 123
Ethiopian People Revolutionary Democratic Front (EPRDF) 117–119; aims 127–128; growth/ transformation discourse 121; official discourse 121; struggle 124

ethnic federalism (Ethiopia) 122–125
Evangelical Churches Fellowship of Ethiopia (ECFE) 120, 125
Evangelical fellowship, challenges (Zambia) 75–76
Evangelical Fellowship of Zambia (EFZ) 75, 139–140, 145
Evangelical Student Union of Ethiopia (EVASU) 120
evangelism 35–36
evil powers, fight 28
*Ewuarde Kasa* (God Will Speak) 60
"exchange of wives" 137
Exodus Apostolic Reformation Church 126

Fabian socialism 135
faith-based institutions 63, 66–67
faith-based NGOs, services 101–102
faith-based organisations (FBOs) 32, 119; social dependency/political legitimisation 102
Family Policy Institute 169, 175
Fantini, Emanuele 115
FESTAC '77 37
"Festival of Ideas" 88
financial integrity (Watoto Church, Uganda) 99
"folk devils" 179; creation 179–184
foreign influences, threat 142
*Four Laws of Productivity* (Otabil) 87
Fourth Republic 67; Nigeria 38, 42, 45
Freeman, Dena 126
Fresh Democratic Party (FDP) 40–41
functional Christianity 154

Gambella region 122
Ghana: charismatic Christianity 50–51; election prophecies 49; election prophecies, upsurge 53–56; mainline churches, perception 53; mainline denominations, impact 53; multiparty politics, return (1992) 49–50; neo-Pentecostal-charismatic Christianity, evolution 52; Police Service, Bempah interrogation 55; political stability 49; political stability, implications 56–57; politics, sacralisation 53–56; population census 51–52; prophetic ministry, salience 51–53; stolen verdict, publication 55
Ghana Pentecostal and Charismatic Churches Council (GPCC) 58
Gifford, Paul 87

Girma, Johannes 126
Global North: decline 23; politics, religions (impact) 15
Global South: charismatic/PC Christians, presence 5–6; politics, religions (impact) 15
Glorious Word Power International Ministries 54–55
Glorious Word Power Ministries 52, 57
God: fidelity 6; inscrutable will 44–45; intentions, reassertion 90–91; kingdom, coming 92–93; national devotion 69–70; power, manifestation 38; relationship 127; revelation 93–94
*God of Israel* (narrative) 52
God the Father, Armed Forces representation 51
Goffman, Erving 180
Gordon, David 135, 138
gospel of John 85
Grand Imperial Hotel, congregation exit 103
"Great Commission" (Cape Town) 168
Growth and Transformation Plan 121
GTP 128
Guatemala, Pentecostal-charismatic churches (prayer) 8
Gusman, Alessandro 2, 177

'hate' speech 158–159
heavenly citizenship, translation 93–94
heavenly commonwealth 83
historical transformation, mode 7
HIV/AIDS 32, 172, 189
"holistic ministry" 126–127
Holy Ghost Congress 42
Holy Ghost Service 42–43
Holy Spirit: active engagement 94–95; baptism 185; gifts 5, 65; impact 28–29; power 84, 170; presence 84, 186
*Holy Spirit*: gifts 55–56; interventions 52
homosexuality: public debates 142, 144; public expression, argument 143
Household of God Church 40–41
humanism (Kaunda) 134–135, 139–141
*Humanism in Zambia and a Guide to its Implementation* (Gordon) 135
*Humanist in Africa, A* (Gordon) 135
human rights-oriented social movements 164

Icamagu Heritage Institute 166
"ideological shock troops" 151
Imakando, Joseph 141
immorality: defeat, conversion (usage) 22; hymns, impact 136; *see also* sexual immorality
immoral public attitudes, supervision 31
Independent Churches of Zambia (ICOZ) 76
independent media, impact 116
individual, remaking 125–126
individual conversion 125–126, 177
Information and Communication Technology (ICT) services 31
Inspector General of Government (IGG) designate 29
institutional Christianity 154
intellectual Christianity 154
Intercessors for Uganda 29
International Central Gospel Church (ICGC) 57, 59, 85–86; Christian community, audience 92
International Criminal Court (ICC) 156
International Monetary Fund (IMF), Structural Adjustment Programme 37
Internet 31, 86
Iranian Revolution (1976) 37
Islam 4, 136, 160; blessing 158; clerics, spiritualist involvement 59; community, nonviolent protests 118; demonisation, rhetoric 42; marginalized, identity (correspondence) 155; movements, attraction 183; presence 115; Satanic religion, Nigerian Pentecostal perspective 47

Jacobsen, Douglas 35
James, D. Willis 96
John Templeton Foundation 46
Jonathan, Goodluck 41–43, 46
Joseph Generation 107
Joshua, T.B. 54, 59, 60
Jubilee alliance party (JAP) 155, 157
Jubilee Christianity, triumph 155–159
Judeo-Christian scriptures, inspiration 40
Justice and Peace Teams (JPTs): goal/formation 72; training materials 73
Justice Party 40–41

Kabalika, Eugene 72
Kabuye, Roland 187, 189
Kagina, Allen 29

Kale Heywet Church 115
Kampala: churches, analysis 12; Pentecostal identity 185; Pentecostal movement, moral mission 181
Kampala Pentecostal Church (KPC) 24, 103
Kapwepwe, Simon 137
Kaunda, Kenneth 134–135; Humanism 134, 139–141; 'Watershed speech' 137
Kenya: Catholic Justice and Peace Commission (CJPC) 67; Christian country, declaration 150–153; Christianity 149; Christianity, placement 152; citizens/traitors/Christianity 149; election, problems (2007–2008) 156; general election (2013), results 156–157; "God fearing nation" 150–151; poverty 155; "social involvement" 151–152; status quo 155–156
Kenya Television Network (KTN) 150, 160
Kenyatta, Uhuru 150, 157
Khayelitsha 164, 169, 171
Kibaki, Mwai 153
Ki-moon, Ban 143
"King Agag" 39
kingdom, citizenship/responsibility (relationship) 90–93
King Jesus Evangelistic Flames Ministry 51
Kingsway International Christian Center 87
Kisaka, Dorothy 29
Kiviet, Noxolo 166
Kobi, Emmanuel Badu 52
Kosgey, Henry 157
KwaZulu Natal 167

Latter Rain Assembly 39
Lenshina, Alice 135
lesbian, gay, bisexual, transgender and intersex (LGBTI) communities: focus 9; healthcare, secular NGO provision 23–24
lesbian, gay, bisexual, transgender and intersex (LGBTI) Ugandans 110–111
Lesbian, Gays, Bisexual and Transgender Persons Association (LEGATRA) 142–143
LGBT human rights, public advocacy 143
LGBTI people, re-integration 32

# Index

LGBTIQ communities (Uganda), punishment 23
Life Line Ministries 24
*Living Hope* (launch) 104
*Living Word* ministry, following 86
Lokodo, Simon 23
*luganda* 188
Lumpa Church 135
Lungu, Edgar 143
Lutheran Evangelical Church (Mekane Yesus) 115

mainline churches, perception 53
mainline Protestant influences 73–74
Makerere Community Church 186
Makerere Full Gospel Church 186–187
Mamdani, Mahmood 10
Mandela, Nelson 38, 166
"Marriage Alliance" 169
Marriage and Divorce Bill, campaign 23
Marshall, Ruth 177
Masupa, David 76
Matale, Susan 73–74
Mau Mau insurgency 152
Mazrui, Alamin 151, 155
Mekane Yesus (Lutheran Evangelical Church) 115, 120
*Meserete Kristos* 124–125
meso-level, influences 68
meso-level religious collective religious institutions, influence 68
Methodist Church 50, 53
Meyer, Birgit 6, 167
middle income country, status 118
Mills, Atta 54, 59
mini-skirt ban 23, 25
"mini-skirt law" 189
miracle-based approach 125
Miracle Centre Cathedral (MCC) 24
"Miracle City" 43
missions 151–152
Mndende, Nokuzola 166
modernity 163–164, 173–174
moral agents, perception 28
moral citizen, production (Ugandan Pentecostal movement) 177
moral decay: agents 182; blame 184
moral imagination, Ugandan Pentecostals (relationship) 179–184
morality: activism (South Africa) 169–172; regeneration 14–15
morally framed public policies, Catholic/Anglican Church promotion 25
moral models, impact 177

moral personhood, sexual morality (importance) 171–172
moral purity, basis 94
moral purity (Zambia), threat 138
moral regeneration, Pentecostal call 116
moral/spiritual lives 136
mother bodies (Zambia) 70–71
motivational speakers 87–88
Movement for Multiparty Democracy (MMD) 70–71, 139, 143
multiparty politics, return (1992) 49–50
*Mulu Wengel* Church 124–125; Pentecostal movement 120–122
*Mulu Wongel* (Ethiopian Pentecostal church) 115
Museveni, Janet 23–26, 29, 32, 181, 188, 189
Museveni, Patience Rwabogo 24, 26, 99
Museveni, Yoweri 188
Muslim religions, perception 155
Mutati, Felix 143
*Mutundwe Christian Fellowship* 187
Mwanza, Pukuta 75–76

Nagel Institute for the Study of World Christianity project 46
National Association of Charismatic Churches and Christian Churces (NACCC) 58
national belonging (Uganda) 21
National Council of the Churches of Kenya (NCCK) 67
National Democratic Congress (NDC) 54–55; revelations, impact 56–57
National Electoral Commission, mistrust 50, 56
nationalism 134
National Mass Communication Policy (1990) 37
National Peace Council 50, 53
National Prophetic and Apostolic Churches Council (NPACC) 52, 54
National Religious Leaders Forums (NRLF), creation 166
National Resistance Movement (NRM), rhetoric 21
national transformation (Watoto Church, Uganda) 99
nationhood 12–13
Ndijo, Basile 133, 136–137
Negussie, Fitsum 121
neoliberal solutions 69
neo-Pentecostal-charismatic Christianity (Ghana), evolution 52

neo-Pentecostal-charismatic denomination, prophetic ministry (salience) 51–53
New Patriotic Party (NPP) 55; opposition 54
Nigeria: born-again movements, evolution 36–37; Fourth Republic 38, 42, 45; Jonathan, accident/miracle 41–42; National Mass Communication Policy (1990) 37; Osinbajo, impact 42–43; Pentecostal citizenship 35; Pentecostal citizenship, problems/reality 43–45; Pentecostal messiah (Obasanjo) 38–41; Pentecostals, spiritual/material realms 8; political/economic shockwaves (1970–1998) 36–38; political participation 35; voters, Holy Spirit guidance 43
Nigeria, Pentecostalism 121; consideration 7; opacity 45
Nkrumah, Kwame 50
nongovernmental organizations (NGOs) 72, 75–76, 172; faith-based NGOs, services 101–102; impact 116; perspective 165; rules, application 119; sacred tradition 167; secular NGOs, attack 23–24
non-Pentecostal Christians, Holy Spirit gifts 5
North America 86

Obama, Barack 150
Obasanjo, Olusegun 36; challenges 40–41; Christian self-advertisement 39; election win 38–39; Pentecostal messiah, self-projection 41; second coming (1999–2007) 38–41
Obote, Milton 25
Ocampo six, accusation 157
Oduyoye, Mercy A. 96
offensive citizens, requirement 26
Ogwal, Joe 105
oil prices, crash (1979) 37
Okonkwo, Mike 39–40
Okotie, Kris 40–41
O'Neill 8, 10, 102
One Love Church 186
opposition parties, impact 116
Oromia region 122
Oromo Liberation Front (OLF) 123–124
Oromo People's Democratic Organisation (OPDO), party cadres (involvement) 123–124
Osha, Sanja 22
Osinbajo, Yemi (impact) 42–43

Otabil, Mensah 57, 85–91, 94, 96; preaching 95; sermon, relevance 89–90
Otchere, Paul Adom 59
other, being 155
Oxford Studies in World Christianity 96
Oyedepo, David 87

para-churches, work (coordination) 127
Patriotic Front (PF): government, public debate 143; party 70
PCV document 46
PDP 40–41, 43
Pentecostal, label (refusal) 5
Pentecostal-charismatic (PC) belief, locating 5–7
Pentecostal-charismatic (PC) believers, impact 8
Pentecostal-charismatic (PC) Christianity 86; growth 32; plurality/incongruity 1; prominence 4; rise 3–7; success 36
Pentecostal-charismatic (PC) clerics: alignment 57; prophetic trends 56
Pentecostal-charismatic (PC) communities: social realms 2–3; social services 109
Pentecostal-charismatic (PC) narratives 21
Pentecostal-charismatic (PC) presidency, running 39–40
Pentecostal-charismatic (PC) property discourses, citizenship (relationship) 94–96
Pentecostal-charismatic (PC) universities, establishment 95
Pentecostal-charismatic churches (PCCs) 99; analysis 22; development/progress, veneer 110; position 11
Pentecostal churches, presentation 186
Pentecostal citizens, Devil battle 27
Pentecostal citizenship (Nigeria) 35; conception 44–45; problems/reality 43–45
Pentecostal citizenship (South Africa), ethics 167–169
Pentecostal ethics (South Africa) 163
Pentecostal faith, impact 123
Pentecostal Fellowship of Nigeria (PFN) 39–40, 45
Pentecostalism: citizenship, relationship 84–85; conversion 126–127, 183; defining 26–27; dominion worldview 86–90; function 4; impact 149–150; relationship 127

## Index

Pentecostal movements 64
Pentecostal resurgence 46
Pentecostals: developmental state 125–129; Ethiopia 115; ethnic federalism 122–125; moral agents, perception 28; political engagement 168; population, density (Ethiopia) 122; types 84; young Pentecostals, behaviour models 184–185
Pentecostal worldview 85
*Pentes* (Ethiopia) 127
People's Budget Campaign 167
Permanent Voters Cards (PVCs) 42–43
Pew Forum 64–65, 160
Phiri, Isabel 140–141
political elites 12–13
political loyalty 110
political participation (Nigeria) 35
political rationality 11
political skepticism/activism 169
political stability (Ghana) 49; implications 56–57
political subjectivity (South Africa) 163
political transformation, mode 7
politics: Christianity, relationship (Zambia) 70–71; Ghana 50–51; interpretation 27; moralisation 22; Pentecostal engagement 168
politics, regeneration 12–13
population growth 35–36
pornography, control 141
post-apartheid modernity, understanding 164–167
postcolonial state, progress/advancement promises 27–28
postcolonial Zambia, sexual citizenship 133; continuity/change 133–134
post-war Guatemala, Pentecostal-charismatics (Christian citizenship concept) 8–9
Prempeh, Agyemang 57, 59
Presbyterian missions 152
private initiative 99
pro-democracy activism 71–72
Prodigal Son, story 91
Progressive People's Party (PPP) 56
prophetic ministry, salience (Ghana) 51–53
prophetic religion, focus 86
prophets of God 136
Prophets of Spiritual Churches Council 50
prosperity, "Jerusalem" 95
prosperity gospel 84–86, 99, 125, 153

Protestant Christianity, emergence 15–16
*Protestant Ethic* (Weber) 149
Provisional National Defence Council (PNDC) regime 50–51, 58–59
public action (Uganda) 21; emotions, impact 21–22
public attitudes, supervision 31
public beliefs 14–15
public communication, networks 66
*Public Faith, A* (Volf) 84–85
public morality (Uganda) 22–25
public/political spheres, moralisation (Uganda) 24–25
public sphere 13–14
pure Christians/Oromo, presentation 123

Ranger, T. 50–51
Rawlings, Jerry Jon 58–59
rebirth 6–7, 156, 183
Redeemed Christian Church of God (RCCG): Camp, prayers/endorsement 42; members, APC choice 43
Redemption Camp 42
redemptive citizenship 177, 188
Refreshing Hour International Church 50
religious community, perspective 165
religious conversion 173; sources 35–36
*Religious Freedom and Citizenship* (charter) 83
religious institutions, impact (sub-Saharan Africa) 63
religious leaders, reflections 71–76
religious mainstream 84
religious sites, testimonies 27
religious traditions 136
renewed Pentecostal citizens, call 119–122
responsible citizenship, African Pentecostal-charismatic discourses 83
restoration, process 91
revival 44, 50, 144
Rubaga Cathedral 24
Ruto, William 150, 156, 158; God declaration 156

Sackey, Emmanuel 7, 13, 22, 49
SACRED International Ministry 121
'safety at risk' 179
salvific vision 40
same-sex marriage, perception (South Africa) 171–172
Sanneh, Lamin 83, 96
Sata, Michael 70

Satan, invasions 158
"Save Nigeria Group" (SNG), establishment 40
Schmidt, Helmut 38
secular NGOs, attack 23–24
secular state, principles 119
self-control, impact 177
self-control (Uganda) 185–187
Senior Advocate of Nigeria (SAN) 43
sexual behaviour, social problems 179–180
sexual citizenship 133; Christian nation 141–144; continuity/change 133–134; longue durée 133; Zambia 135–138
sexual immorality 171; dangers 180
sexuality: attention 133; control 183–184
'Sexuality, Politics and Religion in Africa' (SPRA) 32
sexual morality: importance 171–172; issues 168–169
*shalom* (establishment) 92–93
shared identities (building), folk devils (creation) 179–184
Sharia, controversies 47
Shiraz, Naa Tia Salifu 59
Simmel, Georg 149
Skinner, Gary 103–108
Skinner, Marilyn 103–104, 107–108
SMC 51, 58
Snow, David 180
Social changes, impact 31
social contamination (idea), insecurity (feeling) 178–179
social movements, sacred tradition 167
social realms, interpretation 27
society, regeneration 13–14
socio-economic crises 69
socio-political trends 64
soteriology, understanding 93
South Africa: Corruption Perception Index 167–168; ethics, orientation 169–170; orientations 169–170; Pentecostal citizenship, ethics 167–169; Pentecostal ethics/political subjectivity 163; Pentecostalism, anthropological studies 163–164; political pathways/possibilities 169–172; politics, orientation 169–170; post-apartheid modernity, understanding 164–167; same-sex marriage 171–172
"southern marches," political dignity 123
Southern Nations, Nationalities, and People Regions (SNNPR) 122–123

Sperber, Elizabeth Sheridan 13, 63, 69
spiritual insecurity 163
spiritual rebirth, concept 6
Springs of Joy Ministries 57
Ssempa, Martin 189
state, citizenship (relationship) 163
strangers, being 155
Structural Adjustment Programme, International Monetary Fund (IMF) 37
sub-Saharan Africa: collective religious institutions, role 67–68; democratic backsliding 63; democratisation (struggles), citizenship (construction) 65–70; Pentecostal-charismatic (PC) Christianity, rise 3–7; Pentecostal-charismatic (PC) churches, involvement 11; Pentecostal-charismatic (PC) discourse, perspective 9; Pentecostal movements 64; political institutions, features 68–69; positions, power 68–70; public debate 14; religion, parallelism 2; religious institutions 63; religious terminology 65; states, single-party transition 65–66; third wave democratisation 64
Sundolous African Leadership Training (SALT) 29
Swidler, Ann 164
Synagogue Church of All Nations (SCOAN) 54

Tawiah, Odifour Kwabena 57
"testimonies" 170
'third wave' democratisation 64–65
"thy kingdom come" statement 93
Tigray People's Liberation Front (TPLF) 117
*Times of Zambia* 141
"Town Two," location 169
Traditional Healers Organization (THO) 165
"transformation development" 126–127
true Christian, model (defining) 185
Tumsa, Gudina (killing) 120

Uganda: "Abstinence campaign" 181, 184; actors, emergence 22; anti-homosexuality campaign 180; Christianity 22–25; "Comprehensive Sexual Education Curriculum," change 23–24; consumption

185–187; Destiny Consult, impact 29–30; LGBTIQ communities, punishment 23; "lost generation" 183; Marriage and Divorce Bill, campaign 23; mini-skirt ban 23, 25; moral decay 182, 184; morally framed public policies, Catholic/Anglican Church promotion 25; nation, transformation 108–111; PCCs, citizenship role 99–100; Pentecostal-charismatic Christianity, growth 32; Pentecostal-charismatic narratives 21; Pentecostal movement, moral citizen (production) 177; Pentecostal nation, transformation 29; Pentecostals, moral imagination (relationship) 180–184; power spheres, Devil appropriation 27; public action/national belonging 21; public morality 22–25; public/political spheres, moralisation 24–25; religious sites, testimonies 27; self-control 185–187; sexuality, control 183–184; shared identities (building), folk devils (creation) 179–184; social contamination (idea), insecurity (feeling) 178–179; social problem 179–180; Watoto Church, financial integrity/national transformation 99; young Pentecostals, behaviour models 184–185
"Uganda Anti-Homosexuality Act" 188
Ukah, Asonzeh 12, 22, 35
Unic7000 church 121, 128
*Union Government* (UNIGOV): political reforms 58; proposal, support 50–51
United Church of Zambia (UCZ) 139
United National Independence Party (UNIP) 134–135; control 138
United States 138

Valois, Caroline 1, 13, 99
van Dijk, Rijk 167
van Klinken, Adriaan 8, 14, 133
Vatican 68
Volf, Miroslav 84, 87
Volta Region, NPP campaign 55
voluntary association, structures 66
votes, autopilot 89

*Walking in Dominion* (Oyedepo) 87
Wariboko, Nimi 26, 44, 54
'Watershed speech' (Kaunda) 137

*Watoto Central* rehabilitation 104
Watoto Church (Uganda): Bible basis 106–107; church structure/organisation 104–105; economic responsibility 106–108; financial integrity/national transformation 99; locations 105; origins/perspective 103–104; origins/structures, overview 100–101; study 100; technological expertise 106; weekend service 105–106
William, Duncan 59
witchcraft 95, 139, 154, 163
women, natural beauty (change) 25
Word of Faith churches 92
Word Victory Chapel 57
World Council of Churches 68; umbrella bodies 66
World Miracle Church (Accra) 57, 59
world religion, community perspective 165
worship, territory 27

*Yahweh* (narrative) 52
Yale Divinity School 96
Yom Kippur War (1973) 37
Yong, Amos 140
You-Go City 120
young Pentecostals, behaviour models 184–185
*Your Vote* 88–90; sermon 91–92

Zambia: Catholic Church, activism (example) 72; Christian citizens, formation (Catholic approaches) 71–73; Christian citizenship, making 70–71; as a Christian nation 71; constitutional declaration (Chiluba) 71; cultural values, invasion 138; culture 138, 144; description 73; discretionary support 140–141; elections, freedom/fairness 70; environmentally conscious policies, church commitment 73; Episcopal Conference 73; Evangelical fellowship, challenges 75–76; foreign 'immoral' influences 144; homosexuality, public debate 142; mainline Protestant influences 73–74; moral purity, threat 138; mother bodies 70–71; obscene video, production 141; personality, threat 138; politics, Christianity (relationship) 70–71; postcolonial

Zambia, sexual citizenship 133; poverty issues 74; pre-capitalist past, communal values (idealisation) 135; religious leaders, reflections 71–76; second government 72; state philosophy, Marxist orientation 135; "systematic persecution" 143–144
Zambia Episcopal Conference (ZEC) 139–140, 145

Zambia Humanism 133–135; discourses 142; moral issue, public concern 142; philosophy 134–135; sexual citizenship 135–138; sexual citizenship, politics (example) 136
*Zambian Moral Code: A Programmatic Approach* 135–136
Zenawi, Meles 117–118
Zuma, Jakob 167–168